HR DIRECTIONS

HR Leading Lights On What You Should Know Right Now About Leadership, Engagement, Technology, and Growing Your Own World-Class HR Career

MARTHA I. FINNEY, editor

HR DIRECTIONS: HR Leading Lights On What You Should Know Right Now About Leadership, Engagement, Technology, and Growing Your Own World-Class HR Career

For more information, visit www.marthafinney.global

ISBN# 978-0-9892984-1-4 (eBook)
ISBN# 978-0-9892984-0-7 (Paperback)

Published by: HR C-Suite
Visit our website: http://www.HRCsuite.com

10 9 8 7 6 5 4 3 2 1

Version: 2016.10.09

Table of Contents

Introduction i

About Jobs For America's Graduates iv

1. *Hire a Humanitarian: Bringing the Advantages of Global Experience Into Your Workplace*
   Catherine Carr, Project Coordinator,
   Médecins Sans Frontières (Doctors Without Borders) 1

2. *Leaders Can Be Made: What the Private Sector Can Learn from the U.S. Marines*
   Melvin Spiese, Major General (ret),
   U.S. Marine Corps 17

3. *The Hope-Driven Leader: Inspiring Purpose and Igniting Performance*
   Libby Gill, Founder and CEO,
   Libby Gill & Company 33

4. *Post-Millennial Talent: Steps You Can Take to Reclaim the Future Now*
   Barbara B. Kamm, President and CEO,
   Tech CU (Technology Credit Union) 46

5. *Leader of the Future: Preparing Millennials for Global Roles*
   Jeri Darling, President,
   Darling Global, LLC 61

6. *The Accelerated Millennial Manager: Preparing a New Generation for Leadership Success*
   Devon Scheef and Diane Thielfoldt, Principals,
   The Learning Café 75

7. *Innovative Performance Management: Leveraging Social Media Technology*
Edie Goldberg, PhD, Principal,
E.L. Goldberg & Associates 90

8. *Vision and Substance: The CHRO's Role in Successful CEO Onboarding*
Dan Phelan, Former Chief of Staff,
GlaxoSmithKline 106

9. *The Empowered CHRO: Leading the HR Department as a Company Within a Company*
John W. Sigmon, Chief Human Resources Officer,
AARP 120

10. *The Ten Inflection Points of Coaching; Navigating the Successful Leadership Coaching Journey*
Ian Ziskin, President,
ExecExcel Group 140

11. *Building Belief: The Five Keys to Lasting Cultural Transformation*
Joseph M. Patrnchak, Principal,
Green Summit Partners 154

12. *Blending Cultures: Success Factors in Merging Knowledge-Based Companies*
Mark Walztoni, Human Capital Advisory Services Practice,
Crowe Horwath, LLP 169

13. *Democratizing HR: The Coming Shift in Power to People*
Dean Carter, Head of Human Resources,
Legal, and Finance,
Patagonia 185

14. *The Data Connection: How Keeping Current with Your Impact Players Drives Your Competitive Edge*
Sanjay Sathe, Founder and CEO,
Risesmart, Inc. 199

15. *Building Leadership Capability: How the Suitability Model Simplifies the Way We Think About Talent*
Susan J. Schmitt, SVP Human Resources,
Rockwell Automation 214

16. *Positioned for a Successful Future: Syncing Human Capital Planning With Business Strategy*
Marianne Jackson, President,
3g Human Capital Consulting 228

About Martha I. Finney 242

Introduction

Thirty years ago, I was asked the question that would change my career trajectory forever: "Won't you come write for the American Society for Personnel Administration?" (ASPA would become the Society for Human Resource Management a few years later.) Back in those days, the HR profession was struggling with the same identity challenges it struggles with today. Who are we? And how do we elevate our influence inside the business, within the workplace culture, and, indeed, in U.S. (and ultimately, global) economic and labor policy? ASPA needed a seasoned business journalist in its ranks, one with a nose for news and a certain verve for the language. And so they picked me. And I'm so glad they did. It has been an honor investing my career in the mission of helping HR professionals see the power and potential of their own careers.

In those days I wasn't interested in economic and labor policy (despite my previous years at the U.S. Chamber of Commerce). And, frankly, I didn't care what HR called itself. Personnel. HR. Human capital management. Talent. Whatever. My burning focus was on that critical intersection between human drive for self-actualization and organizational need to achieve mission-critical objectives. While I was reporting on Al "Chainsaw" Dunlap, and the HR impacts of the Oklahoma City bombing by day, I was reading Walt Whitman by night. And every week I religiously tuned in to *CBS Sunday Morning*, to get another infusion of the celebratory cultural legacy left behind by the lyrical, deeply human Charles Kuralt. (If you know what a gandy dancer is, come sit by me.)

It was naïve intellectual nutrition, to be sure. And eventually my palate advanced to Ayn Rand's *Atlas Shrugged* (how could she have been so prescient?) and a true understanding of how elections actually do have consequences. As HR matured, my own understanding of that critical intersection of individuals and organization also matured.

But between yawns at dry professional conferences and symposia filled with Powerpoints and statistical analyses, the question has for decades remained right there on my prefrontal cortex, "Where is the humanity in the HR conversation?" I know HR professionals continue to crave the conversation. The HR profession itself is aloof itself. The belief has been that to go too far down the humanity road is to risk losing precious credibility ground in the business conversation.

I remember one panel discussion on employee engagement that was part of an internal HR annual conference at a Silicon Valley company you know. I was actually on the panel as a featured speaker. To my right and left were brainiacs from the organizational psychology field, each speaking at great length about the statistical justification of certain engagement markers.

There it was, that in-the-wrong-classroom feeling, that dream where in the middle of the narrative you wonder how you could possibly have left the house without your pants. Only this time it was real. When my time to speak came, I had to reassure myself that no, I wasn't dreaming, and yes, I at least had clothes on. But I was definitely in the wrong place. What could I possibly say that would contribute anything to this august collection of high-minded blather? So I just offered the very best of my latest thinking: "I don't know about you guys, but I think that individuals should just love their work. And no one deserves that experience more than HR itself."

The room erupted with applause. That was the moment my deepest belief was confirmed: The HR story is only half-told when the focus is strictly on the quantifiable organizational requirements of its human capital. And individual HR professionals feel the pain of having their humanity denied as keenly as anyone else in the organization.

When I was invited to develop and edit this volume of *HR Directions*, I welcomed this chance to further the HR conversation through the imperative of keeping the humanity aspect an integral part of a rigorous study of HR today. You will find the soaring story of people at work woven throughout these chapters, authored and submitted by some of the profession's leading experts today.

To set the tone for the entire book, I have chosen to open it with two extraordinary perspectives of the passion and power of individuals who are dedicated to their mission beyond their own self-interest. The first chapter, "Hire a Humanitarian: Bringing the Advantages of Global Experience Into Your Workplace," is by Catherine Carr, an HR professional turned project coordinator for Doctors Without Borders, based on her on-the-ground experiences in some of the world's most harrowing locations.

The second chapter, "Leaders Can Be Made: What the Private Sector Can Learn from the U.S. Marines," is a look at the complete selfless dedication of Millennials who are U.S. Marines on the battlefield. Authored by Major General Mel Spiese, who once led the entire training and education command for the Marines, he puts forward the proposition that the same dedication displayed by Millennial Marines at war is within the reach of all organizations, military and civilian alike.

With these two chapters establishing the premise that extraordinary employee dedication invites extraordinary HR vision, this book in its entirety invites you to consider your HR profession as an empowered role that can make a profound difference in any organization daily and over time. I hope it makes you proud to be in HR.

While each of these chapters is written by a CHRO or consultant having come from the senior-most ranks in the corporate world, you will discover that each topic is within your reach to implement. Whether your sphere of influence is your entire corporation as CHRO, or you are just starting out in your profession, this material is adaptable to your scale.

It will be fascinating to see what you do with this wisdom. Please let me know how you incorporate the learnings and insights into your own life, career, and enterprise.

I look forward to hearing from you.

Martha I. Finney, editor
Palm Beach County, Florida, 2016

Martha@marthafinney.global

About Jobs for America's Graduates

A portion of the proceeds of the sales of *HR Directions* will be donated to Jobs for America's Graduates (JAG). JAG is committed to creating "a nation without dropouts:"

Helping resolve our country's dropout and transition problems by expanding state organizations and local programs that help young people greatest at risk overcome barriers to graduation from high school and become college and career ready;

Equipping JAG Specialists with proven programs and unique services for middle school, high school, and out-of-school youth to stay in school through graduation from high school, pursue a collegiate education, and/or enter and advance in their chosen career field;

Developing future leaders for families, employers, communities, states, and the nation.

For more information, visit their website at www.jag.org.

Chapter 1

Hire a Humanitarian: Bringing the Advantages of Global Experience Into Your Workplace

Catherine Carr
Project Coordinator
Médecins Sans Frontières (Doctors Without Borders)

The year was 2014, and it was time to come home. At least for a little while.

In the five years that I had been working with Doctors Without Borders (*Médecins Sans Frontières* or MSF), I had done some interesting work. I had ferociously negotiated a supply agreement with compound guards who were inordinately—and very seriously—invested in receiving their fair share of tea, milk, and sugar. I had held my ground against a corrupt customs official in the Ivory Coast whose French was far better than mine. I had recovered an Australian expat I misplaced in Palo, whom I accidentally put on a helicopter bound for Guiuan, when she really should have been heading to Cebu to catch her flight home to Sydney.

I had found a home for a "polite chicken," and later, working in cahoots with another kind soul, a pet goat that had been slated to be the main course at a farewell party. I had stared deep into the eyes of a little boy with two broken legs, who had been carried to the hospital on his mother's back. I had run headlong into a rebel fighter inside a lonely stairwell in a Syrian hospital, with my hijab most definitely not in respectable condition and avoided an international incident. I had learned enough Arabic so as to avoid causing offense in most reasonably predictable situations. I had learned enough French to keep me out of jail, and just enough Swahili to order beer and make taxi drivers laugh.

I had come to the point when it was clearly time to come home for an extended break. Why now? Because of the gunfire. Not because the gunfire was frightening or too much for my nerves. But rather because it had become an annoying intrusion on my paperwork. And I was beginning to resent it. Resenting the sound of gunfire is not a normal reaction to the thing that usually sends crowds running for their lives.

My mother had always told me, "Be careful with what becomes normal to you, Catherine," and gunfire had become my normal. Thankfully, there was still enough normal within me to recognize that gunfire outside the office compound is not, in fact, my normal. So, after a debriefing session at the Paris MSF office, I got on a plane and began my trip to the small town of Lone Pine, California.

Here was the plan: I would put my suitcase somewhere where my mother wouldn't trip over it. And then I would go to sleep. For a full month (you think I'm kidding?). And then, when I woke up, I'd go into the kitchen and see what she had planned for dinner. And then, since I was planning to be stateside and somewhat stable for at least a year, I would see what I could do about finding a job. Probably something in HR.

But here's what I found out. Friends had trouble knowing how to talk to me. And potential employers didn't know what to do with me. Totally understandable. It's hard for everyone—friends, hiring managers, even self—to find that path to reentry into regular life. I suppose it's like talking to an astronaut. I have no clue what I would ask an astronaut if one walked into the room. "How was the ride?" "Is it hot in that suit?" I have zero context or experience with space travel to ask intelligent questions.

On my side, I usually get, "How was Africa?" "Wasn't it hot?" "What did you eat?" "Do they really need people like you?" (That last question is actually perfectly reasonable. Think MSF and images of doctors—who look remarkably like Angelina Jolie or Antonio Banderas—come to mind. But MSF needs HR and administrative services too. That's where I found a place for myself among humanitarians.)

Before I headed off to Paris in 2009 for a training that would prepare me for my first assignment in Kenya as an HR and finance administrator, I was the HR director for a small Albuquerque-based non-profit. I had an SPHR and everything. I wrote job descriptions. I interviewed candidates. I set up systems that would most efficiently cull out the non-starters and bring only the most qualified people who might or might not be right for the job or the organization's culture. I pushed the buttons, made the phone calls, implemented the policies, worked the networks, relied on exquisitely defined search words, and enjoyed the wonders of online job boards and job fairs.

Then, in 2014, I began trying to find my way back into what was once a familiar world, at least for a little while. But my painstakingly updated resume did not catch an automated applicant tracking system's attention. Key phrases such as "managing the mundane while in complete chaos," "burnout planner," "tea and sugar negotiator," and "livestock relocation specialist" simply don't register. Look, I get it, there isn't much use for those skills in your average workplace.

Before my own MSF days, never once had it ever occurred to me that an employee who doesn't get rattled when the generator goes out, is willing to take bucket baths, or can oversee surgical procedures without running water might be good qualities to look for in a candidate for a First World organization. So I certainly don't expect would-be employers to keep track of my growing list of qualities while I'm out in the world doing things that can't be captured in the SHRM list of competencies.

But here is the thing. I'm not alone. There are thousands of humanitarian workers out there in the world who eventually circulate back to their home country. They marvel at how difficult it is to fall back into pace with the society that used to be their native ecosystem. Not that they come back weirdly changed—although there may be some of that, I grant you—but their resumes don't jive with what recruiters are told to look for. The words on the resume just don't compute.

When you read "adaptable" on a humanitarian's resume, what we really mean is "able to work in complete chaos with minimal complaint." "Problem solver" refers to our ability to "out-MacGyver MacGyver," and "multi-cultural experience" is code for the fact that we regularly spend our days with at least four different nationalities using multiple languages and hand gestures to communicate. "Goal-oriented" translates to successfully getting things done in multicultural teams that, in less *in extremis* circumstances, would be filled with cultural landmines and hair-trigger political, interpersonal responses. The multiple contract dates and locale changes on our resumes are frequently misinterpreted as "jumping around" or "unable to commit." What those details really indicate is that we are "flexible," "go where we are needed," and "able to quickly assimilate into an existing team in a complex environment." But try explaining all that to a computer.

There is no arguing the fact that we are some of the most dedicated, resourceful, creative, mission-driven talent that you could ask for. The problem is, you don't know how to ask for us, and ATS systems overlook us. And we don't know how to step forward, raise our hands, and announce, "I'm right here!"

Fast forward two years, and I can say I did pretty okay for myself. I opted for the non-traditional path of writing and speaking. And now, with some significant amount of sleep and reflection in my system, I'm ready to head back out into the world again.

As I depart, I know that many of my humanitarian colleagues will be returning. We are like the tides. Rolling in and out, passing each other but pausing long enough to say hello and give the highlights on where we have been to ease the other's transition to where they are going. So as I roll out, I'd like to take this opportunity to introduce you to those rolling in. Not one by one, but by the qualities you, as employers, have been crying for.

(As you struggle with the challenges of Millennials coming into the workforce, wondering how you are going to keep up with their ever-increasing demands and expectations, keep in mind that as far as most of us in the humanitarian world are concerned, we're grateful to sit in a comfortable chair. Working Internet and a continuous electricity source are divine. Days without blood, gunfire, or children in pain are also much appreciated. And reliably running water, well, that's nice too.)

Humanitarians Make It Happen

This is what typically happens when the headquarters of a humanitarian organization determines that there is a population in need, security is manageable, and resources are available:

A team of four or five arrives from all over the world to the designated location—invariably remote and extremely devastated. They then stand united, contemplating either an expanse of nothingness or a catastrophe before them. "You see that out there?" the project coordinator says. Heads nod, cigarettes light up, and they shield their eyes from the sun for a better view of what is out there—or what's not out there because mayhem came along and transformed what existed into absolute wreckage. Other than this small group smoking cigarettes, there is not a single human in sight. A collective "Yup" in various mother tongues is heard in response to the question.

"We need a 20-bed hospital, access to water, a secure compound, an office, housing for the expats arriving next week, and qualified local staff members to support the activities," says the project coordinator. In their silence, the team members are already in their various roles getting the work started in their heads. The logistician is accounting for what the project coordinator did not mention: A space for vehicle maintenance, supply stores, and a BBQ pit for the weekends so expats can have some semblance of a social life. The administrator is calculating budgets, creating the organization chart, converting expenses to local currency, and fighting off concerns about slow Internet speeds. The medical coordinator is envisioning patient flow, assessing medical equipment needs, preparing the pharmaceutical order, and handing out malaria pills.

The project coordinator respects the silence, understanding that the team is already making it happen in their heads. This person takes the time to consider security concerns, upcoming negotiations with local officials, and how best to manage team morale in such a remote setting.

More cigarettes are smoked, clarifying questions are asked, and ideas are shared. Soon, the team is nodding in the affirmative, "No problem," they agree, committed to the outcome. The administrator begins handing out local currency to team members so they can purchase needed supplies. The last instruction is a universal one: "Get receipts."

In a remarkably short time, the team achieves the objective. They have created a functional hospital, living compound, and office, all in a secure environment and all out of nothing. Running water may be in the form of staff running buckets back and forth. Roofs might leak, expats might sleep on mattresses on the floor, and Internet might be slow. Electricity might be limited to twelve hours a day, and receipts might be scrawled on the backs of empty cigarette packs. None of this matters because the BBQ pit works beautifully, and, most importantly, patients are receiving treatment.

Translating a vision into the tangible and working in and around limited resources, are inherent characteristics among humanitarians. They can't help it. Further, they are motivated by the challenge. Whether opening a project in a remote location, digging water wells in high-tension zones, delivering food to starving populations, or the thousands of other needs they serve, humanitarians make it happen.

Humanitarians Roll With It

While working in a small village in Northern Syria, medical data started coming in from the refugee camp indicating a potential measles outbreak. No one was surprised. After years of conflict, the country's previously functioning health system was in shambles, and children were no longer receiving routine vaccinations.

A vaccination campaign was planned, and we needed to quickly hire over fifty people for both medical and non-medical support positions. It would be a delicate recruitment to balance getting the skills we needed with having a politically sensitive, diverse representation from the key families in the village. We wanted the new hires focusing on the vaccination campaign and not on comparing the number of positions one family received over another.

We posted job announcements in multiple languages, and within hours we were flooded with "applications." The applications arrived on pieces of paper that had been torn into halves and even quarters. Written in Arabic, potential candidates provided only a name and phone number. Maybe a statement of their desire to work and rarely the title of the position they were applying for.

We rolled with it. This is a country torn apart by civil war. A country where electricity and fuel are non-existent, let alone access to a computer and printer. Even basic supplies like pen and paper are at a premium. In this recruitment drive, those who did have paper were tearing it into pieces to share with family and friends, so they too could submit applications.

It would be impossible to select an initial pool of candidates based solely on the applications we received. So, we invited every single person who submitted a piece of paper to a preliminary group interview. Since phones were also limited, it turned out to be quite easy contacting all those that had applied. Call one person in the family and leave a message for the rest. (How's that for an applicant tracking system?)

After the group interviews, we stepped back into our normal recruitment process. Ranking applicants against job requirements, then holding technical interviews with the hiring managers. Within two weeks, we had sorted through all the pieces of paper, each one holding the hopes and dreams of an individual, and filled the positions in what was a transparent and culturally appropriate process.

Humanitarians work with what is in front of them, adapting processes and expectations to match the constraints of the environment.

Humanitarians are Instant High-Performing Teams

It was November 2013 and we were in Cebu City in the Philippines. Typhoon Yolanda had just destroyed cities and villages on the next island. Here it was, days later, and the world still could not get there to help. Airports were destroyed, shipping lanes blocked, and tons of humanitarian supplies were stacked at the Mactan-Cebu International

Airport, waiting to be transported. It was nearly midnight, and I was in the office facing more hours of work before I could respond to the pleas of my bed calling out for me.

At the same time, right outside my office, was a group of experienced humanitarians who had nothing to do until we found them a way to the devastation. I heard laughter and the unmistakable clink of glass bottles. I did what one does in these situations, I turned the music up on my headphones so I could focus and get to bed all the sooner. It didn't work. I got up to go see what was going on. It was a reunion.

I watched as members of this joyful group caught up with one another.

"Delphine! How are you? Last time I saw you was Haiti. What have you been doing?"

"Oh, Adrien, good, I tell you, good. You know, the usual, working back home to make a living. What about you? I heard you were in Syria. How was that?"

"Great. Horrible but great. Hey, stand still, let me show you a little something the Free Syrian Army taught me."

On and on this group of aid workers went. Laughing, retelling stories, clinking beers, and gearing up for what would be intense work once we got them out of Cebu City and onto Leyte Island.

"Remember when the tent fell on Khalid?"

"And what about the time Matt went out for a six-day trip and ended up staying for six weeks?"

"Yes! He returned and found out we were using his bedroom as storage. Ha ha ha. And oh, oh … what about that bridge we built? Can you believe the villagers still use it?"

"Oh! Is that the bridge Nico worked on in Mzimba? I worked with him in Nigeria and heard all about it. We worked on a malnutrition project together. I'm Natalie. Heard all about you guys from Nico."

People reunited from France, Japan, Australia, the United States, Belgium, Germany, the Democratic Republic of Congo, and more. All coming together again to face another emergency. Medical, logistics, and administrative personnel, all specialists in their fields, instantly forming into a high-performing team. All needing very little direct supervision, except, of course, an occasional reminder about the receipts.

I watched as the scene played out before me, smiling for the first time in hours as they reconnected with one another, remembering the experiences they had shared all over the world and falling in love again with the work that calls to them. And I wondered, "Who is going to hire them when they get home? What are they going to do until the next emergency hits? What company will ever see what I see: Trustworthy, dedicated, spirited, intelligent, and inclusive individuals who bring back receipts…most of the time. What company will hold a place for them and their passion? What employer will let them leave on a moment's notice for a week or two so they can serve others, then return with a full heart and stories to share about what is happening in the world?"

As I turned to head back to my work, I stopped for a moment and thought about it. Why was I worried about them? They seemed to be doing just fine. What I really needed to worry about was what I was going to do after this assignment ended.

Humanitarians Never Stop Communicating

The project for the day was to swap out the old generator. We were in Northern Syria, and the new generator from our coordination office in Turkey had arrived. The only hitch was that we would have to shut down the electricity for a few hours. As the administrator, my job was to not complain with the other expats about the short battery lives on the phones and computers, or wonder how we would live without the Internet. Grumbling and muttering sufficiently accomplished by the rest of the staff, the hospital and office went dark.

A few hours later, Sami and Mohammad, two Syrian employees, walked into the communal office and stood in front of their supervisor's desk. Prior to the war, Sami (who spoke Arabic and English) had been a university student in Damascus studying English literature. Mohammad (who spoke Arabic) had a successful thirty-plus-year career as a car mechanic in his home village. On this day, Sami was working as a logistics assistant, and Mohammad was our maintenance man. Together, the twenty-year-old and the fifty-year-old stood before their supervisor, Thomas, an expat from France (who spoke French and English), to give an update on the generator swap.

Sami: "Not working."

Mohammad: Standing slightly behind Sami, nodding in the affirmative, but not understanding a word.

Thomas: "What is wrong?"

Sami turned to Mohammad and for the next few minutes, those in the communal office watched as they held a discussion in Arabic and our battery lives slowly dripped away. It was a full-on conversation complete with questions, responses, tonal variations, nodding heads, and eyebrows that raised and lowered.

After this extended discussion, Sami, turning to face Thomas, pronounced: "Don't know."

In the office was Aya, also Syrian and also a former English literature student from Damascus University (she spoke Arabic and English), who was now our administrative assistant. AnneMarie, a Canadian doctor (who spoke French and English) was our project's medical director. And I, the American administrator, could speak only English and grammatically incorrect French. The three of us put our computers on sleep mode and sat back to see what would happen next.

Thomas (while peeking at his watch, cognizant of the battery situation) asked again: "What is wrong?"

Sami explained, periodically turning to Mohammad for technical clarification, then to Aya for translation assistance. It went something like this:

Sami and Mohammad (in Arabic): "Blah, blah, blah." They stopped and looked at Aya.

Aya: "Engine."

Sami and Thomas (in English): "Blah, blah, blah." Then a technical question.

Sami and Mohammad (in Arabic): "Blah, blah, blah." They stopped and looked to Aya again.

Aya: "Voltage. I think."

The conversation continued, and before long, Thomas turned to AnneMarie to ask for her help in translating some of the English to French.

In time, someone asked, in some language, the question that is eventually asked when something does not work: "Has anyone read the manual?"

Sami, Mohammad, and Thomas went downstairs to look for the manual. Aya, AnneMarie, and I chuckled and went back to work. Before we had the time to fall back into focus on our work, the office door crashed open. All three marched back in, with Thomas in the lead waving in his hands what could only be the manual.

Thomas (in French and quite loudly): "Merde! Blah! Blah! Blah! Turk!"

AnneMarie (in English and through snorts of laughter): "The manual is in Turkish!"

Sitting down and taking a breath, Thomas picked up the phone to speak with Faruk, the logistics assistant in the coordination office. Faruk (who spoke Turkish and English) happened to have a copy of the generator manual on his desk. Now with six individuals and four languages involved, the team continued to communicate and problem solve. They never stopped. Not even after the new generator was up and running.

Now. Stop and think for a moment about the hundreds of different cultures and subcultures crashing and banging against each other in that small room. The vast differences in customs, religions, genders, generations, languages, beliefs, professions, and educational backgrounds, colliding against one another like atoms gone wild. Each difference a plausible barrier to the restarting of a generator. But electricity in a hospital setting is not optional, and the team was not focused on cultural differences but rather the imperative need to get out of the dark.

Humanitarians Focus on What's Important

A friend told me that one of the questions Facebook recruiters use is: "How many golf balls can fit into a limousine?" Give me a break. Who cares? And who wants to spend precious time discussing parameters, such as make and model of the limo or the exact size of the golf balls the recruiter has in mind? Let me tell you some of the questions humanitarians ask when looking for the skills and characteristics that really matter to their teams.

"Can you be trusted with cash?" Security is the first consideration. Not just with cash, but with all things. And how you treat cash is an indicator of your approach to safety in general. Do you treat cash like you would a stick of dynamite; as a tool that can be used either to your advantage or to your detriment? Do you understand the protocols are in place not to protect the cash or annoy you, but to reduce risk and protect people? If candidates can show they can be trusted with cash, then they can be trusted with all things of value.

"Do you treat others with respect?" Another security-related question, this one aimed at how a person treats other individuals. The concern is not so much how they treat people from their own culture, but how they treat people from different cultures and with different beliefs. When we are working out there, what protects us the most is the support of the communities we work in. And, as we all know, at least intellectually, in order to get respect you must give respect. And respect translates to far safer working, and, in the humanitarians' case, living environments.

"Do you sleep on the job?" Again, another security-related question. In this world, a team's safety depends on their colleagues being awake when they're supposed to be. And not just awake, but acutely aware of the ever-shifting environment around them. Humanitarians operate in chaotic environments and, if not in an obviously violent part of the world, in places where the smallest spark could set off events that might impact generations. Vigilance and attention are key. And to clarify, this question is not reserved for those who work at night. It is appropriate for everyone.

"Can you evacuate with five minutes' notice?" What we are looking for here is how quickly they can organize themselves in times of crisis. When it is time to go, *it is time to go*. Any discussions about evacuation should have occurred long before the need to evacuate. Responsibilities accepted, "go bags" prepared, and multiple lines of communication defined and frequently tested. The answer to this question is also an indicator of an individual's capacity to quickly identify what matters most.

"Do you balk at doing work not included in your job description?" I've seen administrators assist with medical emergencies and nurses manage fuel deliveries. It is incredible the things humanitarians find themselves doing out there, most of it not written down. You want people who do not limit themselves to doing what someone else wrote on a piece of paper. Humanitarians see a situation for what it is, identify how they can pitch in to help, and then do so.

"How do you feel about sleeping under a mosquito net?" If you think sleeping under a mosquito net is exotic or romantic, then you've never done it. It is hot under those things and incredibly noisy with mosquitos buzzing around trying to squeeze through the tiny holes to get to your blood. Best of luck should one actually get inside your net. Any hopes of sleeping are gone for good. Instead of tossing and turning under the unbreathable mesh in the heat of Africa, your night is spent trying to locate and kill the little blood sucker without waking up your roommates. The correct answer to the question, by the way, is: "I don't like it but I do it." Humanitarians know the importance of taking care of themselves. They are no good to anyone if they have malaria.

But the question recruiters should really be asking is: **"You go into a room and see a refrigerator in what you believe to be an illogical place...what do you do?"**

The answer you want to hear is: "I leave it alone until I understand why it is there." If your candidate gives this answer, hire him or her immediately.

Here is the deal. When joining a team, new members are tempted to start marking territory and proving to everyone that they were the right hire. Perhaps they change the font on contracts or highlight the header row in blue rather than the customarily accepted 70 percent gray shade.

They attempt to update policies without understanding the history, call for meetings to reformulate project strategy, or worse, move the refrigerator from the south wall to the north wall. Their intention is to make an immediate and obvious contribution to the team, but in doing so, they fail to understand why the refrigerator is on the south wall to begin with.

Humanitarians have learned the hard way to leave the refrigerator alone. They understand there is a reason why it stands against the south wall, and their job is to find out why. It might be because the south wall has the only working three-prong electrical outlet in the room. It might be the only spot in the room where exterior doors don't bang against it as people go in and out all day long. Perhaps it is there because that particular section of floor doesn't slope or perhaps, because it does slope. Maybe the floor slopes toward the wall just enough so vaccines don't come tumbling out when someone opens the refrigerator door.

Truly, hire the person who waits before changing things. You want people on your team who will leave the refrigerator alone until they understand why it is there to begin with. Not to mention that such behavior indicates the individual recognizes that there are more important things to do.

Humanitarians Offer Perspective

Now I know what you are thinking. "If I hire a humanitarian, they are just going to go back out again, and my company loses out on the huge investments we made with onboarding and training costs." You can focus on the real costs, I suppose, but what if you focus on the intangible benefits? Look at it as the opportunity to hire someone who could inject new perspectives into your environment.

It doesn't take a humanitarian forever to make a lasting difference. They do odd things like ask lots of questions, quickly identify who is really in charge, and show gratitude for the simple things like coffee and climate-controlled environments. That kind of behavior is bound to rub off onto others.

I know the average workplace is stressful, I used to work in one. Having said that, fresh coffee, sleeping in your own bed, big screen TVs, and safe access to outdoor environments can do a lot to reduce stress.

Our First World problem is that we forget to recognize these things as being readily available and fail to take advantage of them in stressful times.

Humanitarians are natural storytellers, and they bring the world to your organization. This is good news for anyone with a corporate social responsibility or community engagement program. Put humanitarians into these positions and watch them find simple and sustainable ways for your company to engage with the world.

Humanitarians are humble and don't take themselves too seriously. They might laugh at inappropriate times but it is usually to blow of steam and put things back in perspective. Besides, especially in the midst of chaos, laughter is important. As are camaraderie, compassion, and finding space to dance with the context.

Chances are your humanitarians will eventually leave to answer a call from somewhere in the world. And when they leave, know that it is not a loss of an investment because for as long as you were able to engage them, you held lightning in your hands. While you gave them time to reconnect to their native ecosystem, they brought you the world and new perspectives. They brought you their passion and commitment, and they gave you their heart-driven best.

So let them go, and I bet, if you invite them to, they just might come back. With their hearts full, some new tricks the rebels taught them, and more stories that make your other employees say, "I never heard of such a thing!" And who knows what great places employees with new ideas might take your company.

Saying, "Sure!" to an unexpected opportunity, in 2009 Catherine packed her MBA, SPHR, a few changes of clothes and an open mind to go on a six-month assignment with Doctors Without Borders. Five years and ten countries later, having served as HR/Finance Manager or Director (the title depending on the organization's needs), she took a break. After almost two years' respite, she has returned to the field.

Prior to joining Doctors Without Borders, Catherine worked in a variety of positions, all of them serving to prepare her for the range of responsibilities she would later hold as a humanitarian: Dance instructor, administrator, temp worker, recruiter, bartender, freelancer, finance and HR director.

Catherine has a Bachelor's degree in Communications from the University of San Francisco and an MBA from Golden Gate University. When she is between assignments with Doctors Without Borders, Catherine shares her insights and experiences with audiences as a keynote speaker.

Follow her at www.catherinecarr.global. To contact her, email her at cc@catherinecarr.global. But be patient. It might take her a while to get back to you.

Chapter 2

Leaders Can Be Made: What the Private Sector Can Learn from the U.S. Marines

Melvin Spiese
Major General (ret)
U.S. Marine Corps

The casual, civilian observer who glances at a photo of a platoon of freshly graduated Marines can hardly be judged for thinking that they all look the same. The uniforms, of course, contribute to the effect. The "covers," or hats. The extraordinary posture and set of jaw that only extreme fitness and rigorous training can support. They are unified by a sense of pride in their singleness of purpose. They have become warriors.

And they are Millennials; young men and women who couldn't have been any more different in background when they arrived for Basic Training. They are ranchers from Montana. Deck hands from St. Croix. Dairy farmers from Iowa. Surfers from Soquel. Hipsters from SoHo. Students from colleges all over the country. Bakers from Queens. High school grads from Canton. Welfare recipients from just about anywhere you can name. And yet, now, they are Privates in the United States Marine Corps. And they know that when they are called, they go.

Their parents are equally and widely disparate in profession and socio-economic standing. They are pharmacists, teachers, physicians, film directors, motel owners, artists, middle managers hoping against hope to avoid the latest rounds of layoffs, meat packers, authors. They couldn't be more different, but they share the same dream for their children: That they have enough to eat; that they get plenty of safe sleep; and that they come home from their career with the Marines healthy, whole, and equipped with the skills and resilience to thrive in the civilian phase of their adult lives.

They are the parents of warriors. And they know that when they are called, *they pick up the phone.*

As a recently retired Major General in the Marines after a 37-year career, I, too, am a warrior. And I am the father of three warriors, a son (King's College 2009) and two daughters (U.S. Naval Academy, 2003 and 2007).

I pick up the phone when it rings.

My son, who goes by the family name MG, was a platoon commander with L Company, 3d Battalion, 2d Marine Regiment when he called me from Helmund Province in Afghanistan. I was the Deputy Commanding General of I Marine Expeditionary Force, driving the bougainvillea-lined California road across Camp Pendleton on my way home one day, when my phone rang. And I answered it.

This particular phone call was the most profound conversation I had ever had, matched only by the call from our daughter just prior to her leaving the large logistics base at Taqquadum on her first combat vehicle patrol in Iraq in 2004. My son had survived his first ambush, and he was calling to tell me about it.

MG, newly arrived in Afghanistan, was slated to lead a platoon that was responsible for six villages around Kurgay and the "rat line" that ran through Salaam Bazaar. He was there in advance of his platoon to familiarize himself with the area, the situation, the local village elders, and the personalities he would have to understand. This mission was accomplished in the company of the out-going platoon, whose last major task was to show him around, so to speak. They would then be going home. Their tour was almost over.

He had already been to five of the six villages without incident. But it was the last village when the squad on foot patrol was ambushed. My son, new to Afghanistan and new to combat, could only observe as the squad activated all their training and experience one last time. He watched as the squad leader, a sergeant still in his 20s, quickly assessed the situation and issued basic guidance to his fire team leaders. The last mission, that point in the Hollywood story line when the narrative typically takes a tragic turn. But they all lived.

What really caught my attention was when my son said, "Dad, the fire team leaders took over the fight. They came up with a quick plan and fought through the enemy." It wasn't the actions of the two corporals or lance corporate fire team leaders that impressed me the most, though. This is to be expected of any Marine leader, even the most junior leader, under the stress of combat. It was their unhesitating action in the face of the enemy less than a week before all the members of that squad would be on a flight heading back to the United States. You know that in many ways they were already home in their hearts. And yet, there they were, in a remote Afghan village fighting for their lives.

Who were these young men? And what was within them that powered their ability to think and decide so quickly under stress, move so rapidly, and act with courage leading their Marines into a fight, all without placing their personal safety before mission and duty?

These are Marines, the graduates of the best leadership development process in the world. But these are also Millennials. This is a generation that causes employers worldwide to obsess day and night about how to keep them retained, motivated, and performing to standards. These are the young men and women who think of home, cars, favorite beer, music, best bars with pool tables, primo surfing locations, favorite secret fishing holes, beloved kitchen smells, the sound of family voices, and all the other passions, obsessions, and joys that come with being a healthy American young adult.

They think about the same things their friends back home think about. Until ambush happens in an Afghan village; and their focus shifts. And their leadership skills and teamwork then bring everyone back to base safely.

These are young men and women who come from the same backgrounds that civilian Millennials do. They become different when they commit to their nation and then submit themselves to the rigorous training that comes with becoming a Marine. Then they are *made leaders*. And that is what we do in the Marine Corps; we make Marines of ordinary young men and women. And then we make leaders of all Marines, no matter the rank, education, or background.

With some adjustment in approach, these are qualities that can be borrowed and adapted for the civilian world to inspire the best from young men and women who yearn to be dedicated to missions greater than themselves, and to perform at the highest of levels.

Leadership Within Reach

> Leadership is intangible, hard to measure, and difficult to describe. Its quality would seem to stem from many factors. But certainly they must include a measure of inherent ability to control and direct, self-confidence based on expert knowledge, initiative, loyalty, pride, and sense of responsibility. Inherent ability cannot be instilled, but that which is latent or dormant can be developed. Other ingredients can be acquired. They are not easily learned. But leaders can be and are made.
>
> General C. B. Cates, the 19th Commandant of the Marine Corps

At the risk of understatement, combat demands specific qualities in a person to simply function effectively and survive. To take responsibility for a mission and for others, to think clearly, to communicate effectively, to expose oneself in guiding others in a confusing, chaotic, and dangerous situation requires the best and the most of people. That the Marines have been producing this in Millennials—recruits and junior Marines not necessarily recruited for previously demonstrated leadership skills—for over a dozen years of overseas deployments to combat is remarkable. That speaks to both this generation—which so many have questioned, doubted, and criticized—and the efficacy of the Marine approach.

The Marine Corps is dealing with the same raw talent that private sector employers must deal with—the same challenges, same problems, same attitudinal issues coming in. The difference must be found in the developmental approach because the Marines end up with fire team members who will take on an enemy ambush. At the same time, in what seems to be a parallel universe on the other side of the planet, private sector employers worry about losing their top Millennial talent because the youngsters might decide one day that for whatever reason, "I dunno, I'm just not feeling it here anymore."

Private sector employers can borrow from the Marines' developmental playbook. Will you get a full-fledged Marine for your efforts? No. But pattern your developmental approach to your talent after what the Marines do, and you will be making leaders who can move you reliably into the next two decades of your company—or even longer.

You will change not only the lives of your workforce, but also the entire culture and atmosphere of your organization.

When it comes to onboarding Millennials, the Marines and the private sector draw from the same crop of talent. And as tempting as it might be to assume that Marines have some kind of advantage when it comes to attracting raw recruits who come in already mission-driven, that's not always the case.

You can duplicate the leadership development experience inside the private sector world (within reason, of course. OSHA frowns on live ammunition). And you can benefit from what we have learned and created over decades of building leaders. You can have these advantages, dedication, and discipline, if you look a little deeper into those in your workforce, invest in their development, and raise your expectations of what the Millennial generation is truly capable of.

The Five Characteristics of a Stellar Leader

As a starting point, the U.S. Marine Corps laid out a list of five pillars that have become the outcomes of leader development in Marine officers. Each must have and be able to demonstrate these characteristics as an essential core of his or her basic nature. These attributes must be installed and demonstrable before any additional technical or advanced training happens to build mastery in any additional skillsets. As I lay each one out, I'll also introduce ways that a civilian corollary can be developed and applied.

A man or woman of exemplary character. Marines have a clear understanding that a Marine commission carries with it "special trust and confidence" and the highest expectations of the American people. They are devoted to the corps' Core Values of Honor, Courage, and Commitment, and possess a moral compass that unerringly points to "do the right thing."

In the private sector, once you give new employees their key cards, their ID cards, even a company credit card, you are trusting them to use a moral values set that you would recognize. You are giving them access to your company's physical interests, your employees' safety and well-being, your enterprise secrets, and reputation. During the selection and onboarding processes, you have found a way to ensure that your new employees share the same ideas of what goes behind the "do the right thing" expectation and assumption.

Devoted to leading Marines 24/7. Marines embrace the "exceptional and unremitting" responsibility to one's Marines and their families. They inspire and instill confidence in their Marines during times of adversity. They adhere to and enforce standards regardless of time of day, location, or duty status. They treat all Marines and Sailors with dignity and respect, and are dedicated to a lifetime of study and learning about the profession of arms.

In the private sector, we often speak of *servant leadership*. Your employees who are on track to become leaders themselves know that their duty is to help their direct reports do their jobs well, not the other way around. The behavior and philosophy of servant leadership doesn't begin and end with the opening and closing of your business day. You count on your leaders to know their team members and treat them with dignity and respect in a consistent manner any time and anywhere. Your leaders also accept the responsibility of developing their direct reports, just as their supervisors are committed to developing them.

Able to decide, communicate, and act in the fog of war. Marines must be able to think critically and operate based on sound tactical thinking that aligns with their commanders' intent. They are able to communicate clearly both orally and in writing and issue clear, meaningful orders and guidance. They hold a bias for action without waiting for the perfect moment or micromanagement from their superiors. And once that action is taken, they follow through on that action with boldness and determination.

War is not commonly experienced in the private sector. But stress and tension are ever-present in a competitive landscape such as free enterprise. The ability to develop and follow through on a plan of action, even when it's fraught with uncertainty, and frequently fear, is essential among private sector leaders, who must also take action in alignment with the company's strategic plan. Once that plan of action is decided upon, the private sector leader mobilizes and manages the direct reports, and the best of them lead their peers as well, consistent with the plan and the immediate supervisor's orders. And there is no dithering. A moment's delay in executing what has already been decided upon can cost the company a great deal financially or in competitive advantage.

Embraces the Corps' warrior ethos. Marines are competent combat leaders, grounded in the basic infantry skills, and characterized by sound judgment and aggressiveness in execution. They are educated in the fundamentals of maneuver warfare, tactics, combined arms, and the time-tested principles of battle. They also maintain an offensive mindset throughout. They are proactive rather than reactive.

How does a warrior ethos translate into the private sector? The private sector is a competitive landscape where there usually can be only one winner. The losers are many, and the loss can be dramatic and devastating. Much has been made over the years about the "participation trophies" that are endemic to the Millennial generation. They get a prize just for showing up. The prevailing concern has been around the likelihood that children don't learn how to lose when they are guaranteed to come home with a bright, shiny present. There's an overlooked hazard to the participation trophy idea: It doesn't teach children how to pursue winning—more to the point, it doesn't teach children how to *let others lose*.

When only one person gets to take home the trophy, the winner shouldn't have to cry in the backseat all the way home because he feels just terrible that he can't share the prize with everyone else.

The workplace is a battlefield of sorts, and the market is filled with winners and losers. Employees are warriors on behalf of your company. Both internally and externally, there are contests every day in which only one person or team can prevail. The winner needs to be *your* organization in the competitive marketplace. The loser is the competitor company that may see its marketplace position degrade in very real ways (loss of market share, downsizing, etc.) as a result.

Our Millennials are our new warriors. And they have one job: To win. To win ethically. And be proud of winning.

Is mentally strong and physically tough. Marines are imbued with a warrior spirit and able to thrive in a complex and chaotic environment and persevere despite the obstacles to mission accomplishment. They possess the self-discipline to push past preconceived limits.

Private sector leaders are unlikely to scale a wall (unless it's at a team-building ropes course), subsist on MREs, kick down a door, intensely negotiate with a local tribal elder, or drag an injured team member out of a building under fire. All before 8:30 in the morning.

And yet the aggressive, high-action demands of the competitive private-sector world require your top-most leaders to retain presence of mind, decision-making abilities, and communications skills under pressure and in uncertainty. This requires a toughness and conditioning that strengthens the leader.

Private sector leaders must develop mental toughness, and evidence shows those who are in top condition are the most likely to feel good, be well-rested, think more broadly and creatively, anticipate, and respond to changing conditions more accurately, and inspire their teams to perform at the same levels of excellence. The private sector desperately needs resilience, courage, and stamina. These qualities are accessible in leaders who are both mentally and physically in top condition.

Those attributes are built into Marines through instilling and developing within them a codified set of "leadership traits and principles." The methodology of the Marine Corps' process is certainly unique and structured to the mission and culture of the Marines. However, their validity, utility, and adaptability are universal. When you consider these traits and principles, ask yourself if there is any reason at all why your company doesn't deserve to have Millennials with these characteristics as well.

Leadership Principles	Leadership Traits
Know yourself and seek self-improvement.	Integrity
Be technically proficient.	Courage
Develop a sense of responsibility among your subordinates.	Judgment
Make sound and timely decisions.	Justice
Set the example.	Decisiveness
Know your people and look out for their welfare.	Knowledge
Keep your people informed.	Dependability
Seek responsibility and take responsibility for your actions.	Initiative
Ensure assigned tasks are understood, supervised, and accomplished.	Tact
Employ your team and organization in accordance with its capabilities.	Unselfishness
Manage and train your people as a team.	Loyalty
	Endurance
	Enthusiasm
	Bearing

Granted, the lists are long, and the items should come as no surprise. Lists of leadership qualities are common, and of course, debatable, although in the end, they seek a common outcome and often tend to look alike. I have defaulted to the Marines because their lists are codified and proven to be successful, forged in that most basic and dangerous crucible of combat. They are proven to work in scenarios where failure is not an option.

Some of these traits, such as *Courage* and *Integrity*, instantly stand out. Those make every list in one form or another. With the Marines, there are several less-expected traits, but critical traits in the relationship of power of one over another. This is where an essential difference is made: The Marines understand that leadership is all about relationship—upward and downward through the organization.

If a courageous and honest leader displays poor relational qualities, that can negatively impact his or her effectiveness and the atmosphere and culture of the organization as a whole. So those "lesser" traits speak to a relationship of respect of one over another, knowing that the leaders who respect and value their direct reports will be much more effective.

It's not just the traits that bring success to the Marines' leadership culture. It's also the principles—the basic leadership practices that the Corps has codified over time. Within those principles, the Marines have identified several that are a leader's obligations to him- or herself, such as knowing self and seeking self improvement, in addition to basic practices relating to the leader and those being led.

The Marines have developed a very sophisticated, comprehensive, and holistic approach to leadership development. And the components are predictably universal in nature and applicable in all walks of life. Adopted and practiced, they transform lives and relationships. In doing so, those people, those leaders, will transform cultures, working atmosphere, and organizations. In the military and on Main Street.

Does Your Company Deserve the Made Leader?

Granted, while the U.S. Marine Corps recruits some non-starters and eventual wash-outs periodically, by and large this branch of the armed services attracts the cream of Millennial America for one over-arching reason: We have *earned* it.

As much as we expect from our Marines, we also owe them the training, the loyalty, the patience, the equipment they require to get the nation's job done. Young recruits come into the Marines naturally uncertain, nervous, and maybe even second-guessing their decisions (if they don't second-guess that decision at least once during Boot Camp or Officer Candidate School, we're letting them down). But they also know that if they give themselves over to our training and discipline, they will emerge from the experience fit, dignified, professional, proud, and capable of bringing themselves and their team mates home alive to the extent most reasonable. They know this because of our track record of success, and because they're surrounded by examples of graduates who personify the leadership ideal. Among the many emotions the Marines puts these young adults through, inspiration through role modeling is one of them.

First they have to trust us. So we have to earn that trust through kept promises and a reputation of being their best possible choice. We constantly work in alignment with our own leadership traits and principles to make sure we are always giving them what we're expecting them to give back to us.

Let me turn the eleven Leadership Principles around into questions to consider for yourself and your organization. This is now presented to you as a self-assessment in deciding whether you and your company have earned the right to attract, recruit, and deploy the best made leaders that are available to you. As you glance through them, you might think, "This is just a rehash of a generic employee engagement list." I invite you to look at it through a different lens. Employee engagement is about how your people experience their work with you within your company. This list challenges you to look at actions *you* can take to attract and secure the best Millennials who choose your enterprise as the locus of their commitment:

Do I know myself and am I committed to self-improvement? What is your own program for self-development? Assuming you are working within a "learning organization," and you want to attract high-quality talent that is equally committed to growth and development, you must commit to the same level of personal expansion that you're expecting from those around you.

Am I technically proficient in the skills I want to pass on to my leaders? Are you keeping up with the latest developments of your profession? Can you speak to your organization's objectives with the authority and confidence of someone who is still active and on top of his life's work? If you suddenly had to step into your direct report's role, would you be able to keep up with the sudden set of demands, both physically and intellectually?

Do I regularly develop a sense of responsibility among my subordinates? Do you delegate everything that you can so that your subordinates can learn to step into your shoes when the time comes for you to move on to your own next promotion and assignment? Do you reward initiative and follow-through? Do you make it safe to make honest errors so that everyone can learn from the mistake?

Do I make sound and timely decisions? Can your team count on you to be decisive so they can take the right action in a safe, effective manner? Are they confident that any time they must spend waiting for a decision or direction is absolutely essential time you need to consider all the ramifications and gain necessary input from other sources? Do they trust that you're respecting their own time and their bias for action?

Do I set the example? You must keep the faith with your direct reports, especially when their work calls for them to put their own self-interests on the far back burner. Whatever standards you or your organization set for your leaders—and, for that matter, the rank and file—you must be prepared to meet them. Ideally your standards should surpass those you have set for your subordinates. Your behavior will inspire your team to reach for greater achievements.

Do I know my people and look out for their welfare? Do you take the time to know your direct reports by name? Do you know what their personal concerns are? Do you look for ways that you can extend extra support to them on a personal, one-on-one basis? As you do, they will take that role-modeling and extend the same caring and consideration downward throughout the entire organization.

Do I keep my people informed? It has been said that the army travels on its stomach. But I believe that nothing moves without full information necessary to get the job done. There are, of course, certain kinds of proprietary and confidential information that can't be shared. But Millennials want and need to know more than less. Beyond the immediate "what" and "how," it's increasingly essential for high-potential Millennials to understand the context that a decision is made in and how it is relevant to other moving parts.

Do I seek responsibility and take responsibility for my actions? Millennials need to see their own leaders reach for stretch assignments, take on new opportunities and responsibilities. And then own their mistakes when appropriate. When it is safe for you to fail and for you to own your errors, they will take on the challenge of growing to new levels of their own abilities as well.

Do I make sure that assigned tasks are understood, supervised, and accomplished? Vague assignments set your direct reports up for failure, and ultimately burnout. Yes, your company's day-to-day activities are engineered to further the interests of your company's customers and stakeholders. But each activity can also be used as a training and development opportunity for your leaders. When assigned appropriately, you are growing your replacement. But you must be clear and committed to supporting their success. Even when they make mistakes in the discharge of that assignment.

Do I employ my team and organization in accordance with their capabilities? There are stretch goals, and there are impossibilities. As their leader, it's your responsibility to make sure that their assignments are well within their reach—even if they have to extend that reach just a little beyond what is comfortable and feels natural to them. However, overwhelming them with assignments too massive or too difficult will break the trust agreement between the two of you that you will develop them and they will allow themselves to be developed...by you.

Do I manage and train my people as a team? In my son's initial experience in the sixth Afghan village, none of them would have made it out alive had the squad not trained, worked, and lived together for months beforehand. They were of a single mind, a single body of movement, plan, tactics, and looking out for each other. That level of intense movement as one comes from dedicated training to not only develop the individual but also to build the heart of a team.

This team-oriented spirit is one of the greatest gifts Millennials bring to any organization they join—whether it's the U.S. Marine Corps or a private sector operation that wants to tap into the heroic heart of this generation's best.

Conclusion

All across the United States, employers worry about the newest generation coming up from college and moving out into the workplace. They consider the characteristics commonly ascribed to these young adults—spoiled, unreliable, over-protected, unethical to varying degrees, undisciplined, detached from the realities of free enterprise—and employers understandably worry about what's to become of their companies if this is the raw material the foundation of the future will be built on.

You may be surprised to discover the Marines worried about the same things in the early 2000s when the order came from Washington to rebuild our forces to prepare for an invasion in Iraq, which would commit this nation to an extended armed engagement with no defined ending. Naturally, there were some sterling individuals who recognized their nation's need for their dedication and passion and stepped right up immediately. But overall the population we had to draw from was by and large known for its indolence, its selfishness, its materialism, its addictions, and its struggles as young adults mostly unprepared to take on the task of ordinary American life—never mind the rigors of life in the Marines. Who among these people would even volunteer for service, when there was so much to give up right here at home? When "can't someone else do it?" was a well-thumbed page in their playbook of Getting Out of Stuff.

But they surprised us. Then and now, wave after wave of young men and women present themselves to us, their eyes lit by a fresh dawning of what it takes to be an adult in America today. They take on the sacrifices, and willingly exchange their toys for an M16, body armor, seventy-five-pound backpack, and long walks in tough conditions. These young Americans report for duty, and then return to duty, despite their own devastating losses of their closest friends on the battlefield and the innocence in their young American hearts that had been raised in shopping malls and on video games and flat screen TVs showing *The Bachelor and The Jackass.*

The ones who come home safely personally know young friends who don't. And yet they still return again and again, deployment after deployment, knowing full well what they have gotten themselves into.

This is also the character of the young Millennials. No matter where they work. Not every Millennial who presents him or herself to you for a job opportunity will be able to rise to the challenges and opportunities that your company might extend to them. Likewise, not every young Marine recruit makes it through our rigorous program either. But the qualities are there in more young adults than you might expect. They may be dormant, as General Cates observed. But you have what you need to awaken them and inspire them into action.

Take on the mindset of Marine leadership and borrow the best training principles from the nation's best young men and women. Expect dedication and mission-driven commitment from your talent. Work hard to make sure you and your organization have earned their devotion to excellence. And you will uncover vast bands of extraordinary leadership deep inside your organization in the most unexpected places.

Melvin Spiese, Major General, U.S. Marine Corps (ret), recently retired from the Marine Corps after a 37-year career. Joining the Marines at age 21, his last role at age 58 was as Commanding General of the First Marine Expeditionary Brigade and Deputy Commanding General of I Marine Expeditionary Force (I MEF), where he ran the training and development, readiness, crisis response, and combat deployment of a 55,000 Marine organization.

Before his assignment with I MEF, he served as Commanding General of the Training and Education Command, overseeing the development of all 200,000 Marines throughout the Corps. Other career highlights include overseeing the revision of the US European Command military strategy across 92 countries, and representing the United States in bilateral and multilateral programs with over 36 countries—many of which were highly sensitive politically.

Today he advises large international companies on how they can import the Marines' traditions of leadership excellence and discipline into the private sector—with a special emphasis on engaging Millennials. His private sector consulting has taken him to Kuwait, the United Kingdom, Canada, and Australia.

Mel has also been a national security advisor on the campaigns of two presidential candidates.

Contact him at 571.765.0410 or mel@leaderscanbemade.com.

Chapter 3

The Hope-Driven Leader: Inspiring Purpose and Igniting Performance

Libby Gill
Founder and CEO
Libby Gill & Company

When poet Emily Dickinson famously said, "Hope is the thing with feathers," she neglected to mention that it is also the thing with talons. Soaring and magical, hope lifts our sense of what is possible, but it also gives us the tenacity to hold tightly to our vision despite the obstacles. Since I began writing about this topic in 2001, I've thought of hope as the jet fuel for the journey of work and life. And for the nearly thirty years that I've been involved in helping shape excellence in the workplace, first in the corporate world and now as an executive coach and leadership consultant, I've observed how hope, or the lack of it, affects performance.

Willpower and Waypower

The word *hope* is derived from the Old English word *hopian* and literally means to "leap forward with expectation." Hope plays such a pivotal part of our lives that scientists have endeavored to define its role in what's known as *hope theory*. The concept was pioneered by C.R. Snyder, PhD, a professor of psychology and, from 1979 to 2001, director of the graduate training program in clinical psychology at the University of Kansas at Lawrence. Encouraged by the noted psychiatrist Karl Menninger, MD, who once spoke about hope at a conference of the American Psychiatric Association, only to have his concepts derided by his colleagues, Snyder became intrigued with the significance of hope and its role in helping us reach our goals.

Snyder defined hope as based on both willpower and waypower, where one is able not only to create the pathways to realizing a vision, but also to sustain the mental energy and perseverance to travel those pathways effectively. He likened this process to the old adage of "where there's a will, there's a way," citing both elements as critical to success. Today, with the workplace focused on ideas and innovation, rather than merely output, the most successful employees are often the most hopeful. One of the primary reasons is because they see multiple pathways, rather than the only way, to arrive at a successful outcome.

Among the advantages of having a high level of hope (not to be confused with *optimism*, which is a generalized outlook on life independent of one's actions and circumstances), Snyder's research showed that hopeful people are more likely than non-hopeful people to:

- Set a great number of goals
- Have goals which may be more difficult to attain
- Be more successful at reaching their goals
- Have less distress and greater happiness than low-hope people

Belief and Expectation

Adding to the pioneering work of Snyder is Harvard-trained oncologist Jerome Groopman, MD, one of the world's leading researchers on cancer and AIDS. Author of *How Doctors Think* and *The Anatomy of Hope*, Groopman believes that hope is based on two key components: Belief and expectation. More specifically, belief that change is possible, and the expectation that actions of an individual can result in a better future.

As a clinician, Groopman learned that when he gave cancer patients too much information regarding their prognosis, he often robbed them of hopefulness, which he and other scientists believe is instrumental in the healing process. On the other hand, when he gave them too limited information, he ran the risk of creating the false impression that they had little about which to be concerned. It was the challenge of finding that delicate balance between *true hope* and *false hope* that propelled Groopman to advance the research in the field of hope theory.

How Belief Drives Behavior

Although Snyder and Groopman approached hope theory from different perspectives—medicine and psychology—it is clear that both saw it as a combination of feelings and actions. Or, as I witness it in the workplace, it is the interconnection between beliefs and behaviors. If you believe that change is possible and that your actions will have a positive influence on outcomes, you're less likely to defend the status quo and more likely to take positive risks, inspiring others with your behavior. Conversely, if you believe the opposite is true, that change is impossible and it makes absolutely no difference what actions you take, you're apt to stay stuck in mediocrity. Or, as Henry Ford famously put it, "Whether you think you can or think you can't, you're right."

So why are some companies eternally energized with a sense of hopefulness, while others are perpetually stuck in the hope-starved doldrums? Why do some leaders naturally inspire an anything-is-possible confidence in their teams, while others struggle to keep employees even marginally engaged? How do we as leaders learn to systemically foster the positive beliefs that result in effective behaviors? And how can we possibly explain the seemingly squishy subject of hope in the context of leadership and workplace engagement?

Like everything else in the workplace, creating a hope-driven culture starts with the individual influencers, often HR leaders, who have the commitment, credibility, and communications skill to instill these concepts within a broader swath of the organization. Yet, despite numerous studies on the subject of hope and hope theory (as well as its emotional cousins, happiness, and optimism), it's not easy to introduce a subject that has bottom liners and cynics alike spouting, "Hope is not a strategy." Utterly useless.

In my ongoing observations of hope in the workplace, I see a clear pattern emerging, highlighted by the following:

- Most professionals see hope as an essential element of leadership.
- Some professionals feel that they intentionally feed hope in their workplace.
- Few professionals believe that their organizations inspire hopefulness among their employees.

The disconnect is all too obvious. While professionals see the relevance of hope—especially when defined as positive beliefs driving positive behaviors—they're not sure how to spread hope within the employee base, and they certainly don't believe that their organization's leadership is doing a good job inspiring it in any overall sense. So how do we, as change agents, close the hope gap?

The Hope-Starved Culture

For me, it all starts with communication. No surprise, perhaps, since my entire professional background has been focused, either directly or indirectly, on effective communication and the use of language as a workforce motivator. Nowhere was this more apparent than when I was recruited to head media relations and corporate communications for the worldwide television group at Universal Studios. I joined the studio shortly after it had been purchased by Seagram, the spirits company. A massive reorganization was underway and in a span of approximately two years, every business unit—music, motion pictures, theme parks, television, and consumer products—had new management in place.

That was a lot of change for people who had previously worked for the longest-running leadership team in Hollywood history. The divisions had been famously siloed and the reporting lines often had more to do with historic relationships than logic. At my first staff meeting where I centralized the communication functions from five different areas, I discovered a number of my direct reports had worked at the studio for more than twenty years, and yet never met their counterparts. Even though they worked just a building or two away all that time. I was astounded that they had not gotten together for a cup of coffee out of curiosity, at least, if not to share strategies and resources.

But it was when I tried to network outside of my department that I truly hit the brick wall of hopelessness. Throughout the organization, people were so used to keeping their heads down, doing their jobs, and protecting their turf, I had an uphill fight just to get acquainted with my new colleagues. Undeterred, I got in my golf cart—the optimal mode of transportation on the massive Universal back lot—and went out to introduce myself to producers, directors, HR staff, costume designers, and finance executives—essentially, anyone who had a stake in the success of the television group and was willing to spend a few minutes with me. What I discovered was a workforce in the throes of transformation fatigue: Tired of all the management changes, unclear about the future direction of the company, and fearful of the stability of their jobs.

But I also found that, with a bit of encouragement, most people were willing to reignite that spark of hope in the form of engagement and collaboration. They wanted to be on a winning team, even if there were all new players on the field. Once a relationship was established with my studio colleagues, trust and respect weren't far behind. For example, it wasn't long before my team and I were able to convince our theme park counterparts, with their built-in audience of entertainment aficionados, to float a five-story banner from the top of the Jurassic Park ride to promote the premier of a television series. Or to host a swag-filled TV Night for the Universal Studios tour guides so we could update them with fun factoids about our shows that they could pass along to the captive fans on the tram tour, thus increasing audience viewership and loyalty. With some shared success behind us, it was far easier to chart a mutually beneficial course into the future—a course that crossed all departments, functions, and business units.

In a Gallup poll of more than 10,000 workplace participants, the four traits cited most often as what followers wanted from their leaders were compassion, stability, trust, and hope. Needless to say, absent those leadership qualities, as is often the case in the midst of reorganization and ongoing change, employees are often not at their most productive. When Gallup asked workers if their managers and leaders made them feel hopeful about the future, among those who said yes, 69 percent also scored high on a scale of engagement in their work. Of those who said their managers did not instill a sense of hopefulness about their futures, only 1 percent scored high on the engagement measure.

What I understood instinctively in my early days of leadership and what propelled me to solicit face-to-face meetings even with less-than-enthusiastic participants—the critical need for fostering trust and creating a shared plan for the future—has been backed up by numerous research studies. According to Shane Lopez, PhD, business professor at the University of Kansas and author of *Making Hope Happen*, leaders must do three things to create a hope-fueled workplace:

- Create and sustain excitement about the future.
- Remove existing obstacles to goals and avoid creating new ones.
- Reestablish goals whenever circumstances necessitate.

Language of the Hopeful Leader

There's an old joke: "If you're leading and nobody's following, maybe you're just taking a walk." Not so funny, perhaps, if you're the one attempting to create some followership. I've found that creating specific leadership language that is authentic to your style and culture can go a long way to establishing an engaged following and collaborative culture within the organization. Here is a basis for building hope-instilling leadership language that I recommend to my coaching clients. It is easily customized for specific situations with this as a foundation.

"Here's the Vision."

Hope begins with an over-arching purpose and shared dream that everyone holds in their heads and hearts—knowing they can count on each other to pull together in the same direction. That vision has to be so rich in detail that it's imagined by all the team members in a similar way, even as interpreted through their unique perspectives. It has to be so vividly imagined by the way the leader describes it and the way the employees see it in their collective mind's eye that it's already real on some fundamental level. What exactly does success look like? How do your stakeholders (employees, customers, partners) feel about this success? How does success improve their lives, the way everyone works together, the array of exciting new choices and opportunities that result from the accomplishment of this vision?

Don't let that vision go stale or become so taken for granted that it loses its vivid power to focus your team members' commitment. You have to be the constant evangelist of this vision, returning business conversations to the vision regularly to keep it refreshed, alive, relevant, and consistent in everyone's minds.

"This is the Plan."

Along with the vision, hope-driven leaders have a plan, whether they implement it themselves or hand it off to others. Look one year ahead, if not several, and create a specific and detailed picture of the future. Next, start working backwards, quarter by quarter, month by month, week by week. What are the results you're looking for? Be clear and concise about action steps and anticipated outcomes. Set your high-level objectives, critical tasks, milestone markers, and project ownership. Avoid ambiguity and corporate-speak. Everything needs to be crystal clear to everyone on the team. Let your team or task leaders concern themselves with the details of the process and how to meet expectations.

"What Do You Need From Me?"

Check in regularly—at least as often as the milestone markers you've established—to make sure everyone is on task and on time. Know what your people do well and tap into their talents. Find out what each team member needs, directly or through your managers if you're in a large organization, to get the job done effectively. Resolve conflicts quickly and give feedback frequently. Blend kindness with candor but don't waste time sugar-coating reactions or pussy-footing around problems. You will make things worse, and you'll teach others to follow your conflict-avoiding behavior.

"How Can We Improve?"

As a leader, you want to share your perspective on the competitive landscape of your industry with your team as often as possible. When you're an open book, including sharing some of your own mistakes along the way, people feel safe to offer suggestions.

Keep a "we're good, but we can always be better" attitude and encourage everyone to regularly contribute strategies and suggestions to improve the workplace. Sometimes referred to as *kaizen*, literally meaning "change for the good," after the Japanese auto manufacturers' practice of encouraging workers at all levels to offer ideas to offer ideas for increased quality and productivity, ongoing improvement should be part of your organizational DNA.

"Woohoo! Let's Celebrate!"

Celebrate success along the way. Not just the big scores, but also the small wins, including meeting your milestones. Institutionalize celebrations that fit your unique culture. A great example is the Sacred Boomerang Award that Milwaukee-based design firm Kahler Slater uses to welcome back former employees who've returned to the company after time away. Or the FANATI Award, given by web hosting company Rackspace to its own clients that it wants to recognize for outstanding customer service. Even a good old Friday afternoon beer bash just for the heck of it can increase collaboration, camaraderie, and hopefulness.

The Compassionate Culture at Work

In my book, *Capture the Mindshare and the Market Share Will Follow*, I describe one of the most hope-infused organizations I've ever come across in my research. On a daily basis, the staff at the New Mexico hospital, San Juan Regional Medical Center (SJRMC), demonstrates the hopeful principles of excitement about the future, removal of obstacles, and ongoing establishment of new goals. The spirit of hopefulness runs so deep in its corporate culture that you can actually hear it in the hospital's brand language. Its conversations and even its website are so rich in reverence for human beings and their inherent value, it's not hard to see how SJRMC inspires a sense of purpose in its staff that is matched by the hopefulness among its patients. Take a look SJRMC's listing of its core values, which seems to focus almost as much on spirit as it does on science:

Sacred Trust: Everyone who works at the hospital, in any capacity, is considered to have entered a covenant with the patients, patient families, and each other to "do the right thing no matter what." This integrates hope through its commitment to high standards.

Personal Reverence: This value states that each person—whether patient, family, friend, or staff member—must be treated as a unique and valued being. As that happens, tolerance and respect are elevated to a level of "reverence." According to their code, healing implies not only a connection between caregiver and patient, or art and science, but between head and heart. This integrates hope by placing a high value on all human life.

Thoughtful Anticipation: SJRMC thinks of preparation as part of their commitment to excellence. They are continually involved in the process of innovation and problem solution, as well as learning from everything they do and have done in the past. This integrates hope by tying present actions to future success.

Team Accountability: This is the crux of SJRMC's sense of stewardship and obligation to patients, employees, and community, as they believe that teamwork and quality are inextricably linked. This integrates hope by making excellence non-negotiable.

Creative Vitality: More than mere awareness that needs will change and best practices will evolve, Creative Vitality calls for a blend of enthusiastic exploration and rigorous science to answer not only the *how* questions but also the *why* questions. This integrates hope by demonstrating the will to think deeply and act boldly.

"It took us a whole year to come up with those five values and their definitions. And then we spent another year working on how we would hardwire them into our organization," SJRMC's Vice President of Marketing Catherine Zaharko said. Now the values are put to daily use in matters ranging from patient care to housekeeping. Added Beth Volkerding, SJRMC's director of Workforce Excellence, "The values were put together to help us make decisions. For example, Sacred Trust is doing the right thing for the patient—no matter what. We also developed service standards, so if there's a conflict in the value piece, our service standards are like a decision tree. Our service standards are stewardship, efficiency, courtesy, and safety. And you work from the bottom up. So, we would sacrifice money first. We would sacrifice being efficient second. And if we had to sacrifice being courteous, we could, but we never sacrifice safety."

While it's not unusual to hear hospitals and care providers talk about values and service, SJRMC has a deeper sense of purpose at the core which manifests in some very unusual ways. Named a Top 100 Hospital of Choice by the American Alliance of Healthcare Providers and Solient Health's Sixth Most Beautiful Hospitals in the United States, SJRMC recognizes that the physical environment plays a significant role in the hospital's culture. When faced with the need for expansion, it worked hard to help them blend multiple cultures into a workplace that could serve the needs of its patients and staff.

Because SJRMC services not just the Four Corners area where New Mexico meets with Colorado, Utah, and Arizona, but an entire region of vast Ute and Navajo reservations, hospital personnel interact with a wide and culturally diverse population. Many of the Navajos, for instance, live in such remote regions that they may have never set foot inside a hospital before an illness—theirs or a loved one's—brings them to SJRMC. Another group populating region is made up of Christians, mostly Caucasian or Hispanic, many as steeped in their traditions as the Navajo are in theirs. Balancing the needs, beliefs, and social systems of these two very different cultures—both represented in the workforce and among the patients—was a constant juggling act.

One of the issues of greatest concern to the staff, especially since their Sacred Trust value states that "no one here should ever feel unconnected or alone," had to do with the Navajo traditions surrounding death. According to their belief, when a member of the Navajo tribe dies, the spirit of the departed passes out of the body with their last breath. If the spirit—including its most negative traits—has no physical route by which to escape, it will attach itself to someone present. Since there was no exit for trapped spirits within the hospital rooms at San Juan, the Navajo patients preferred to die alone, often with family members and staff waiting down the hall. While the families were accepting of the tradition, the hospital staff found it very difficult not to be ministering to the needs of their patients in their final hours. But the limitations of the hospital's physical layout, along with their patients' dying wishes, left them few options. That is, until the hospital brought in Kahler Slater, with whom they could collaborate until they reached a successful, if challenging, outcome.

The SJRMC team was looking for more than a design for a new hospital wing. Looking for a bridge between cultures and a pathway to a better future for all their constituents, the team members from SJRMC and Kahler Slater met regularly for visioning sessions, along with members of the local community. Their goal was to create an environmental experience that would not only meet the physical needs of patients, but also would be true to the values of the hospital staff. In addition, they wanted a design that honored the spirit of Native American tradition without infringing on the culture and beliefs of the Christian community.

Thanks to open dialogue based on mutual respect, even where very different matters of faith and belief could have made it difficult to cross the cultural divide, many concerns were brought to the forefront. Where there might well have been a battle based on lack of trust and competing agendas, there was genuine respect. When the financial stressors might have killed the aesthetic elements so crucial to the result, the teams worked together and got a sales tax surcharge passed by a community that recognized the value of the project. Jennifer Schlimgen, architect and "Experience Designer" at Kahler Slater, recalls that there had previously been two referendums for the community to share in the costs of the hospital expansion and both had failed.

"It was their third try at getting the tax passed. They created a video with a professional videography, basically making the case for the community as to why the hospital was important. Then they went out to Rotary Clubs, Kiwanis, Chamber of Commerce meetings and sought people out. They did a ton of work to engage the community."

On the third try, the referendum won in a landslide. The result was a new wing with a beautiful spa-like atmosphere including a piano in the entryway, bright sunlight, open spaces, water features, graceful curved walls, and environmental touches not often found in a hospital. There is even a beautifully landscaped meditation garden constructed over the loading dock.

The showcase feature of the new wing was based on the sacred structure of the hogan, which literally means "home place," and in the Navajo tradition, is a circular one-room dwelling. The four posts of the hogan are oriented to the north, south, east, and west. The hospital's hogans were built at intervals throughout the addition. Symbolic of the Navajo traditions, to the Western or Christian eye, they are simply beautiful structures that allow people to gather comfortably for prayer, ceremonies, conversation, or classroom instruction. Said Schlimgen, "We picked the circular form and the four cardinal points in the oculus at the top based on the hogan, but if you didn't know anything about Navajo culture, you would just think it was a pretty, round room. So it satisfies the Navajos, but there is nothing particularly Native American or Navajo about it. It's just how it is."

Another issue that was solved by the new structure was one that had long troubled Navajos who work at the hospital. According to their religious beliefs, they may not pass by a morgue where dead bodies are housed. Yet in the older structure, there was no way to avoid that.

Kahler Slater accommodated this by creating an entrance that only those people who were intentionally entering the morgue need access and others could easily bypass.

Even more remarkable, the collaborating teams were able to determine how to deal with the thorny issue of Navajo tribe members being forced to spend their last moments on life alone. In their ingenious plan for the new wing, Kahler Slater was able to create private rooms with screened-in balconies that open directly to the outside to allow the departing spirits to move heavenward. With that change, both family members and hospital staff could be bedside in the last moments of a patient's life. Thanks to Kahler Slater's skillful design and willing collaboration of SJRMC's engineering staff, they were able to build the overhanging balconies to shade the desert-facing rooms below, keeping the energy costs of cooling and heating the balcony additions manageable.

Although the hospital describes its culture in terms of "Sacred Trust" and "Personal Reverence," it's clear that they mastered Lopez's three tenets of hopeful leadership by sustaining excitement about the future, removing obstacles to success, and establishing and reestablishing goals as needed along the way. From the treatment of staff and patients to the building of screened-in porches, it is clear that they fueled their path to success with an abundant supply of hope.

The last stanza of Dickinson's beautiful—and infinitely hopeful—poem states:

I've heard it in the chillest land
And on the strangest Sea
Yet—never—in Extremity
It asked a crumb—of me.

As an HR leader, hope is arguably your most important deliverable. Hope asks for nothing from us. It is accessible to all, available in abundant supply, and overhead-free. Most of all, it meets humankind's most fundamental hope of all—to know that we are not alone in our efforts to live lives of purpose.

After a successful career at Universal, Sony, and Turner Broadcasting, Libby Gill founded executive coaching and consulting firm, Libby Gill & Company. A sought-after media guest, she has appeared on CNN, MSNBC, NPR, The Today Show, *and in* BusinessWeek, O Magazine, Time, The New York Times, The Wall Street Journal, *and others.*

An award-winning author of four books, including You Unstuck *and* Capture the Mindshare *and* Market Share Will Follow, *Libby's work has been endorsed by business leaders, including Zappos CEO Tony Hsieh, Ken Blanchard and Sony Pictures Television President Andrew Kaplan.*

Her clients include AMC Networks, Avery Dennison, Cisco, Disney-ABC, Kellogg's, Microsoft, Nike, Oracle, PayPal, Royal Caribbean, Safeway, Warner Bros., Wells Fargo.

Libby can be contacted at libby@libbygill.com, or call 310.440.4400.

Chapter 4

Post-Millennial Talent: Steps You Can Take to Reclaim the Future Now

Barbara B. Kamm
President and CEO
Tech CU (Technology Credit Union)

Take just a moment to consider your current staffing plan—especially the recruitment of entry-level candidates. Does it fill you with confidence? Are you certain that as each current entry-level employee is promoted to the next level, thereby vacating the beginner's position, you have a deep enough bench of future candidates already in play somewhere out there in the world—high-quality, qualified young people eager to compete with each other for the opportunity to get their start at your company? And grateful enough for the foot in the door when they do land a job at your company that they will treat the opportunity with respect?

Or is the hum of worry that you may soon not get the talent you need getting louder? While these are entry-level positions, they are still essential to the running of your business. You need an ongoing fresh supply of candidates whom you can count on to respect themselves, their careers, their employers, and your customers. But what are you receiving when you put the word out that you're hiring?

While this chapter is about casting forward to a post-Millennials generation, the Millennials make up our current crop of entry-level employees. So let's take a look at what we're dealing with in terms of generational characteristics, capability, and work ethic:

- A marked sense of individualistic entitlement
- An indifference to conventional performance and workplace standards, such as being at work on time and staying throughout the entire day, focused on the task at hand
- A weakness in basic math and language skills
- A pronounced preference for fun and team activities over the solitude of individual achievement
- A lack of understanding about the competitive, proprietary interests of companies and their secrets
- Short attention spans, exacerbated in many cases by substance abuse
- Finally, the added knowledge, skills, communication, and cultural conflict challenges presented to employers by immigration surges—the effects of which will show up within the decade.

Of course, not every Millennial should be painted with the same brush. But these are trends and commonalities that are all too often used to describe an entire entry-level generation. And we can only look at the future generation *en masse* at this point; it's too early to start picking out the individuals as exceptions to the trends. As employers, can we really expect things to get better unless we take active steps now to prepare future generations for the eventuality of them one day presenting themselves as candidates at our workplaces?

As a society, we have historically assigned the job of preparing children to become productive citizens (which would include becoming dependable employees) to parents and schools. Employers were busy developing the current crop of workers, relatively confident that year after year the social contract would deliver yet another cadre of reasonably equipped candidates for starter jobs. Companies would grow. Society would grow. Generations would be absorbed into the work world, and decades would roll on—with only the usual ebb and flow of projected labor shortages and overabundances that seemed to work themselves out over time.

But now it's different. The struggles we're having as employers to integrate a whole new mindset into our workplace cultures is in large part due to the fact that we have still been assuming the parents and schools have been raising children to be prepared for their adult working lives. Not just skills and work habits, but also attitude and responsibility to an organization larger than themselves and their personal interests.

As it turns out, that is not always the case any longer. What we're experiencing now is an advance warning of what's to come if we don't take a more active role from the very beginning of a child's preparation for adult life.

The struggles you are having right now in this area are the direct result of your predecessor naturally assuming that society will always deliver a reasonable selection of candidates to keep your company running. What will you be dealing with five to twenty years from now? Whether it will still be you personally coping with the recruitment challenges of the day, or it will be your predecessors, you can take steps now to change the future.

Collaborate With Other Employers

As counterintuitive as it may seem, your best advantage in laying down a long-term, community talent development strategy is the very group you may one day compete head-to-head with for those candidates—the other major employers in your community. Looking ahead five to twenty years from now, many of the most valuable steps you can make in advance workforce preparation are geared to creating a community that attracts high-quality workers and their families. You want to prepare an attractive environment that offers people affordable housing, efficient transportation, excellent education, and an array of employment options for spouses and their entry-level working children. No single company can do it alone. For this you need the collaboration and cooperation of your fellow employers, especially if you are a relatively small employer in a field of big, brand name workplaces.

At Technology Credit Union (Tech CU), we may only have 230 employees, but we are long-term partners with many of the big-name, high-tech companies that are the global stars of Silicon Valley. We collaborate under the auspices of such groups as the Silicon Valley Leadership Group (SVLG) to determine what is essential to create a better community overall in the future. We recognize that we all share the same stake in creating a healthy, vibrant, attractive, affordable place to live for both singles and families. Being successful as a region means that we have the right kinds of people to employ in all our companies, that they are happy living here, and that they come home to content families who are also happy to be here—as opposed to yearning for Austin, Miami, or Manhattan.

As a group at SVLG, we identify eight to ten public policy issues, and then we work together to address them through initiatives, special events, studies, awareness campaigns for our politicians, who have come to regard us as an objective brain trust and expert resource. One of our public policy initiatives, for example, has been to find ways to give the educational advantage to underprivileged children in the region. As employers we understand that if we want to have an educated, capable workforce in the very near future (twenty years go by very quickly), we have to help these children now.

No company, no matter the size, could, by itself, take on this kind of large-scale social endeavor that will require fifteen to twenty years to deliver a return on its investment in the community. Nor should any one company be expected to take on this burden. But it's exquisitely appropriate for employers throughout the region to undertake this vision collectively. No single employer takes on all the risk; all employers stand to benefit from the fruits of the vision in due time.

Collaborating with other employers raises our visibility on all fronts in the community. It's impossible to have an effective parade of one. A small company, trying all by itself to get something started in its community, can be easily overlooked—or ignored altogether, for that matter. For instance, an individual employer trying to capture a politician's attention around the fact that California needs 60,000 new baccalaureate graduates every year to stay competitive both nationally and globally might easily be brushed aside. Likewise, no single employer would have much clout in the struggle to allow highly skilled foreign-born students to stay in this country, giving them the opportunity to apply their U.S.-acquired knowledge to U.S. companies (as opposed to our direct competitors abroad). No single employer could expect to successfully lobby for additional funding for STEM (science, technology, engineering, math) programs. But as a collective, a lot can be accomplished.

Working as a team with all the community's significant employers raises even the smallest employers' visibility merely by association. For example, in addition to your own ongoing hiring processes, join a regional job fair where you are able to introduce your own employment value proposition to the assembled job seekers. Throw in with even lighthearted corporate-sponsored community events, such as fun runs and health fairs, and your company's name and logo will appear on banners and t-shirts, raising your company's visibility. The child who sees your logo year after year at the same community event involving Easter egg hunts or turkey trots will one day grow up to be the adult job candidate standing at your door.

Get Involved in Politics

You may be thinking, "If I wanted to get into politics, I would have been a lawyer." But it's been said that even though you might not be interested in politics, politics is most definitely interested in you. This is especially the case in the sphere of the employment world because the workplace is being used as a lever for social change. And it appears that the pace of political intrusion in the workplace is not going to slow down. The legislative decisions that are being made today are molding the individuals who will one day present themselves to you as candidates for a career in your organization.

In HR, every aspect of your work is governed by the outcome of some political battle in the past:

- Wage and hour laws

- Immigration status and the employment of skilled foreign-born employees
- Healthcare
- Internships
- Recruitment, selection, termination
- Retirement
- Education
- Workplace safety
- Environment
- Taxation

Even the cost of regulations of other aspects of your business also impacts your ability to grow your workforce. If, for instance, you have to choose between hiring an additional employee or paying the hardscape tax based on the square footage of your paved parking lot for some obscure EPA water run-off regulation, you will be forced to forgo that additional employee. It's time for you to get familiar with the marble halls of your state and national legislative bodies.

No matter what side you may be on philosophically and politically, your workplace is a social battleground. So while you may not be excited about making the rounds of the elected officials' offices in your state capital and in Washington, you can be fairly certain that "the other side" is making very good use of your politicians' time and attention—and leveraging the fact that you are focused elsewhere. Ultimately the politician will vote on an issue based on his or her understanding that might have been molded by your opposition, without having a clue that that policy position might be antithetical to the best interests of business or your community.

So, like it or not, if you want to have any say in what kind of future workplace is going to be available to you, your employees, even their children and grandchildren, you need to become actively interested in politics.

Your first responsibility here is to make sure your politicians understand the impacts on enterprise that their decisions will have. We can't assume that our representatives fully comprehend the nature of our business—or even the essential pillars of free enterprise. If the competitive, skullduggery nature of politics intimidates you, simply consider yourself part of a consultative team of colleagues who ensure that their elective representatives are fully equipped with the knowledge they need to make a wise, balanced vote. Spend some time in your state capital and in Washington, DC, if you can. (If you can't, visit your officials' local district offices. You are likely to find one near you.) Invest some time courteously educating them on the impacts of pending legislation on your business. Go with like-minded business colleagues, so that you can take advantage of the strength in numbers, as well as gain moral support.

(Don't be disappointed if you end up speaking with staff, and not the principle politician him- or herself. The aides are the ones who are typically crafting the representative's policy anyway. So you will be most effective by educating *that* person. It may not be as glamorous as the chance to talk with the representative, but you will achieve your purpose.)

It's often not appropriate to use your company's clout or coffers to support the campaign of an individual candidate. Identify and support organizations whose activities support your company's best interests. Your local or state chamber of commerce, for instance. Political action committees sponsored by your trade or professional organization would be other choices. Make sure they are serving your best interests, however. Over the years, even trade and professional associations can have their agendas almost imperceptibly hijacked by the political opposition. So don't simply assume by the name of the organization that it has faithfully remained in alignment with the historic position of your profession and industry sector.

Reach Out to Overlooked Populations

If your company currently relies on conventional recruitment mechanisms to source promising candidates for open positions, you may be taking care of your immediate, short-term needs. But five to twenty years from now, those sourcing practices will likely skim over vast numbers of wonderfully qualified, high-potential, would-be candidates who simply needed an extra assist right now.

The HR executive who is thinking ahead is wondering *now* how to identify high-potentials while they're still in grade school, even, and help position them for those first-rung opportunities when they're old enough to compete for the starter jobs. Where will these people acquire the necessary experience for even the most entry-level positions, so that one day the automated tracking system will be able to spot those necessary experiential keywords? Wise business leaders are exploring ways to reach out to young people now to prepare them for the job market that they will eventually join.

Who might those populations be? Children of economically stressed families (immigrants, families on food stamps, foster families, homeless families); high-potential young men and women who need extra mentoring and guidance in navigating the workplace culture; the disabled who would benefit from the new technology and understandings that will lower the barriers between them and career opportunities; military veterans who have much to offer in skills, leadership, discipline, but who need help translating their military experience into civilian offerings; even older men and women who need to extend their careers for a variety of reasons, and need to update their skill sets.

All these groups represent significant promise of talent and drive for the employers. They just need a little extra thought and effort to integrate them into the working population. The return on investment for you: A qualified population of prepared candidates to draw new job candidates from. And those you don't hire will be employed elsewhere, creating a thriving economy that is good for all businesses.

You have a selection of avenues into these populations already in place. Your local chamber of commerce, for instance, is the perfect centralized organization to hold initiatives geared specifically to reach out to these populations on behalf of the entire business community. If your local chamber doesn't already have these programs up and running, as an employer in your community it is appropriate for you to take a leadership role in that endeavor.

In Silicon Valley, we employers support a variety of initiatives both financially and through opportunities for exposure and mentoring. For example, TeenForce is an organization that helps foster children who have aged out of the system at 18 years and must now find their own way—often without any guidance and support at all. TeenForce helps these young people prepare for and land their first jobs. It also provides housing for many of these young adults who are all too often homeless because the state no longer provides financial support to their foster families. Employers help themselves develop a cadre of trained entry-level workers by helping TeenForce with funding, training opportunities, mentorships, etc.

Breakthrough Silicon Valley is another organization we support, which helps disadvantaged youth who don't have a strong and supportive home life. With the help of employers, this organization identifies specific students who have demonstrated an extra desire to achieve and improve their lives. It follows these students through high school, giving them age-appropriate training and experience in becoming promising employees when they graduate.

Employers can and should also work with local community colleges and vocational tech organizations to provide the necessary education to equip young adults with the specific skills needed for jobs in their communities. We are seeing that generic liberal arts degrees often have limited value in helping graduates compete for entry-level openings that have very specific skills requirements. On-the-job training is part of the entry-level experience, of course, but we employers still need candidates to come equipped with at least some of those skills that will help us sustain our competitiveness.

Employers should work in concert with curriculum developers to make sure that graduates enter the work world capable of keeping our local economic machine running. Some regions have an emphasis on specific industries or professions: Farming; healthcare; in the case of Silicon Valley, technology. In addition to the highest levels of education required for the most advanced positions in these fields, there are also millions of jobs requiring the "middle skills" of technical proficiencies that can be provided through a collaboration between employers and educators.

Even though we're primarily focused on Millennials and post-Millennial populations, employers and educators shouldn't overlook older individuals as a population to reclaim for the future. Baby

Boomers and older Generation Xers are working deep into years when previous generations might have been retired. These people are continuing to work for a variety of reasons: They haven't put aside enough money to retire fully; work continues to add relevance and significance to their lives; they're staying busy while they wait for their younger spouses to reach retirement age; they love to stay active and involved in their profession.

These older workers offer companies a wealth of advantages that you want to retain as long as you can. They hold decades of institutional knowledge and invaluable wisdom that can only come from experience. Their work habits and discipline set an example for younger workers. They can provide formal and informal mentoring to the rest of the organization that could mean the difference between keeping highly desirable talent or losing them to your competitor.

Because this chapter is about reclaiming future employee groups, it might seem counterintuitive to "reclaim" a future employee group who would appear to be more grounded in the past. But these older workers have different needs moving into the future. So you want to reclaim them in the context of what will keep them engaged in upcoming years. Give them the training they need and want to keep their skills up to date. When and where you can, provide them with flexible scheduling options, or part-time employment, if they prefer it. However, don't confuse the status of part-time with low-value. These people are likely to be your in-house industry experts and thought leaders. Keep them engaged on the level commensurate with their experience and expertise.

Finally, of course, we have hundreds of thousands of military veterans returning to civilian life. As a population they are reporting difficulty translating their military experience into skills that promise competitive value for civilian employers. Communities that are adjacent to military bases naturally have a high density of veterans to reintroduce into the civilian workplace. But you will find veterans in communities, large and small, throughout the country. Because of their nature as individuals, combined with very valuable training and experience, they uniquely bring discipline, responsibility, attention to detail, respect for hierarchy, dependability, and wonderful leadership acumen. As many of them are Millennials themselves, they offer great role-modeling opportunities to help their civilian peers understand what it means to be responsible in the workplace.

You may be missing out on the advantages they bring to the workplace if you depend on automation to deliver likely candidates to you for consideration. Automated applicant sourcing and tracking systems are typically loaded up with keywords that describe the job at hand, and the necessary job-related skills and experiences to make the average civilian qualified for the position. However, if you know you would benefit from the characteristics common among veterans—and are willing to train for the skill sets upon hiring—you won't be able to count on getting too many veterans' resumes delivered to your inbox.

Use less technical methods to open the channels of conversation between you and the veterans in your market area. Work with the career counselors of your community colleges to help you find potential candidates on campus; hold job fairs and assign recruiters specifically to talk with veterans; open dialogs with the military bases in your state or region—or even nationally—to let them know you welcome conversations with service men and women looking for ways to return to civilian life.

Adjust Your Workplace Culture to Appeal to Future Generations

It is a given across the board that younger generations typically want a different workplace experience than their predecessors. And they feel that they can reasonably expect accommodations to suit their expectations. For instance, they are not so impressed by hierarchies driven by seniority, or even leadership. Respect is earned in their world, rather than conferred by rank. They also have differing opinions about such trivial matters as arriving to work on time, whether they have to show up at all, and protecting intellectual property.

As the employer, you are still the adult in the room, and future generations of employees deserve to develop their careers in workplaces that help them build discipline and maturity as they gain professional experience and skill sets. But there is a balance that must be struck between sustaining standards of behavior and service delivery and becoming open to changing needs and expectations of future generations of employees.

Preparing your workplace now to be an attractive environment for future generations of employees—even the generations starting now—is an opportunity for you to decide what standards really are non-negotiable, and what can be relegated to the past.

The change in standard operating procedures should stand to benefit everyone, not just simply to pander to the preferences of younger generations. For instance, when I assumed the CEO position at Tech CU, complacency ruled the culture. Many employees had been there for a long time, and just their length of service conferred upon them some kind of "can't touch this" celebrity. There was no special sense of urgency in their workdays. Performance suffered, as well as customer service. This culture demoralized our finest employees who naturally assumed that their best efforts were squandered energy.

We had to change our cultural attitude from one that seemed to exist for the benefit of the "one big happy family" expectation of employees to one that focused on serving the customer first. To that end, we had to replace the stagnant non-performers with employees who would work; who would think; who would put in maximum effort; who knew what they were doing; and who wanted to grow and develop in their careers. Employees were given the chance to improve their work habits. But those who passed on the chance were eventually counseled out of the organization.

The necessary mindset shift throughout the culture of the credit union naturally had to incorporate a change in compensation plan. We not only had to change the way we rewarded people, but we also had to use that change as a device to attract the kinds of employees we wanted to work for us.

Prior to the transformation, the company had a tradition of an annual bonus that dictated that 5 percent of an individual's salary would be paid out to everyone if the credit union hit its goals. It was very egalitarian and applied across the board, regardless of performance. We replaced that plan with a pay-for-performance bonus structure that directly rewarded the high performers. Poor performers were eased out over just a few years. As a result, morale among high performers, engagement, and our capability mix became significantly better quickly.

We also had to infuse and reward innovation in our culture. As I look ahead to future generations of prospective employees and essential talent, I have to remind myself that we're in a disruptive marketplace. A third of the younger generation believes that traditional banking institutions (including credit unions) are irrelevant to their lives from the outset. Online money management services such as Apple Pay, prepaid cards, LendingClub.com, etc., are throwing our market offerings into upheaval. So we have to attract younger talent to help us envision ways to stay relevant to our members.

And to do that, we also need to eliminate such expressions as, "We've never done it that way," "We tried it before and it didn't work," and "We've always done it that way." We need a culture that promotes cutting edge thinking, innovation, the bandwidth to change ourselves before change is forced upon us and makes us irrelevant.

To accomplish that transformation toward a more innovation-friendly culture, we have to be willing to revisit standard operating procedures. But that doesn't mean that we give up our position as leaders of our culture. Even though in other workplaces it may be acceptable for younger employees to shuffle into work after they are expected, it is most emphatically *not* acceptable at Tech CU.

We try not to be a hierarchical company, and we welcome innovation from all ranks in the organization. We acknowledge that younger generations value transparency—which is appropriate because we are counting on them in return to contribute to the credit union from a position of owning the future prospects of their workplace. If the credit union is to prosper into the future, the burden of excellent performance is on their shoulders. Everyone owns the responsibility to the future. Nothing is guaranteed or automatically assumed to be secure.

You don't have to give up your performance standards in the spirit of creating a welcoming workplace for a group of people you want to attract in the future. The high standards themselves are a wonderful invitation to your workplace—for the kinds of people you want to attract.

Conclusion

Back in the mid-1980s, when most of today's HR professionals were still children themselves—counting on the adults around them to prepare a world for them to thrive in one day, which would be today—several quotes emerged from popular culture and science that reminded us of our power to exert our influence on the future.

In 1984, the first *Terminator* movie was released. And its organizing theme was this: "The future is not set. There is no fate but what we make for ourselves."

Two years later the space shuttle Challenger exploded upon launch. Among its crew was the young Christa McAuliffe, who had famously said, "I touch the future. I teach."

Companies have always been key in shaping the future of individuals, communities, and countries. There is no aspect of modern life that is not touched in some way by enterprise. Likewise, as employers, we touch the future too. We have within our power to change the fate of individuals—ideally for the much better—as they have the opportunity through us to set goals and realize their potential.

As employers, we touch the future too. We teach. We influence. We change lives. We activate hope in individuals, in families, and in communities. We just have to start doing it sooner.

Barbara B. Kamm recently retired as President and CEO of Tech CU (Technology Credit Union), a $1.9 billion financial institution that serves the technology ecosystem in the San Francisco Bay Area. She has had a long and accomplished career in financial services, including as Chief Administrative Officer of Silicon Valley Bank and as consultant to entrepreneurs, start-up businesses, and venture capitalists on financial, strategic, and operational issues. Among her consulting clients was New Resource Bank of San Francisco, where she advised the Board through a CEO transition and *became a member of their Board, chairing the Directors' Loan Committee and sitting on the Audit Committee. She has a BA from Stanford University and an MBA from Thunderbird School of Global Management. She is also a graduate of the Pacific Coast Banking School and Stanford's Directors' College for Venture-Backed Company Directors.*

Barbara can be reached at bkamm@kammventures.com.

Chapter 5

Leader of the Future: Preparing Millennials for Global Roles

Jeri Darling
President
Darling Global, LLC

Leadership is a changing game. The world we find ourselves in bears little resemblance to the one that spawned scientific management theory and five-year strategic plans. Global is the new normal, and the world is more complex than ever. The term VUCA (volatility, uncertainty, complexity, ambiguity), used in the 1990's by the military to connote an unusually dynamic environment, is now the water we all swim in. It drives what leaders must contend with on a daily basis.

As a result, leaders need new characteristics and skill sets. According to Development Dimensions International, global executive talent development is viewed as the most important business challenge related to globalization. PriceWaterhouse Coopers reports that 60 percent of the CEOs it surveyed plan to increase the number of international assignments as part of their HR strategy. And the United Nations Global Compact reports that 76 percent of the executives interviewed identify global leadership development as critical to their organizations' future success.

This skill set is increasingly required as the norm, but not everyone has it—and it takes a while to develop. The most capable global leaders have typically achieved it through many years of experience. In most companies there are not many of them—which was fine when only a handful were needed. Now, however, we need many. And we need them soon.

These new leaders are likely in their 20's and 30's. As Baby Boomers retire, their roles are increasingly being filled by Millennials—half of whom are already in leadership roles. Without the proper support, these young leaders could easily crash and burn. This chapter explores the changing requirements of leaders as global complexity increases and how to prepare those who will fill these roles in the very near future.

Globalization 2.0 Drives the Conversation of Futurists

Enterprises around the world have become accustomed to operating globally over the last few decades. Most companies source components from overseas manufacturers in multiple locations, service overseas customers, take products to new markets with distinct cultural identities and traditions, participate in globally distributed design teams, negotiate contracts, and make deals with investors and partners around the world.

However, the steady movement of goods, services, finance, data, and people, has reached unimagined levels. One in every three goods now crosses national borders, and more than a third of financial investments are international transactions. By 2025, what the McKinsey Institute calls *global flows* are expected to triple to $85 trillion. To meet the demand of this transformational level of interaction, we need a new level of globally capable talent.

The futurist firm Z-Punkt also predicts several additional fundamental changes that directly speak to the changing context for leaders:

Globalization 2.0: A constantly changing global economy resulting in numerous opportunities and threats as a new middle class materializes in emerging markets.

The digital era: Living and working with digital technology is shifting power from organizations to consumers and employees—particularly younger digital natives—and breaking down divisions between personal and professional life. This will generate unprecedented transparency and compel leaders to act with full sincerity and authenticity. It also supports greater portability and autonomy, as employees can work anywhere, for anyone, at any given time. Currently, 80 percent to 95 percent of knowledge worker time is spent on email, phone calls, or in meetings (both virtual and face-to-face), and the diversity and volume of collaborative demands have doubled due to globalization, matrix structures, and technology.

Demographic changes: A burgeoning and rapidly aging population will transform markets and place pressure on social structures and welfare systems. This will create a shrinking global workforce and drive a war for talent on an unprecedented scale. HR leaders will also face the ever-evolving demands of an intergenerational and multicultural workforce with increasingly diverse attitudes and needs.

Technological convergence: Progress in fields like nanotechnology and biotechnology will transform many areas of our lives, with the greatest advances emerging from the combination of technologies. This will place huge demands on companies to stay ahead of the curve and collaborate closely with competitors on a variety of initiatives, including complex research and development initiatives.

Environmental crisis: Critical natural resources are becoming scarcer, causing leaders to fundamentally rethink their operations to compete.

Individualization and value pluralism: Growing affluence in emerging markets will drive individualistic attitudes in more parts of the world, increasing consumerism and an increasing diversity of needs and preferences.

Observing the new "geography of talent" influenced by these trends, a report by Oxford Economics (a commercial entity of Oxford University's business college) identifies four broad areas where skills will be in greatest demand around the world: 1) Digital skills, 2) agile thinking, 3) interpersonal and communication skills, and 4) global operating skills.

Additionally, a recent multi-country study aimed at helping global organizations understand the most important characteristics of the leader of the future by Accenture Consulting and the Alliance for Strategic Leadership asked high-potential candidates what they see as the future leadership skills that will be required by C-suite leaders. Characteristics such as vision, integrity, focus on results, and ensuring customer satisfaction were seen as factors that have been critical in the past and will continue to be so in the future. However, five key qualities are also viewed as being clearly more important in the future than in the past: 1) Thinking globally, 2) appreciating cultural diversity, 3) demonstrating the intelligent application of new technologies to help the organization, 4) building partnerships and negotiating complex alliances and networks of relationships, and 5) sharing leadership across a fluid network of stakeholders.

These trends all speak to the changing nature of both the "hard" and "soft" aspects of leadership. The global leader's job description is changing quickly along with this evolving context. In response, leaders will need what some have described as a *meta skill set*—one that goes well beyond the standard set of traditional competencies. They will need to function in a very different way. The dominant leader who knows everything, gives direction to everyone, and sets the pace, is over. Leaders now need to reach across cultural divides, connect with individuals who don't necessarily share frames of reference, priorities, or social norms, and bind them with shared goals and solutions that benefit all.

Highly adept global leaders are thus curious, motivated to learn, flexible, respectful, open-minded, and resourceful. They have a true global mindset, a tolerance for ambiguity, resilience, strong cross-cultural competence, and experience in multiple countries. They have what I call *global fluency*—the ability to move natively throughout the world (even if that world is only in cyberspace) and work seamlessly with people of other countries, values, and languages. They listen actively to others and are emotionally open and strongly empathetic. Most importantly, they know themselves well and are able to self-reflect and quickly self-correct.

They increasingly need to be able to function in the moment and figure out very quickly what information is important and what to do with it. They need to be hyper-alert to what is happening around them, be flexible and aware, process information, and make quick decisions if needed. They also need to make connections, know how to get the right people in the room, and be able to influence the thoughts and actions of others indirectly, through influence and support. They need to build trust and create a learning environment. And, in an unpredictable world, to maintain stability and help people stay focused in unexpected situations.

Implications for Millennial Leadership

Companies need globally astute leaders with this unique skill set. In the face of this need, Millennials are the largest demographic group behind Baby Boomers (in fact, 9 percent larger) and will continue to increase as a percentage of the workforce. They now represent 36 percent—and by 2030, will constitute 75 percent—of the workforce. In the immediate term, Generation X is, of course, a feeder pool for global leadership roles, but this is a significantly smaller group. As a result, Millennials will be in line for these key roles very soon, and at an earlier age. They will need focused support and preparation in order to be successful.

The good news is that they are well educated, achievement oriented, and in a number of ways, uniquely qualified for these roles. At the same time, in spite of their advanced educations, many have had a hard time finding the right (or any) job during the recent global recession, or may not have had steady or progressive work experience, or any focused development.

As a generation, Millennials are marked by particular characteristics that make them a very good fit for leadership in companies all over the world, as well as bringing a valuable global worldview to domestic companies with a local focus.

They are tech savvy, team players, and good communicators. They were born onto the world stage, with easy access to information and experience with diverse cultures. They want responsibility and involvement, and want to make a contribution. They care less about where they are on the org chart than they do about an interesting job, with flexibility and autonomy. They are most motivated by access to learning and development, and prefer a coach to a manager. They are also motivated by a larger purpose in the world and believe that their efforts matter.

Millennials also want time for their personal and family life. They represent a shifting of values, away from overwork to a more balanced lifestyle with more meaning and purpose. They come to work more interested in creative contributions and personal fulfillment than in climbing a pre-defined corporate career ladder. They have witnessed that ladder collapse under the feet of their older siblings and parents, and recognize that a self-determined career path, full of experiences that foster growth, will be the best approach for building skill sets that remain relevant over time.

The through lines are systems thinking, relationships, creative collaboration, and acting with the larger community in mind. This represents a shift of focus to what is needed in the larger system, and supports the innovation culture that is so needed today.

Here are a few unique aspects of Millennial "fit" with the requirements of global leadership:

Millennials prefer openness, transparency, and diversity. These are critical attributes that serve global leaders well. This generation commonly has found a way to accommodate cultural differences. Global leadership requires reaching across cultural divides, connecting with individuals who don't share the same frames of reference, bringing together talent from disparate backgrounds, and finding solutions that contribute to the well-being and common interests of all. Because they have grown up in a culture that supports diversity in gender, race, and sexual orientation, Millennials are ideally suited to lead across multiple cultures—national, ethnic, generational, and organizational.

Millennials are accustomed to working within a relational context, and like to work in a collaborative, connected way. The days of the dominant leader who derives power from position are over. The new leader doesn't have to know everything, provide direction to everyone on the team, set the pace, or be the smartest person in the room. In fact, in many circumstances there are no team leaders at all, with leadership coming from everyone in the room. The focus has shifted from a power-based structure to relationship-based leadership where effectiveness is drawn from the ability to be intellectually receptive to ideas from anywhere, emotionally open, and strongly empathetic. In collaborative global teams, the issue is not who is sitting at the head of the table as there is no table. Leadership comes from those who can create the conditions in which others can shine and do their best work.

Millennials thrive in flatter organizations with plenty of opportunity for involvement and influence. They are able to make connections that create new approaches and ways of thinking that challenge the belief systems of their seniors. They don't take no for an answer. Their need to be valued, to grow, and to have a voice means that concrete, specific, and honest feedback—skillfully delivered—should become a regular feature, as opposed to the conventional annual performance review.

Millennials easily establish rapport and trust—even in virtual relationships with people they have never met in person. They are at ease establishing far-flung networks and fostering connections between team members. They want genuine engagement, connection, involvement, and feedback—for themselves and for others.

The role of trust in leading globally is also critical. While trust tends to decline with distance, the adept use of networking technologies demonstrates that challenge can be managed. The ability to build social capital lies in the individual who is a great connector and is most active and generous in sharing ideas, leads, and insights. The ability to establish trust across distance and differences is one that Millennials comfortably master.

Millenials are globally oriented, want to lead, and believe they can make a difference. A Telefonica survey indicates that 61 percent are optimistic about the future, and 74 percent believe they can make a difference in the world. Many are entrepreneurial and have started their own businesses. They are used to embracing diversity, using social media to make new—and stay in touch with old—friends and contacts across the globe. Their business and personal worlds become seamless and support each other.

Strategies to Develop Millennials for Global Leadership

In principle, Millennials are well-positioned to provide the type of leadership that is needed. The opportunity is there to ensure that the elements are in place to get the best from talent within your reach—as your company's reach expands. There are a variety of ways to accelerate their readiness for global leadership roles:

Promote a global mindset across your organization

As noted earlier, there are few organizations that are not global, either in terms of suppliers, customers, resources, financing, data, and/or people. Every company with a website is a global company. However, many do not take the time to make this visible and explicit. Actively formulating internal and external communications from a global perspective, and ensuring that employees are well versed in the global activities of the company, is a start. Take every opportunity to embed your company, and employees, within a truly global frame of reference, including initiatives as basic as attending international conferences and building a network of contacts who can provide you with global information and perspectives. And, make these accessible to your Millennials. Articulate the ways in which your business fits into the larger global matrix of sourcing, manufacturing, marketing, and selling.

Even if your company is relatively local in terms of its services and sourcing, your operations are influenced by other economies and cultures in unexpected ways. If they aren't now, they will be. Perhaps it will be a new community of employees that you will need to access. Or an unforeseen regulation will require collaboration with another country. Or you will source an essential material abroad because it will no longer be available domestically. Or you will enter into a joint venture to take advantage of growing demands for your products and services in an emerging market.

Announce your intentions to create global fluency in your organization

It's not enough to simply operate globally, with the expectation that your people will pick up on this. As a group, Millennials like to know what's going on, why, and what specifically it has to do with them. They also respond to explicitly defined announcements set in a context that will be immediately meaningful precisely to them. Even if your global initiatives may be relatively modest, make them obvious, unmistakable, and irreversible. Offer your communications in multiple languages, delivered across a diversity of platforms so that your message can be accessed the way different cultures want to access it (rather than merely the way *you* want to deliver it).

Help Millennials build career "portfolios"

Global skills can be developed by providing multifaceted developmental strategies and activities over time that escalate in complexity and sophistication. The most effective development experiences for global leadership take place via hands-on experiences, such as expatriation, short-term international assignments, conference travel, participation on teams and task forces, global virtual teams, and domestically working on projects with people of diverse backgrounds. These can be relatively short-term projects and put together in a variety of combinations, adding up to the overall skill set that is needed. This approach also offers much-needed flexibility in terms of cost and efficiency, as the nature of available projects and assignments becomes more *ad hoc*, as well as offering the ability to tailor development to individual needs.

Bearing in mind that Millennials like to understand the context of what they're doing, not only in terms of company needs but also from the perspective of their career path, give them thoughtful developmental assignments that make big-picture sense for both purposes. Again, the word *explicitly* comes into play here. They need to be confident that their next assignment isn't a random hole in the org chart that needs a warm body to plug into. Each new position should carry with it some intrinsic value, even (or especially) when it is a lateral move.

When there is a global component to a new assignment, it's all the more critical that the Millennial and his or her boss focus on what the international aspect entails and what it will mean to the employee's future prospects. Whether they stay with the same company throughout their career (which is unlikely) or take that portfolio with them to future, external opportunities, they will need to be able to tell the story of all their assignments in a way that demonstrates their understanding of the organizational value of their work.

Provide interesting and challenging gigs

Millennials want to move quickly and are hungry for development and direction. "Fascinate me" could very easily be the slogan of this generation. Although some of this distractible energy might be dismissed as the impatience of youth, we do ourselves a disservice if we neglect the fact that they were raised on video games and TV shows with stories that were resolved in 30 minutes, instant texts and tweets, and a world of choice at their fingertips. If they don't like what they see, they need only type in a few keystrokes to serve up something more interesting on a mobile device, or check out what your competitors might be up to.

Maturation toward complex executive roles takes time—no matter how badly Millennials would like to rush their career growth, hitting milestones in rapid succession like a game of connecting the dots. Developing global leadership skills requires more real-life experience than classroom hours. It involves a fundamental transformation, as opposed to simply adding incremental new abilities to the required skill sets. It is only through experience that a new leader can develop the sensitivity, judgment, and savvy necessary to lead in a complex global context.

Provide support for the long haul

The only way high-potential Millennials can develop their full potential is through first-hand exposure to multiple cultures and challenges, and to different world views. And time in job and depth of experience are two of the best predictors of high performance. With international assignments—especially multi-year assignments that require relocation—commitment to the job through to completion is critical. Consequently, the development of global leadership skills should be a combination of real-time and structured learning, including mentoring by senior advisors whom Millennials trust to have their career interests at heart. This trusted relationship will reassure them that they are not languishing out of sight in a far-flung outpost. And senior-level mentors are best positioned to create meaning and context within projects and assignments to ensure that their mentees can see their next career goals and how to get there. Typically mentors will also evangelize on their behalf, which helps ensure that there will be a meaningful position available upon their return.

Also keep in mind their social and emotional needs while abroad. It's not uncommon for loneliness and frustration to set in once the novelty gives way to day-to-day reality. Look for ways to help meet the need for social connection, mutual support, spousal career support, etc., when they are on international assignments.

Provide opportunities to develop emotional intelligence and self-awareness

To deal with the demands of global business, leaders need to know themselves well—their strengths, their weaknesses, their limitations, their triggers, and how others respond to their behavior. They need to be practiced in the parallel abilities of thinking and behaving strategically while managing the relationships and motivations of the people they work with. That kind of self-awareness can take years to ripen.

Global leadership introduces additional layers of complexity. Global leaders need to have a keen sense of timing, an acute awareness of unwritten cultural rules and cues, and be able to achieve results in conditions that are fluid, with a variety of points of view and under unpredictable conditions. They need to be able to re-form and reframe relevant knowledge from previous experiences to generate new and creative solutions, and to deal with complexity and uncertainty on an ongoing basis.

As much as Millennials might crave the opportunity to quickly expand their experience, their emotional intelligence (particularly self-awareness and self-management skills) may not be their best strength yet, and may be an area that requires focused development. As a group they will recognize that these opportunities are coming to them at a younger age than they did for their older counterparts. They may also find themselves in the uncomfortable position of supervising older colleagues in countries where age and status are still very much tied to power.

While a certain amount of emotional intelligence and self-awareness can only be acquired through time and experience, accelerated development strategies can be put in place to support Millennials in finding their way in this critical aspect of leadership. Self-assessments, personality profiles, 360-degree feedback, global leadership assessments, coaching, and other methods of building and accelerating self-awareness are very important. Here again, mentors—particularly returning expats or global executives—can provide a critical perspective, and one that they will value. To their credit, high-potential Millennials as a group are inclined to recognize this developmental need that will require more depth and even emotional risk than the simple accumulation of skills and years. They are typically humble enough to acknowledge that they will benefit from this specially focused coaching and developmental support.

Provide global experience right here at home

Frequently employees and business partners from other countries come to headquarters or regional offices for temporary assignments, meetings, or projects. This can be a great opportunity to start building global awareness among Millennials who aren't necessarily slated for international assignments themselves, or if global projects are not available.

Even when companies say they are "global," there is still often a tendency to mentally place a pin at headquarters, around which everything else is oriented. In fact, the way international employees are welcomed and integrated to headquarters and other key offices can be the difference between a successful engagement and an abject failure. For instance, non-US employees commonly complain about the experience of isolation and loneliness when on assignment in the United States. Americans often eat lunch in their office at their computer and go straight home after work—except for younger staff who might socialize with each other before heading home to an empty apartment. This isolation can come as a shock to visiting colleagues used to livelier meals and after-hours gatherings with friends and colleagues.

Start the preparation of your Millennials before they begin their passport application process by creating ways to support their global awareness at home. Develop a buddy system so they are directly responsible for the orientation and easy entry of international staff at their location. This will allow them to vicariously experience the assimilation process into a new culture. Assign them to projects and task forces working with co-workers from other countries. Encourage development of global relationships online. Put them on projects that require international reading and research. Actually, they probably won't need much encouragement and likely have contacts all over the world already. In this respect they might be way ahead of the company. If so, it will be up to you to catch up with them, and you might benefit from a bit of reverse mentoring.

Show your expat Millennial that they have opportunities to come home to

"Out of sight, out of mind" is an expression familiar to every professional who has had to find a job following a global assignment. That worry can be very distracting when young talent is abroad working hard for your company. As the HR leader, you can implement a thoughtful re-entry program so that you don't lose high-value talent returning with superb experience, that represents a big investment for the company. Your home-based employees will also observe the re-integration of key employees in a way that makes sense. So when their turn comes, they can depart with every confidence that they will receive the same support to re-establish themselves upon their return. You will build their trust, and hopefully their loyalty, as they travel the world on your behalf.

Conclusion

Companies increasingly need experienced and adept global leaders who can deal with the complex and unpredictable world we live and work in. Not only are Millennials the primary candidates for these roles in the future, they are particularly well suited to them. Committing your company to enable them to take on global leadership roles as early in their careers as possible will give you a head start in positioning your enterprise and your emerging talent to compete effectively.

The importance of building a culture that supports the preparation of new leaders is too often underestimated by those in charge of high-potential development. The required skills are best developed in situations that force young leaders to think and act using global competencies, and to internalize them in a way that becomes automatic. They need to develop a global mindset *now* that will allow them to leverage opportunities to open new markets, tap new talent, and address problems and opportunities as they occur.

Traditional executive education settings in which lecture, case analysis, and Socratic dialogue are the primary vehicles to develop these advanced types of leadership skills simply do not work—particularly among Millennials, for whom hands-on and real-life learning, with the close support of caring mentors and coaches, are most effective. Complex skills can only be developed in *experiences* that offer immersion in a global context and enable them to think and act with global perspectives and skills.

Some companies hope their high-potential talent will figure it out on their own. However, this *laissez faire* approach can risk significant misunderstandings, lost business, and a damaged reputation—not to mention a decreased ability to attract and retain young talent. CEOs and HR leaders can get ahead of the game by building a global mindset and creating focused strategies that provide the opportunity for Millennials to become the leaders of the future that we need.

Jeri Darling is President of Darling Global LLC, a firm providing strategic coaching and consultation to achieve outstanding leadership, talent, and organizational performance. She is a trusted advisor to leaders and senior teams focused on developing successful global leaders and excelling in a complex environment.

Jeri has led successful transformation initiatives with diverse global companies and has held senior roles at TRW, BAE Systems, Mercer Delta/Oliver Wyman, and Work in America Institute. She is executive director of the Global Talent Innovation Network, a board member of HR People & Strategy, and adjunct professor at American University. She holds a MA, MBA, and a Professional Coach Certification.

Contact Jeri at jeri@darlingglobal.com or call 301.949.9491.

Chapter 6

The Accelerated Millennial Manager: Preparing a New Generation for Leadership Success

Devon Scheef and Diane Thielfoldt
Principals
The Learning Cafe

Time has a way of getting away from us. And children have a way of growing up before we know it. As HR leaders, that shock hit home with many of us when Millennials began appearing with their job applications and beginner resumes. Really?? Was it that time already? Maybe so, because there they were, in the reception area—with their parents.

Then we returned our focus to our work. When we look up again, they are presenting themselves to us for consideration for leadership roles. How can that be? They haven't been in the workforce for very long, and now they want to be leaders in our organizations? It would appear so, because there they are, with that ambition in their eyes.

No. Correction. It's more of a confident look. A look that says they know they're in demand, even in a rough job market. And if we want to keep them, and keep them engaged, it will have to be up to us. Because they can walk. And they know it. They're well-educated, they're skilled, they're competitively recruited. They are deeply and widely connected, thanks in large part to all the social media that's second nature to them.

If you are like many employers around the world, you are coming to the conclusion that assigning leadership roles to Millennials might actually be a good idea. In fact, you probably have. Fifteen percent of Millennials in the workplace are already in formal leadership roles. They do have value to offer in terms of positioning a company to be competitive in the immediate future. They will help you anticipate and design products and services specifically for history's fastest-growing marketplace—their own. And they will help you attract and keep talent just like them to sustain your organization's competitiveness for years to come.

While it's ill-advised to assume all members of any generation share the same qualities, this younger generation of high-potential performers could benefit your enterprise if you fast-tracked their career path somewhat. Your high-potential Millennials are at home with almost any kind of consumer-level technology you can think of (and some that have probably escaped your notice). Their presence inside the social media world is already deep and broad. They are uniquely driven and self-motivated. They are eager to learn and hungry for coaching. If they are particularly passionate about your specific industry, they are likely to hold a highly energetic, even entrepreneurial interest in the direction your organization is going. And they want to be a part of it in some very meaningful way. If there was ever a generation marked with a shared drive to "have impact" early in their careers, it's this one.

The Millennial candidates you would want to consider for promotion are probably sophisticated beyond their years when it comes to applying their business and industry-specific technical acumen to the forward-moving strategy of your organization. Given the right roles and responsibilities, they can take your company far into a future that they may see more clearly than even you can. And, as far as they're concerned, that's actually okay, because that future is going to be their responsibility soon enough. So they see no point in waiting for some unclear time when someone will deem them seasoned enough to take on a leadership role.

As members of a specific point on a national—even global—timeline of human events, the oldest of this group feel a shared sense of urgency informed by the historic time when they first became aware of their world. They have felt the economic and political roller coaster more acutely than even the Baby Boomers did while growing up. Born between 1977 and 1998, they had parents who likely felt the impacts of the first national rounds of lay-offs, either first- or second-hand. For them, however, the Clinton and GW Bush years rolled under them like gentle ocean swells, with an ever-increasing sense of economic optimism and even entitlement. Remember the New Economy, with its upward line that didn't seem to show any signs of moving downward again? While they may not have understood it directly, they certainly rocked in the soft lap of its luxury. Their older brothers and sisters were bringing home mind-blowing paychecks. And they were waiting for the time to come when it would be their turn.

But then the economic collapse of 2000 was followed by the attacks of September 11, 2001. The attack embedded in their cultural DNA the reminder that nothing is guaranteed. Not even tomorrow. Some parents, brothers, and sisters lost their jobs. Some of them deployed. Some never came home again. At the same time, the parental focus on the Millennials' self-esteem and elevating their children's expectations has created a generational approach to work, commitment, and reward that's historically unique.

All of these events created a "get it while the getting's good" mindset. Combine that with a razor-sharp entrepreneurial attitude and optimistic confidence that comes from driven, encouraging parents. And you have a generation of high performers who aren't so likely to wait ten, fifteen, or twenty years until someone older than they pronounces them "ready" to take on the role of leading others. They want it now. But they also know their limitations. So they want coaching on how to do it. *Now.*

What's in it for employers to accommodate and adapt to a new generation of desirable Millennial managers and keep them on an upward career trajectory?

The aging population is the first answer: Baby Boomers are moving toward retirement. Or they don't expect to retire, but they want to ratchet back their job obligations. Gen Xers are still moving through their career lifecycles. They certainly haven't lost their relevance. Yet. These are the people that Millennials might want to cultivate long and deep relationships with over time. But these are also the individuals who are likely to be moving forward on their own career paths, perhaps changing companies, eventually retiring. So that sense of a long-term return on relationship investment isn't as relevant as it once was for earlier generations who expected to stay with one company their entire careers. Whatever these people have to teach Millennials, Millennials want to learn it now.

The Millennial group is also uniquely suited to anticipating and serving the needs of its own marketplace. That marketplace is rapidly becoming an essential consumer group, with its own purchasing and decision-making ecosystem—made up, of course, of Millennials.

Multiple Strengths of Millennial Managers

Millennial managers are valuable for many reasons. Respondents to our survey rated the following traits as top strengths of this generation:

- They are tech-savvy digital natives who will fearlessly change how we do business.
- They are effortless multitaskers, and can juggle several tasks at the same time. (However, they expect the same of others, which can be challenging.)
- They seamlessly connect and network, and can motivate, inspire, and connect at a personal level with each team member.
- They are adaptable and flexible; they handle changes in direction or plans without negative attitudes or nay-saying.
- They are creative and innovative, and always looking for ways to create new, simpler methods—and they do this in collaboration with others.
- They are inclusive. Millennial managers are sensitive to diversity; they embrace it and value it.

- They are collaborative. Millennial managers are all about cooperation and teamwork. For them, asking for help is an effective use of resources, not a sign of weakness.
- They are go-getters. They work fast and get things done.

As someone who owns the human capital aspect of your organization, you owe it to the future of your company and its people to prepare your youngest for the leadership roles they want and can uniquely fill, even now. Our research has shown, however, that accelerating a Millennial's career isn't exactly a plug-and-play situation that might have been your experience with advancing your more mature talent into managerial roles. Millennials benefit from special handling. To their credit, they know it too. And they welcome added support.

Where Millennials Need Most Support

To fully grasp exactly where Millennials required the extra support in their development, and how their expectations met with the needs of their colleagues and companies, The Learning Café conducted a Millennial Manager Research survey, encompassing over 400 Millennial managers, their managers, peer managers, and team members. HR and business leaders participated, as well. The responses represent the perceptions of all four workplace generations: Silent, Baby Boom, Gen X, and Millennial. Information was gathered via survey, focus groups, and interviews. Participants came from corporations, federal government, not-for-profit, and industry associations.

This quote most succinctly summarizes the findings overall: "Contrary to popular belief, we Millennials are not a group of entitled, narcissistic, technology-obsessed (well, maybe a little technology-obsessed), wave makers. We have been told we have the power to change the world—and we do—and we are changing the world (the green movement, the organic/healthy living trends, the quest to end modern-day slavery and human trafficking, marriage equality…the list goes on). We are a group of individuals who believe we can achieve more than ever imagined and are not afraid to risk everything trying to do so. We are unashamedly discontented with the status quo."

What do you notice about Millennial managers and how they lead?	What comes easily for Millennial managers?	What's difficult or challenging for Millennial managers?
#1 Inclusive and appreciate differences Millennials are sensitive to diversity, embrace it, and value it. They accept the differences among people. *Quote: "We prefer a diversified workplace and are more accepting of differences—our generation is open to non-traditional behaviors and cultural diversity."*	**#1 Understanding and using technology** Millennials are tech savvy digital natives who are changing the way we do business. *Quote: "We have endless resources to learn and apply new concepts. We can do business anywhere. It's not a big deal."*	**#1 Managing older team members** Millennials face a challenge with authority and communicating with older generations, especially when the occasion calls for more structured or formal communication. *Quote: "Smart Millennial leaders incorporate the experience and wisdom of previous generations with the ambition and resourcefulness of their own generation."*
#2 Collaboration and teamwork Millennials exert a greater push for cooperation; they view asking for help as an effective use of resources, not a sign of weakness. *Quote: "My generation of leaders loves teamwork and is willing to spend more time building relationships with our teams. We motivate each other to achieve a common goal."*	**#2 Rapid attention switching (multi-tasking)** Millennials can juggle several balls at the same time, and expect the same of others, which could be challenging. *Quote: "If we can't chat while punching keys, well then we can't gab about the weekend."*	**#2 Gaining credibility and respect** Millennials managers are advised to get organizational tenure and experience before they can make a significant impact. *Quote: "We do not want anything handed to us. We want to prove ourselves and earn our leadership position."*

What do you notice about Millennial managers and how they lead?	What comes easily for Millennial managers?	What's difficult or challenging for Millennial managers?
#3 Go-getters with a sense of urgency Millennials are focused on getting things done, achieving milestones. They are go-getters. *Quote: "We want to make a notable difference in the company in which we lead."*	**#3 Connecting and networking** Millennials are social as a group. They motivate, inspire, and connect at a personal level with each team member. They are comfortable mixing fun with work. They care for the team. *Quote: "This is the generation of communication, exploring, and sharing."*	**#3 Fundamental management skills (delegation for example)** Millennials must still be taught some of the basics: How to conduct a performance review, delegate, and solve conflicts for example. *Quote: "We are all about self-improvement. We are making strides to understand and personalize our leadership style to improve our contributions to our teams and the business."*
#4 Flexible life balance Millennials value life balance, and they try to ensure everyone enjoys it. *Quote: "Contrary to popular belief, we are not a lazy or entitled group."*	**#4 Adaptability and flexibility** Millennials aren't rattled by changes in direction or plans. They can turn on a dime without negative attitudes and naysaying. *Quote: "We see the old way of doing things as a good starting point but certainly not how to sustain the future. We have a strong hold on adaptability."*	**#4 Understanding hierarchy, bureaucracy, and status quo** Older generations view Millennials as resistant toward existing systems and bureaucracy. *Quote: "We want immediate rewards, fast change, and not waiting to pay our dues. We ask for the change we want."*

What do you notice about Millennial managers and how they lead?	What comes easily for Millennial managers?	What's difficult or challenging for Millennial managers?
#5 Informal and casual Older colleagues view the working style of Millennials as casual with informal communication to their superiors and subordinates, too. *Quote: "We reject hierarchical leadership. We consider ourselves to be more on a level playing field with all levels of the organization."*	**#5 Creativity and innovation** Millennials challenge the existing systems, innovate, and create new and simpler methods. They do this in collaboration with others. *Quote: "We will not accept the way things have always been done. It's just too much fun figuring out new ways to do them!"*	**#5 Patience** Millennials are in a hurry. They don't want to wait for results. They seem to get bored pretty easily. *Quote: "We are hungry; we are ready, ambitious, and willing to work."*

These are general characteristics that are unique to this group of employees and their relationships with their coworkers. Depending on the nature of their particular workplace culture, these traits can be problematic to their older colleagues or supervisors. But they aren't insurmountable either. They just require awareness and specific strategies for addressing them as they present themselves as actual problems at work.

Constantly double-check your assumptions. Up until most recently, the acquisition of professional and organizational knowledge typically went hand-in-hand with the accumulation of life experiences that helped a successful employee become a mature leader of people. Granted, no one would ever assume that all senior executives who come up the traditional way are paragons of maturity and emotional intelligence. But let's face it, we tend to expect more considered wisdom from people with senior titles. So when the reverse happens, when people get the senior leader titles before moving through the decades accumulating wisdom that only life experience can bring, we tend to expect a little more maturity from them than we would if they were still in the age-appropriate apprentice levels of their profession and your organization. It's natural for there to be some unexpected disconnects between their professional abilities and their people skills. While everyone needs leadership development and refresher courses throughout their careers, don't forget that your

Millennial managers may have had no management training coming into their new roles.

Bear in mind that they're also open for learning. Since, as a group, they appear to recognize this deficiency in their own skill set, you can count on them being receptive to your coaching.

Raise their visibility internally with specific communication and development initiatives. According to Ernst & Young, there has been a significant shift in younger workers moving into management roles. In the years 2008 through 2013, 87 percent of the Millennial managers surveyed had moved into a management role, versus 38 percent of Gen Y managers and 19 percent of Baby Boomer managers. However, only 5 percent of Millennials are perceived by their colleagues as being prepared to lead. Our own survey confirms this: Millennials need some support in gaining credibility and respect in order to be accepted as leaders.

It's up to the human capital management side of the business to bridge that gap. If you have identified key talent whom you want to develop into leadership positions in an accelerated way, make sure they are known and accepted by the entire organization well in advance of their game-changing promotions. Leverage their energy and enthusiasm to learn. Consider assigning them powerful mentors in leadership levels. But also make sure those mentors are actively sponsoring them for key, visibility-raising projects. Encourage your senior leaders to put Millennial names forward whenever appropriate opportunities arise.

Also consider reversing the relationship by looking to Millennials as potential mentors of their senior leaders. One of the reasons why Millennials are so valuable to your organization is that they bring new knowledge and fresh perspectives. Activate that knowledge by giving them the chance to push it upward as they're acquiring the time-proven leadership and emotional intelligence insights from their leaders. For instance, send them to conferences and other industry meetings where they can gather and then report back the latest information. This approach puts Millennials in front of their senior colleagues, who will benefit from their instruction in a context that is received as reasonable all around. Then, when a Millennial's accelerated promotion is announced, it will make sense to the senior leadership. And they will make room for the Millennial's continued learning.

Raise their visibility externally. Chances are you already know who your high-potential Millennials are, long before you are ready to promote them to their new leadership positions. By the time they attain that promotion, the world is going to want to Google them and get more substantial results than simply their Facebook activities. So use that interim time to develop them as externally recognized key contributors to your organization.

Assign client-facing projects to them, which will introduce them to your customers and external industry partners. Have them work with your public relations team to write white papers and industry journal articles about some cutting-edge aspect of your company's work. Train them in public speaking, and slowing build up their presentation experience so that they're ready for appropriate venues as they move up their own career ladder.

This way, when you announce the promotion to the world, you want the reaction to be, "What a great strategic move." Not, "Who's that?"

Leverage their eagerness to learn for on-the-spot, on-the-go coaching in short spurts. The Millennial generation is marked by its eagerness to receive feedback and learn how to improve on an almost moment-by-moment basis. The time it takes to walk down the hallway with your Millennials could be just enough time to praise for a job well-done, with a quick tip, action step, or insight that will help them improve their performance next time.

If you manage Millennial managers, check in with them more often than you might your more experienced managers. They'll appreciate it, and they probably want to discuss some things. Be specific with your feedback. Newer managers seek directed coaching and specific skill acquisition. Coach them on situational context, too. New managers are more receptive to advice when they understand why. Make sure they understand context, history, and factors they don't yet know about. Help them comprehend that their role is greater than team "lead," friend, or buddy. Get specific, and work with them to create their personalized leadership style.

Teach them how to give and receive feedback in more formal settings. High-potential Millennials are learning on multiple levels, especially in performance feedback meetings. Not only are they learning what you have to teach them, but they're also watching you teach and give feedback. Make sure you model the performance you want them to duplicate. Teach Millennial managers how to ask for feedback. For example, when a Millennial's boss says, "Great job!," make sure the boss is ready to discuss what was especially on point, or what should the Millennial remember to do again the next time a similar situation arises.

Remember that Millennials tend to learn differently. This is a generation that grew up in front of computer and television screens. While older employees might have succeeded with books and manuals, this is a group that does very well with short training videos, a sixty-second YouTube clip on a specific, isolated topic, or infographics. Make it real for them by giving them examples of what to say and how to say it. Scripts and role modeling help them see how a whole manager/direct report conversation can play out from beginning to end. Or even simple tasks involving paperwork that might seem self-evident to us.

As HR leaders, we do our newer managers a disservice by mandating process and supplying forms, but not making sure Millennial managers know how to use them. They're looking for much more specificity and are grateful for (not insulted by) directions and coaching.

Bridge the generation gap. Millennials may need some coaching in working with, and managing, older generations. They tend to question authority, and their informal, team-based approach can be hard for older generations to swallow. They can be seen as resistant toward existing systems or bureaucracy—which is basically true. All parties may need some guidance in finding common ground when it comes to change or lack of change.

Revisit your expectations of how and when work best gets done. According to research by Cisco Systems, on average, 69 percent of Millennials believe that regular office attendance is unnecessary. They might actually be right. Remember how the school year was designed to meet farming needs? The children needed to be available to their families in the summer for chores and harvest. Likewise, the standard 9-5 work day evolved during the industrial era.

It's probably still important that you have your workplace staffed during specific set hours. But it would also be a good idea to take a fresh look at how your work gets done, and whether being present in one's permanently assigned cubicle seat really is essential to productivity and effectiveness.

Some work habits are more conducive to the night shift, which might ultimately be advantageous to your business—especially if a global footprint is part of your strategy. Or you may return to the conclusion that a conventional 9-to-5 schedule works best for your company. But a fresh revisit of the question now and then couldn't hurt. And it will help you articulate your reasoning when your Millennials ask you why; which they will.

Be sure that your fast-tracked Millennial managers receive basic business training that they may have skipped over in their speed to rise professionally. In addition to issues around daily work schedules, you may need to impart some fundamental management skills, such as delegation, conflict management, or even how to conduct a performance review.

You may also discover that you need to address confidentiality, intellectual property, proprietary concerns that you would have expected to be self-evident to any high-potential employee smart enough to be tapped for the fast track. Keep in mind that this is a sharing generation that characteristically feels more at home in a group situation. So they are dynamite in rallying a team around a company project, making everyone feel personally invested in group success. But they are also flummoxed to discover that the CEO is upset that they posted company news on their LinkedIn page before the PR group has readied the press release.

According to the gamification company, Badgeville, 70 percent of Millennials have "friended" a manager or coworkers on Facebook and are "friends" with at least sixteen coworkers. This is the GoToMeeting generation. They grew up using MySpace, then Facebook, FourSquare, SnapChat, Kickstarter, and crowd-sharing. They can wreck a company's reputation or destroy their own careers with one inappropriate post. Without explicit directions not to, this is a generation that might think nothing of taking a picture of the schematics of your latest, very expensively created, design and post it online for group input—the group being members of an external special interest group that may or may not include your competitors. In some geographic areas densely populated with competing companies (Research Triangle and Silicon Valley, for instance), it's not uncommon for young married couples to find themselves working for competing companies. Whoever expected regulating pillow talk to be a mandate for HR?

Don't just assume that they will be mindful of what's secret and what's for public consumption. Be very explicit about what may be discussed outside the walls of the company. Remember the next generation iPhone prototype that was left behind in a Silicon Valley bar and found its way into the pocket of a tech blogger? That can happen to you, too.

Be explicit. And be repetitive. As new people enter your workplace, everyone needs to hear the company policy about discretion and proprietary information again and again, like they've never heard it before.

Encourage innovative thinking, even if it has to mean listening to the same ideas that were rejected fifteen years ago. Every young and enthusiastic high-potential is motivated to put forward ideas for improving the business. And every seasoned, been-there-done-that coworker has probably heard them before. So the exchange that concludes with, "We tried it fifteen years ago; didn't work then, won't work now," has historically been a hard bump in the rites of passage for young up-and-comers throughout the centuries. Things are different now.

The idea that was rejected fifteen years ago might have just been ahead of its time. And now conditions may have changed so much that the newly presented old idea is just the right thing at the right time for moving the business forward. A summary dismissal of the freshly proposed old idea could rob the company of an essential differentiator that's perfect for now.

Instead, encourage your senior leaders to allow ideas to percolate a little bit. They are the ones most likely to have heard those old ideas before, so they are most likely to cut them off with the well-intentioned purpose of saving the company time. (Additionally, they might still be smarting from having their own youthful ideas rejected way back when. Young, confident, fresh Millennials presenting familiar ideas could inadvertently press some long-forgotten emotional buttons.)

Your senior leaders are also the most likely mentors to help the Millennial high-potential with specific tips and strategies for developing an idea into a solid business presentation. Maybe the idea is even worthy of a pilot project or a new line of business in a marketplace that has transformed over time. That old idea that has come and gone repeatedly throughout the years may just be the idea whose time has finally come.

Recruit Millennials' endorsement for organizational initiatives and major decisions. Studies have shown that employees of all ages will accept a difficult business decision if they have been in on the decision-making process from the beginning. As true as that might be across the generations, it is even more markedly so among the Millennials. As a group, they grew up accustomed to being included in many major family decisions. In school, they were typically focused on team and group consensus. They have carried this trait and expectation into the workplace.

Since many Millennials are still at front-line supervisory level at this writing, it is especially important that they be given the chance to align themselves with whatever initiative may be coming from the very top. This way they can evangelize it to their direct reports with authentic enthusiasm. If they are left out of the early decision-making process, it's possible that their resentment will overpower their business judgment, even if it's unconsciously. Their ability to own the organization's initiative and support it could be compromised.

Employees who prefer the command-and-control method to this approach might criticize it as a pandering continuation of an especially pampered childhood. But whatever the origins of this expectation of inclusion may be, wise leadership will regard it as an attribute to be leveraged. Millennials' managers operate within a culture of community and team spirit.

Use that trait wisely and you'll be able to cultivate the support and commitment you need to activate the initiatives you want. Help them feels as though they hold part ownership of the initiative from the start, and they'll see to it that the entire team is rallied around the decision.

Finally, keep your culture going. A youthful corporate culture is one that relishes curiosity and ongoing learning. This is the differentiating key to a competitive enterprise, no matter how old (or young) its executive staff might be.

One trait that Baby Boomers characteristically share with their Millennial counterparts is a youthful outlook on life. This is the common ground that will help all age groups help each other along in everyone's development.

Unify everyone in the shared purpose of your company's mission. Give your entire team opportunities to have fun together—especially in meaningful activities such as community volunteering. Look for ways to dissolve the age group silos, and you will take your company culture far in offering everyone a collegial environment where everyone learns and grows. And everyone recognizes your workplace as their best opportunity to achieve their full potential.

Diane Thielfoldt and Devon Scheef are co-founders of The Learning Café. They channel their business expertise and up-to-the-minute research into exceptionally practical and user-friendly tools, training materials, and presentations. They work with clients to bridge the workplace generation gap, develop outstanding leaders, use personal branding as a unique career development tool, create successful mentoring initiatives, transfer mission-critical knowledge, and grow top talent.

The Learning Café's presentations, training materials and learning experiences have educated thousands of managers and employees. They have proven success in nearly two dozen industries and over 100 organizations from aerospace to insurance, manufacturing to pharmaceutical, and the federal government. Their work has been published or cited in over 80 publications and a college textbook. For more information, visit www.thelearningcafe.net.

Contact Diane Thielfoldt via DianeT@thelearningcafe.net or call 843.471.2374.

Contact Devon Scheef via DevonS@thelearningcafe.net or call 805.494.0124.

Chapter 7

Innovative Performance Management: Leveraging Social Media Technology

Edie Goldberg, PhD
Principal
E.L. Goldberg & Associates

Around the world, millions of workplaces large and small share the same annual or semi-annual dreadful routine—the performance review, which may or may not be expertly linked to a performance management process, which the managers may or may not respect. This exercise in unproductive awkwardness is almost universally despised. It's handled in a variety of ways, from being completely ignored ("We can't slow down long enough to have this discussion now, we're in the middle of a big project.") to being abused ("I can barely remember last week, let alone a whole year of your performance. I tell you what: You write out your own review, and if I agree with it, I'll sign off on it. Don't expect much of a raise this year, though.").

In any case, conventional performance management systems (and their attendant performance review process) typically depend on a single, vertical channel—the relationship between the employer and the manager. The assumption is that the relationship is a stable one, built on mutual respect, trust, communication, and accountability. A secondary assumption is that employees only care about what their manager thinks. Finally, it is assumed that the manager interacts with the employee on a regular basis and is the best (and only required) source of information about the employee's performance. You can see right away what the embedded problems are: These assumptions are flawed echoes of a past workplace culture.

A small handful of employers are pioneering new methods of keeping their employees engaged in a meaningful way, harnessing their energies and intellects to the service of achieving the company's goals. The solution: Social performance management, a technology-based approach to performance management that fosters an ongoing dialogue among all of the company's employees to facilitate sharing of goals and progress against those goals, and timely feedback and recognition from anyone within the company. In this chapter, we'll discuss how organizations can leverage social technology platforms to manage performance in a way that is more meaningful and valuable to the employees and, not coincidentally, more beneficial to the organization.

Why Conventional Performance Management and Review Systems Are Counterproductive

Before we turn our focus to the benefits of social performance management, let's consider the specific reasons why conventional performance management and performance reviews have become anachronistic and fallen out of favor. To be concise, these long-established tools are based on assumptions that are no longer applicable.

They assume that setting goals once a year is an effective way to manage the business.

Traditionally, goals and objectives are set with six- or twelve-month timelines. This may have once been appropriate for a slow-moving company, with lumbering moving parts and deliverables. An employee's job might have the exact same set of requirements over a year's time. In contrast, today's most competitive companies must be agile, even project-oriented, with completions due monthly or quarterly. In fact, according to the *High-Impact Performance Management Research Report* Q3 (2011), by Bersin & Associates, companies that set or adjust goals quarterly or more frequently demonstrate better financial performance than companies that do so less often. High-performing employees consider goals that are set twelve months ago are "so last year." And they crave a rate of feedback that tracks most relevantly to the rate of change within their profession, company, and industry.

They assume that the employees should set goals independently of one another.

While team-based work has been around for centuries, the complexity of work has driven an increase in the amount of collaboration in the contemporary workplace. Organizations are becoming flatter, leaner, and more agile. At the same time, jobs are becoming more complex and more global in scope. All these factors make it more difficult for any one person to do a job in isolation from teammates.

Nearly all organizations employ teams in some manner; whether they are project teams, standing committees, task force, quality circles, self-directed work teams, customer teams, or emergency response teams. The importance of feedback and regular communication within and across teams is magnified by the fact that these teams are often operating both virtually and globally. Some team members may never meet each other in person, which makes it all the more essential that they are confident that they are on track with their individual deliverables that serve team goals.

They assume that the same manager is going to be in place twelve months from now.

Job stability and security are relics of the past, not only for individual contributors but also for their bosses. There is churn throughout every org chart, on all levels. Employees often report that they have several managers over the course of one year. The current manager is asked to track down input from past managers (if they are still with the company), but this *ad hoc* process leads to a review that usually reflects performance for a small portion of the year.

They assume that the manager knows more about what the direct report is doing than the direct report does.

That might have been so when leaders had worked their way up the ranks. But in the modern enterprise that must always hold an entrepreneurial edge in a knowledge worker culture, it's not uncommon for intact-team employees to know more about their work than their newly installed manager, who may be just passing through. Many of those employees—especially Millennials who are more valuable because of their expertise than their years invested in any kind of apprenticeship model of promotion—may actually leapfrog over their boss today to become their boss's boss tomorrow.

They assume that any given employee is working for just one person.

That might have been true in the past. But in today's matrixed organization where cross-functional teams are commonplace, the employee's direct manager will have one perspective on performance, but the other matrixed-manager's opinions are equally important and valid—and may be quite different. How are these opinions taken into account in the traditional review process? Likewise, today's employees may be working more for their colleagues than any formally identified boss up the org chart. In team settings, it's far more important for coworkers to be in sync with each other and each others' needs than to be in the good graces of a distant manager.

They assume an annual or semi-annual pat on the back, or performance correction, is sufficient to motivate employees and retain them.

As hard as it may be to imagine, there are still managers who will tell an employee, "I'll tell you if you're screwing up. If you don't hear from me to the contrary, assume you're doing a good job." That attitude was never an inspiring way to manage high-quality employees. And it certainly won't engage Millennial employees, who famously require ongoing feedback to keep themselves on track and assured that their efforts are well-invested. This is a generation that is used to getting information when they want it; their life has always included the internet, and they expect immediate access to information as a matter of course. And, let's face it, employees of any age are constantly making a stay/leave decision because they have other opportunities. How frequently they are recognized for their work, or getting information about how to have a greater impact, will drive their motivation and desire to stay with the organization.

They assume that employees only care what their manager thinks about their performance.

Today's knowledge workers may be eager to please their immediate bosses. But they are equally—if not more—passionate to know how their peers and other leaders regard their performance. Millennial employees are comfortable asking anyone for feedback, regardless of status. They are a very inclusive generation that values the input of others. They do not see their manager as the only true source for feedback. Furthermore, often managers may not be physically with all of their direct reports. Thus, peers may have much more accurate and specific information about an employee's performance than the manager.

They assume that the managers are reflecting on the performance of employees during the year—and taking notes.

Is the manager really tracking the employee's performance and accomplishments throughout the year? Does that boss really hold the employee's self-interest top of mind as the completion of each project rapidly segues into the next? Or does it all become a blur, which must be forced into focus in time for the next performance appraisal?

They assume that we need to "manage" the performance of knowledge workers.

Performance management is a process that was born out of the Industrial Age. Knowledge workers of today are more educated than ever and have a very different relationship with work. These smart and competent employees want to be inspired, and they want to have an impact. Their needs are quite different from employees in previous generations. Thus, companies need to change their mindset about how management interacts with their employees. In the words of Debbie Cohen, former Chief of People at Mozilla, who has adopted social performance management, "Employees want to be inspired and know they are having an impact. We need to create a dialogue regarding performance. It is about helping them move forward."

So, rather than managing and controlling their employees, leaders need to share their vision with their people, help them to understand what they are trying to achieve and how they can make a difference. Leaders need to provide their direct reports with on-going feedback to help them have the impact everyone desires. Contemporary leaders need to loosen the reins on the command-and-control hierarchy and respect their employees for the value they can bring to the workplace. They need to provide employees with the tools, resources, training, and information they need to do their job well.

They assume that employees will trust that they've been treated fairly upon evaluation.

Somehow low-performing employees still get promoted. Given the small merit increase budgets provided over recent years, high-performing employees are puzzling at the measly raise reflected in their next paycheck. The outcomes of these highly stressful annual events are rarely meaningful, perceived as fair, or welcomed by anyone forced into the conversation.

As with most business processes over the last forty years, automation was considered to be a solution to the resistance that employees and their managers alike felt toward performance management systems. It was assumed that it would speed up a slow, time-consuming process.

True, automation might have helped managers capture a performance record in real time, assuming they stopped what they were doing to make a note of the incident. However, in most cases, it simply reduced the printing of paper forms and improved the ability of HR to track the process.

But automation did nothing to address the real weaknesses of the conventional performance management system. Managers still dread the process of sitting down, writing the review, and then coming face-to-face with their employees as they have to give the feedback in person. Likewise, employees are squirming in their seats, as they feel judged by a manager whose opinion is perhaps not the only opinion they care about. So while automation is nice to have in place, it has not solved the problems of the flawed process that does not engage and motivate employees throughout the entire year.

But social performance management systems do. They have the best potential of leveraging the available technology today—technology that employees use voluntarily, such as Facebook, LinkedIn, Yammer—to address the performance management and engagement needs of today's employee. They offer a platform for ongoing dialogue in real time where employees can ask for, and receive, truly relevant feedback about their performance in a way that's meaningful to them and capturable by the organization's management.

While it may be normal to assume that this is especially attractive to younger workers, it's not exclusive to Millennial employees. It can be perceived as valuable to all employees who see themselves as part of mutually dependent teams, and whose resumes are more portfolios of project accomplishments than job titles.

It's fashionable to look at workplace trends and innovations through the lens of keeping the younger employees engaged in organizational objectives. But let's first look at the characteristics of the 21st Century knowledge worker of any age. Regardless of their age, it's fair to say that high-performing employees know that their career track is not a simple one in which their job security depends on their own high-quality performance and the wisdom of a single person—their direct boss. Anyone in the workplace today is all too familiar with the experience of lay-offs or other shocking changes that are beyond their ability to directly control. And almost everyone—at least among knowledge workers—has at least some experience in social media sites like LinkedIn and Facebook. This technological territory is not the turf of just the Millennials—it's likely to be embraced by knowledge workers of any age.

Naturally, the rise of Millennial employees in the workplace is accelerating the desire to update and upgrade performance management processes. Their native-born familiarity with computers and facility for establishing authentic relationships online feed their demand for more frequent feedback and recognition for the work they do. That said, we shouldn't underestimate the value of these systems to older workers as well, who are equally invested in making sure their performance is up to expectations. While they may not be as demanding of such frequent feedback, high-performing talent of all ages will see the advantages of social performance management to their careers.

Unlike their predecessors who were paid for their time and output, knowledge workers are compensated for their vision, innovation, and the way they use their knowledge to enhance their company's competitive, differentiating factors. And so, as engagement studies have shown, it's essential that they have a line of sight between a clearly articulated company mission and their own efforts within the organization. While their efficiency and effectiveness are still evaluated, they are judged in different ways than an easily quantifiable productivity score. Ongoing feedback, especially meaningful acknowledgement of excellence, when deserved, goes a long way in increasing engagement that shows up in improved innovations, relationships, interdepartmental communication, and mutual support. Today's knowledge workers need that ongoing communication and support from their colleagues.

A positive, communicative team culture, based on trust and respect, gives them the confidence they need to continue growing and providing even more competitive advantages for the company. Knowing that their activities are on the right track and in alignment with the organization's goals is good for the enterprise's competitive interests and reassuring to the employees themselves.

Social Performance Management Replaces Conventional Performance Management

Social performance management allows managers and employees to establish and share goals with each other and track against those goals in real time. It enables individuals (managers, peers, direct reports) to provide feedback and recognize each other when that recognition is most relevant—enabling spontaneity to capture pertinent records at the moment, rather than six to nine months after the fact.

By its very nature of intuitive navigation and the experience of individual ownership of the system, social performance management can be linked to Facebook, LinkedIn, and other social media platforms that individuals use voluntarily, even joyfully, in their discretionary time. Transfer those experiences of real-time dialogue with people whose opinions they care about (team members, project partners, etc.) and your employees will have a resource that will enhance the team culture, promote collaboration, as well as provide a lasting record of their performance against goals and development for future review.

In the context of social performance management, individual contributors working in the same building, or spread around the world, can work closely in a collaborative, transparent culture, where honest on-going feedback and meaningful recognition are given authentically and taken seriously. Recognition made possible with this system drives employee engagement because when individuals are acknowledged for their performance in real time, they feel more valued and are more likely to continue engaging at a higher level of performance.

While social performance management is software-based, and, by necessity, must be supremely easy to use, setting up and implementing such a system is far from *plug-and-play* from the perspective of the C-Suite. Certain critical considerations must be thought through and weighed against your cultural realities before implementation. As with any initiative designed to align employees with the company's goals and provide on-going feedback and recognition, if done poorly you could create more damage to the organization's culture and employee morale than improve the company's performance.

These are the essential questions that will help guide you in making your decision to implement a social performance management system:

Is your culture conducive to a social performance management system?

Size of the company or number of employees in your population are not the issue. What is essential for social performance management success is a culture that is already based on transparency and openness, where people willingly share their goals with others. If you have a hierarchical, closed structure that drives its employee performance through a command-and-control managerial style—or if you have a highly politicized culture where employees must compete with each other for advancement—social performance management is not going to solve your performance management challenges. A low-trust environment will not lend itself to people openly sharing information or provide feedback to improve performance.

On the other hand, some cultures are so relationship-driven that feedback is not often provided for fear that it would damage personal relationships. In these cultures people are not only willing to provide positive feedback and recognition for work well done. This need not be a deterrent from using a social performance management system, but the purpose and intent of providing feedback should be addressed first, before implementing a new system.

If you have a high-trust culture, you can build a frame of reference that helps employees (and managers) understand that constructive feedback comes from a positive place where the individual providing feedback cares for you and wants to help you be as effective as possible. With this frame of reference and a positive intent, social performance management can become a well-utilized process. You must be willing to open your company's culture, communication, and—to some degree—strategy to your employees so they can understand how what they do serves the larger organizational mission. And, for that matter, how the way they help their coworkers do their work enhances collaboration across the organization.

What is the viability of the performance management system that you already have in place?

Do you already have culture alignment and uniform clarity around what your employees and their managers are working to achieve? Or are you, perhaps, thinking social performance management might be the solution to the wrong problem of mutually conflicting organizational strategies and objectives? How well does your current system work today? And precisely how do you expect social performance management to *enhance* it?

Do you know what you're trying to achieve by making your performance management process more social?

When you have the answers to this question, you will be able to clearly decide who "owns" the system. The most cutting-edge solutions in the marketplace allow for employees themselves to own their data in such a way that their records go with them to their next jobs throughout their career. Who gets to see the feedback employees get from their peers? Just the employee? Employee-identified co-workers? The employee's manager?

Does the new system have endorsement from the most senior leadership?

It's not enough for the CEO and other senior leaders to send the message, "Here is your new system, I expect you to use it." They must be willing to use it themselves, even to the point of receiving feedback on their performance from deep within the organization. If they're not using it, people will assume that it's not really important, and it will be consigned to "flavor of the month" status before long.

The CEO and other senior leaders must be able to demonstrate their endorsement of the system by publicly recognizing not only the high performers who have emerged as a result of the system, but also the individuals who are using the system to acknowledge and support each other. Set a recognition system in place that not only calls out the high performers who are hitting their goals or living out the company's values, but also the managers who are using the system the most to develop their direct reports.

The CEO and other senior leaders must also be patient and allow enough time for the change in performance management to take hold. They should expect a two- to three-year implementation process for the use of social performance management to become ingrained as part of the culture. It is more than just a function of habit and frequency of use. It's also a matter of making social performance management a tool used by as many people in the organization as possible. According to a study by Stanford University, an 80 percent participation rate is ideal for being able to expect to see a significant transformation in the company's performance as a result of this new system. So you need to allow time for the entire organization's population to become habituated to the system before you can expect to see a significant transformation in your company's performance. A culture shift takes both time and critical mass.

Is there clarity around the rules of engagement?

This consideration has two components: There should be as few rules as possible. And those few rules should be articulated so that everyone understands.

This system must be owned by the entire workplace population, where they are inspired to develop, share, and support goals that align with corporate priorities. Burdening the social performance management system with rules issued from high up in the org chart effectively takes the system away from the employees and discourages their voluntary participation. Management cannot overestimate the sharing of feedback or recognition, because this form of control will make the system inauthentic. Micro-management would soon lead to censorship and attempts to game the system. Consumer services, such as Amazon, are already experiencing this in their attempts to crowdsource opinions and feedback on their products. As a result, the reviews that accompany many of their product descriptions (especially in the books department) are now taken with a grain of salt.

Human nature being what it is, management imposition of control over the content of social performance sites could easily lead to a certain amount of editing of the feedback content to play the system for political ends and engineer reputations.

How simple can you make the system's accessibility and usability?

Part of the power of this system is that it enables employees to freely and spontaneously support each other in their personal development and goals. Accessing the system should be as easy and as intuitive as sending an email or jumping on Facebook or LinkedIn to participate in a discussion. Any additional level of difficulty takes the energy out of the employees' enthusiasm for contributing. Even if you have employees who have been using computers since they were five, or even younger—as most Millennials will tell you is their experience—your social performance management system has to be easy to use. It should be accessed in just a matter of two or three clicks. Make them go through screen after screen and click after click just to get to the feedback system and you will quickly lose your employees' passion for contributing.

How can you build momentum around the system?

Depending on the size of your company or nature of its industry, you might not be able to roll out your system to the entire company all at once. So how do you give it its best chance of success by starting it out correctly?

Seek out internal evangelists to help you build steam and get the system culturally integrated throughout your organization as quickly as possible. Pick employee groups that are most likely to contain early adapters—departments with a young population, for example, or business units that are based on technological innovations. Look for groups where stories around quick wins can most quickly be created and then disseminated throughout the rest of the organization. Don't overlook the power of "connectors" or "mavens," those individual opinion makers scattered throughout the organization who have a knack for influencing employee opinion.

In addition, you need to ensure that this is not a system that stands alone on a desert island. If the process has no connections to your other talent management processes, it will not be seen by either your leadership or your individual contributors as important and useful. Just as with any performance management process, social or not, this process should link to learning and development, compensation, promotions, etc. Should you incentivize participation through gamification?

This is a subject of much debate. On one hand, the general assumption is that people are especially motivated and excited by the challenge of a fun competition. On the other hand, an argument can be made that turning critical workplace practices into games treats adults as children and cheapens the overall perception of social performance management as a valuable organization and culture tool.

Instead of unifying a company culture across departments, even around the world, toward a shared goal, gamification could conceivably create dysfunctional behavior by having employees compete for "badges," or gift cards, or other tokens of recognition. This would be at the expense of the real focus of getting the work done and meeting company goals through improved individual and team performance.

High-performing talent is intrinsically rewarded for making an impact, achieving challenging goals, and being recognized by their peers and leaders for their accomplishments. By focusing on extrinsic rewards, as is often done with gamification, you run the risk of turning off these intrinsic motivation factors and exciting passion for the prize rather than pride of performance. Quality knowledge workers—the ones you want to attract, retain, and motivate—are not simply turned on by money or gift cards. They have a strong achievement drive. Acknowledge and reward that.

Conclusion

A 2012 study of McKinsey Global Institute reports that two-thirds of the value creation offered by social technologies lies in improving communications and collaboration within and across enterprises. McKinsey estimates that by using social technologies such as those involved in social performance management to increase communications about goals and collaboration in the achievement of goals, companies could see a rise in productivity by knowledge workers of 20 to 25 percent.

This insight comes at a time when researchers are deepening their understanding around the way Millennials as a group crave ongoing feedback on their performance and clear line of sight around their own career path. Combine that emerging need with the ongoing need to keep older high-performing employees engaged, relevant, and functioning at a high capacity, and the potential value to a company that social performance management tools offer becomes apparent.

How we interact with others and share information has changed dramatically with the new technologies available today through both mobile and social applications. We build our professional network on LinkedIn and share our social selves on Facebook. We review local businesses and that dinner we had last night on Yelp. We talk about our latest adventure (or misadventure) on Trip Advisor. We rave about the latest spy thriller on Amazon. And we do it voluntarily and happily. Some might even say addictively. So why not bring that energy into the workplace?

Tools like Yammer and Chatter are bringing social communication to the work environment to increase efficiency and ensure that everyone is working on the most critical priorities. They help companies build agility because employees can see how they're progressing toward goals, and anticipate change because they are more informed. Social performance management helps to provide visibility to individuals regardless of where they work and helps create a sense of accountability to the team and organization when goals are shared.

Goal-setting has long been recognized as a key ingredient for high performance. But today goals are often shared, and it is difficult to know how you are progressing against a goal unless progress is posted publicly for all to see. Social goals setting lets employees share goals, follow and support the goals of coworkers, and collaborate for ongoing efficiency and mutual success.

Through real-time, authentic, mutual goal setting, and support via social performance, co-workers may be able to provide the feedback or recognition that will motivate individuals and entire teams to achieve their goals.

Will this time completely take the place of the more conventional annual performance review and ongoing top-down performance management systems? Probably not, at least not right away. But it will make those conversations more productive and relevant.

Between the changing expectations of the workforce and the fact that organizations are more matrixed and more collaborative than ever before, we simply need new processes to reflect today's business realities. True, technology is only a tool. Used correctly, this technology helps facilitate the many changes in performance management necessary for the process to be more relevant to the employee today and to help drive organizational performance in a dynamic business environment that requires to-the-moment responsiveness and frequent shifting of priorities.

Edie Goldberg, PhD, is the principal of E.L. Goldberg & Associates in Menlo Park, CA. She has specialized in talent management and organization development for over twenty-five years. Her practice is focused on designing HR processes, and programs to attract, engage, develop, and retain employees. Edie has published and presented at numerous conferences on performance management, building management capability, career management, and succession planning. She earned her PhD in Industrial/Organizational Psychology from the University of Albany, SUNY; and her BA and MS in Psychology from San Diego State University. She has served as Chairperson for HR People & Strategy (HRPS).

Contact Edie at 650.854.0854. Or email edie@elgoldberg.com.

Chapter 8

Vision and Substance: The CHRO's Role in Successful CEO Onboarding

Dan Phelan
Former Chief of Staff
GlaxoSmithKline

It was on an overnight flight en route from Philadelphia to London, in the muffled hum of the company jet, when my CEO looked up from his reading, studied me for a few seconds, and then said, "Let's do your performance appraisal."

There seemed to be only one reasonable response, given the circumstances. So I said it, "Okay."

"Do you know what I'm paying you for?" he asked.

"For my judgment," I replied, trying to conceal my unease as to whether this was actually a trick question.

"Right," he said. "I don't care how you run the function; I don't really want to hear about it. I just want it to run smoothly and not hear any complaints about it."

Given my position as CHRO of SmithKline Beecham, his expectations of my role in the company were spot on. But the word *judgment* carries with it multiple responsibilities both deep down into the organization and upward in the extraordinary opportunity to serve as CEO confidant. HR professionals on the career track that will one day bring them to the C-suite discover early in their careers how essential it is for them to demonstrate their strategic acumen, their ability to predict and consider all permutations of any potential decision—especially the ones that aren't obvious to anyone else—and, of course, their absolute trustworthiness and discretion when it comes to being the trusted advisor of their senior leaders.

This is one opportunity to proactively secure the success of the newly appointed (or promoted) chief executive that appears to be overlooked all too often. That opportunity would be assuming the responsibility to start the chief executive on the right foot from even before Day One. The same posture that we assume taking the role of trusted advisor with the CEO can also be duplicated earlier in HR careers as we help onboard new leaders throughout the organization. While the tactics might be slightly different, the principles are the same when it comes to helping senior leaders organize their new roles to the benefit of the company, their organization within the company, and their own careers.

While this isn't necessarily a rare opportunity to influence the future direction of a department, business unit, or entire company, it's an opportunity that is seldomly maximized. And it seems that seizing the opportunity to intentionally and systematically assist the incoming executives gets rarer further up the org chart the potential partnership goes.

The failure rates of new CEOs speak to the need for someone to take ownership of helping them begin their tenure with every chance of successfully guiding the company toward its immediate future. With all the time, focus, and financial investment dedicated to searching for a new CEO ideal for taking the company into its future, one would think that the Board would take special pains to ensure the CEO's success. But according to the *2011 Global CEO Succession Study*, conducted by Booz & Company, companies would do well to take a more proactive role in ensuring the success of their newly placed CEOs. According to the study, 20 percent of CEOs promoted into their new position from within their company aren't successful. And CEOs hired from outside the company are almost twice as likely to be forced out as those promoted from within. Between 2009 and 2011, companies dismissed 35 percent of "outsider" CEOs.

Clearly someone needs to proactively exercise his or her judgment, step up, and assume that relationship with the new CEO—even before that CEO officially takes up the new position. What better person than the CHRO?

The CHRO's influence can begin as early as the actual initiation of the entire search process. If you are in the position to anticipate the pending retirement of the current CEO several years in advance, you can be the one to engage with the Board to develop the succession plan and then search for that CEO's replacement. In that case, you are also perfectly positioned to already have a relationship of trust in place by the time the new CEO assumes the role. (See "Picking the Right Insider for CEO Succession," *Harvard Business Review*, by Dennis Carey, Dan Phelan, and Michael Useem.)

The senior-most HR executive should be valued for his or her judgment, and therefore should always look for opportunities where that judgment can be sought, applied, and valued as essential input in moving the company forward on the best possible strategic path. By taking the proactive initiative to help properly orient the CEO, you will provide the immeasurable value of protecting the company's investment of time, money, and reputation. And you will position yourself as the CEO's trusted advisor who will then routinely seek out your judgment over the course of your working partnership.

As the statistics have shown, there is a big gap to close for the incoming CEO that is critical to the CEO's success. As the CHRO, the role of closing that gap is absolutely appropriate for you to assume, even starting well in advance of the new CEO's first official day. In my experience of onboarding CEOs, I have identified seven crucial areas that the CEO needs to be fully conversant in as he or she takes up the role of the company's chief executive. The sooner you can begin focusing your new CEO on these seven critical areas of vision and substance, the better positioned the new chief executive will be to start his or her tenure with your company on the right foot, consistent with the strategic vision for the future.

Your initial substantive conversations should cover all this ground, naturally. But additionally, an onboarding memo comprehensively attacking each of these subject areas will serve as a roadmap for a focused, one-on-one, onboarding program that results in a deep understanding of the company, its critical stakeholders, the new CEO's strategy for addressing key initiatives, and envisioning the future that the executive is now tasked to deliver.

The Board

CEOs often overlook the need to cultivate strong relationships with the Board members in a positive, proactive way. Likewise, Boards don't always consider it to be their responsibility to ensure the CEO's successful assumption of their role. But they will be the ones who will vote the CEO out if thing don't go well. So, if the CEO doesn't get these relationships correct from the very beginning, nothing else will matter. If the CEO doesn't have great relationships with the Board members on an individual basis, he or she won't have the relationship strength and trust already in place when the need comes to work together to handle the really big issues and crises.

The days of viewing the Board as a necessary evil to be worked with are long past. Using your position as advisor, strategize with the CEO about how best to communicate with the Board members between meetings, to build relationships with them as individuals. How does each Board member want to be communicated with so they feel attached to the CEO as a collaborative partner investing their energies toward shared goals? (Time flies and the next Board meeting has a way of coming up very quickly, without any relationship-building conversations in the interim. To address this for one CEO I worked with, we created a simple checklist with the directors' names in the left column and boxes to tick off every time he made a call to them between meetings. This at-a-glance approach to tracking such a simple task turned out to be very effective in cultivating individual relationships in a balanced way.)

Also work with the CEO to gain an understanding of the Board's composition. Be the one to help the CEO understand in a confidential context who the individuals are: Their sensitivities; their pet concerns; any hot buttons that would affect the CEO's ability to work successfully and adroitly with the Board members themselves. As the CHRO, it's absolutely within your role to appropriately have these conversations with the CEO.

Who is the chairman and what is his or her top issues? Who is slated to retire from the Board soon or within a few years? Who might be ideal candidates to fill those seats when the time comes? Is diversity (race, gender, geographic distribution, industry representation) at the preferred balance? Should the new CEO put succession planning on the docket to work with the Board proactively?

Finally, while helping the CEO understand the Board and its individual players, use this opportunity to brief him or her on the potential crises the Board may be facing. What industry trends are on the horizon that will dominate Board conversations in the upcoming meetings? Is there a merger/acquisition in the works? Is a controversy involving the company about to break into the public arena? Is there contention around a pending decision to enter or leave a particular business or market?

Granted, the CEO should be aware of these last issues before agreeing to accept the position. But by using your confidential one-on-one meetings to invite further discussions on these matters, you are setting the stage for deeper inquiry that the CEO may not feel comfortable exploring with the Board before being fully fluent in all the issues facing the company.

Shareholder Relations

This is the time to brief the CEO on your assessment of shareholder issues, especially in how they might intersect (or collide with) the interests of your employees. Increasingly shareholders are transforming themselves beyond investors with an active interest in the company's financial well-being into activist players in the company's performance—at times contrary to the company's financial best interests.

Know who the big investors are, what their investment strategies tend to be (growth? value?); and what activist issues might be on the immediate horizon. Are investors expressing an increasing interest in human capital issues, such as labor relations? Are they taking an extraordinary interest in executive pay, especially as compared with the median pay in the company? Are you seeing growing evidence of social activism among your shareholders that could scuttle any strategic plans developed within the safe confines of the C-suite?

Brief your CEO on any shareholder concerns, with special attention to the ones that directly impact any executive policies that, in turn, impact the employees.

Senior Management Team

By now, of course, the new CEO will probably have formally met the senior management team. But, just as with the Board members, there are some things that only the CHRO can appropriately say about the individuals in the context of your role as the confidant. Your onboarding conversations are perfect opportunities for the CEO to consider the current composition of the senior team players, how they have worked together in the recent past, and whether this is the configuration and system of executive interaction that the CEO wants to carry forward.

For instance, the expression, *senior management team*, is often a misnomer in that the members report to the CEO from the same level of the org chart, but they may not necessarily collaborate with each other as a team toward mutual goals. They are responsible for widely disparate—often rigidly siloed—functions. The wise CEO often looks for opportunities for this group of individuals to work together toward shared, multiple objectives.

If that's what the CEO wants, then fine. But this is the time to be intentional about the composition of the group that makes up senior management, how the CEO wants them reporting to him or her, and working together.

Other changes in the senior management team are also to be expected. With the introduction of a new CEO, there is a new personality thrown into a previously established group of people who had found a way to work with the previous CEO. With the new leader, the agenda is going to change. Personality issues will arise. The CEO may decide that some members of the current team were excellent for the previous CEO's priorities, but, for some reason, inadequate for the new agenda. Or the CEO decides that what is really needed is an infusion of fresh thinking—with the assumption that new appointments to the team will provide that new energy. That may necessitate the departure of some members on your current senior management team.

This is not just a situation where the new CEO has the luxury of having a selection of mature, considered, senior executives all pulling together for the sake of the company. There is a wide variety of other interplays going on. People will resign, or start planning their exit over the course of the next year or so. In your consultation with the new CEO, you may discover that within a set amount of time, the company's leadership levels must contain certain skills or profiles that don't currently exist. And the two of you will strategize together how you shift the talent balance at the top to help move the company in the direction of future growth.

Clearly, another conversation around succession planning is in order. Make a list of the people who are on the team today, along with their immediate career plans, so that your new CEO can tell at a glance who is within five to ten years of retiring; who is likely to move on because of the new chief executive and who might not be on board with the new directions the company will be taking as a result of the new appointment. What skills, abilities, and expertise must be introduced into the senior mix; and what needs to be removed.

This is also the time for you to identify the up-and-comers who will almost inevitably take their place among the senior ranks. Work with your new CEO to determine how large the future senior management team will eventually be, what its composition will be, and who deep inside the ranks of the organization should be groomed specifically with the goal of preparing them for taking the role you have planned for that person. Don't overlook the opportunity to identify people who are not currently in your company, whom you will want to actively recruit and then place on the path to the senior management team.

Communications

Communications is a great lever for change; it must be used with as much strategic thought as every other component of the new CEO's program. This is the opportunity for the new CEO to create his or her brand, as well as brand the new administration with a menu of specifically designed ideas and themes. People will want to know who the new CEO is, as well as what the new priorities and direction will be. Before your CEO utters a single word beyond the boardroom, use your influence in this onboarding process to engineer the initial communications plan—working in collaboration with your senior-most communications executive.

At the very least, your new CEO will be breaking from the past in some way by the mere act of assuming the new role. What will be the new leader's major themes? Will they be a complete departure from the predecessor's? A celebration of the company's tradition of specific values? A new destiny, with a transformed mission? Even a different set of stakeholders? Identify four or five key themes at the most and create your CEO's messaging around that limited grouping of new ideas, so that all stakeholders can absorb and retain the critical core messages over time.

This is the CEO's opportunity to demonstrate that he or she considers all employees to be business partners who deserve to be spoken to candidly. In addition to framing up the company values, as well as the employee value proposition (what the employees can expect from the company), this is the opportunity for the new leader to demonstrate through actions and messaging that indeed all employees are to be respected as adults in charge of their own career decisions and destiny.

Don't overlook the power of actions and symbolism in ensuring that messaging is consistent throughout the employees' experience of the company and its new leadership. For instance, does the CEO speak passionately about everyone having an equal voice and being equally valuable to the organization, and then retreat to a clubby, carpeted, freshly decorated top-floor executive suite, with its own private dining room and full-time chef? While everyone else must work in a noisy, echoing rabbit's warren of aging cubicles? Is trust a core theme of the new leadership, but freshly laid-off employees are escorted off the premises by security guards? Look for the messaging disconnects in these kinds of experiences, and work with the new CEO to close those gaps.

Finally, bear in mind that communication is also about languaging—and languages. However excited the new CEO might be about the new strategies that are about to be launched, your position as the CHRO is to take care of the feelings of the people tasked to activate those strategies. No one wants to be told that everything they worked for up until the moment when the new CEO took over was worthless or outdated. No one wants to be told that they're "yesterday's news." Even words such as "legacy," seemingly benign, even elegant and dignified, carry the subtle message that this group of employees belongs to yesterday. You know that, and your communications leader knows that. This onboarding process is your chance to make sure that your new CEO watches his or her vocabulary in public pronouncements.

Likewise, the assumption that English is the global language of business risks alienating essential talent throughout communities and markets all over the world. Wherever your company has locations, C-suite messaging must be distributed in their preferred languages.

Incentive Systems

As the CHRO you know that incentive systems drive certain specific behaviors. Those desired behaviors may also change when the new CEO takes the helm and creates a new strategy, goals for a transformed corporate culture, new R&D objectives, or opens new markets. Any shift in strategy almost automatically renders the current incentive system obsolete to some degree. Or at least it creates the occasion for the CHRO and the CEO to consult with each other on how best to make sure the incentives promote the desired behaviors to achieve the new set of strategic outcomes.

Rare is the company today whose fortunes are completely independent of employee initiative. Therefore, if variable pay isn't already in place, this is an excellent time to implement a program that rewards desired behaviors throughout the entire company, from the shop floor all the way up the org chart to the senior leadership team. It's healthy for everyone in the organization to have some pay at risk because it gives them "skin in the game," and makes them feel that they are actually contributing to (and directly benefitting from) the success of the company.

How you implement variable pay depends on your objectives. You can tie the rewards to individual effort, team collaboration, company profits, and mutual support instead of internal competitiveness. Do you incentivize new customer acquisition? Or customer retention? Do you reward performance as measured against your competitors in the industry? Do you reward the individual achievement of such ancillary initiatives, such as smoking cessation or weight loss?

Regardless of what is officially pronounced from the communications department and the C-suite, how your employees are paid trumps any other message coming from the corporation. This CEO onboarding process is the perfect opportunity for the CHRO to review with the new leader which programs might be counterproductive to the new strategy. Work with the CEO to determine what measurements will support the new set of desired behaviors, right attitudes, and supported performance styles to promote the new brand. Subsequently use your expertise, created in collaboration with your CFO, to develop an incentives program that will be consistent throughout the entire company, from the factory floor to the C-suite.

Human Capital Metrics

Many companies don't do a good job measuring what's important to them, not only in the human capital arena but also in their industry space. The questions just don't get asked: How does our performance look versus our competitors' or against other businesses similarly situated (industry, geographically, nationally, lifecycle, etc.)?

Come to the initial CEO onboarding meeting with hard business metrics that provide an unimpeachable snapshot of your human capital profile. This serves to give your CEO rapid understanding of the current state of your employment experience. It also serves to dispel any misperceptions about the health of the engagement culture in your company. (People will want to fill your chief executive's ear with their own stories and spin on the condition of the company culture, naturally in favor of their own best interests. Metrics will help strip away the politics and allow the CEO to quickly understand the state of affairs as objectively as possible.)

- What is your profit per full-time employee (FTE)?
- What are your sales per FTE?
- What are your total compensation costs?
- What are your absenteeism rates?
- What are your costs per hire?
- How much are you spending internally and externally to bring talent aboard?
- What are your turnover rates? Voluntary? Involuntary?
- What are your current engagement scores overall, and how do they compare with the previous set of scores?
- How do these results compare with your competitors' results? How do they compare with your desired results?

If you have an effective human resources information system, you should have this data easily available. If not, use whatever advance notice that you have to gather as much of this information as possible. Pulse surveys administered immediately before the CEO's arrival will also provide that absolute latest snapshot of employee attitudes and opinions.

Ensure that your metrics report is tailored to the CEO's personal interests by researching past press releases and articles or books with his or her byline. If, for instance, in the CEO's last position, there was a CEO-endorsed wellness campaign, find a way to statistically capture the current state of wellness or health habits of your people. Even if this isn't a burning issue for the CEO in the new role, you are demonstrating through your actions that you're independently anticipating what might be top areas of interest.

Be sure to share this information with your employees, as well as with the CEO.

Leading Change

It's been said that change is the only constant. And CEOs don't wait for a company to have achieved some level of stasis before taking on the corporate leadership role. They just step right into the rapidly moving stream of corporate change. As their confidant and advisor, you can take on the role of easing them into the action, with as little disruption as possible.

If the new CEO has been appointed from within, you can be confident that he or she is already aware of the change initiatives in motion—and most likely concurs. An outside CEO, however, may be tempted to jettison the change plan, driven by the ego need to make a mark early and unmistakably. As the advisor, your job will be to talk that person down from that ambition—at least until the fundamentals of trust, understanding, and context comprehension are in place.

By the time the CEO is in the chair, the change initiative that had been activated before has already been discussed with the Board. As a result, there is tacit acceptance of whatever plan is in play, at least to some degree. Help the new CEO to embrace the change already in motion but to also brand it with his or her own languaging, initiatives, and symbols.

You want to help the CEO experience a transition that's smooth and grounded. And you want to help the CEO deliver that experience to all the stakeholders, within only a few months' time. This is the time to brief the CEO on the change plan that's already in motion, what the status is in terms of the talent management aspects, and what components of the program might actually conflict with the new CEO's long-term vision. Use this time to make the CEO aware of what potential friction points might exist and how they can be finessed over time to move the company in the right direction without being too immediately disruptive, alienating the employees.

Finally, for a smooth transition to take place, it's essential to have the outgoing CEO enthusiastically supportive of the incoming CEO and vice versa. The messaging from both parties should be broadcast to the stakeholders that there's mutual respect and collaboration in the handoff. The outgoing CEO should warmly welcome and endorse the new

CEO. And, in turn, the new CEO would be wise to graciously share initial ideas and plans with the predecessor, who could have important inside intelligence to pass on to help the successor achieve that essential transition that keeps the company moving forward.

Conclusion

At first glance, these seven agenda times might seem overwhelmingly comprehensive to HR professionals who have always considered the people side of the business to be their main purview. However, we should never overlook the fact that the HR leader's role (no matter where the person sits in the company) is also to serve as the senior-most executive's confidant. And so, it would follow that it's HR's responsibility—and opportunity—to take an active role in ensuring that leader's successful onboarding.

This is especially the case with CEOs. It would seem counterintuitive that the most powerful executive body within any company that is tasked to be strategic routinely drops the ball in the matters of proactively ensuring the success of the expensively recruited new CEO—whether he or she is promoted from within or recruited from the outside. This is, at best, a puzzling abdication of an essential initiative to help the company stay on track for the immediately foreseeable future.

This is an ideal opportunity to take your place as the CEO's trusted advisor even before the position officially commences. You will demonstrate your proactiveness, your ability to think outside the confines of the people department, and anticipate the larger picture needs of your chief executive.

You will demonstrate your judgment. And that is, after all, what you are paid for.

Dan Phelan retired from GlaxoSmithKline in December 2012 after 31 years. He was Senior Advisor to the CEO from 2011 to 2012. From 2008-2010, he was Chief of Staff with global responsibility for Corporate Strategy and Development, Human Resources, Information Technology, Real Estate and Facilities, Environmental Health and Safety, Security and Aviation. He was Senior Vice President, Human Resources from 1994-2008, a member of the Corporate Executive Team from 1994-2010, and has been an advisor to three chief executives.

He is a member of the Board of Directors of TE Connectivity (formerly Tyco Electronics) and is Chairman of the Management Development & Compensation Committee. He is a member of the Board of Directors of Indivior plc (formerly Reckitt Benckiser Pharmaceuticals) and is Chairman of the Remuneration Committee. He is also a member of the Health Care Advisory Board of Computer Sciences Corporation and the Advisory Board of RiseSmart, which offers next-generation outplacement solutions leveraging cloud-based technology.

Dan can be reached via email at dan.j.phelan@gmail.com

Chapter 9

The Empowered CHRO: Leading the HR Department as a Company Within a Company

John W. Sigmon
Chief Human Resources Officer
AARP

In October 2014, Korn Ferry's managing partner Ellie Filler, and her coauthor Dave Ulrich, professor of the University of Michigan's Ross School of Business (and a renowned analyst of the future of the HR profession), gave HR quite the year-end gift. In the white paper they published through the auspices of the Korn Ferry Institute, *CEOs and CHROs: Crucial Allies and Potential Successors*, they drew compelling correlations between the personality characteristics essential to world-class CEO performance and what characteristics are commonly found among equally world-class CHROs. Those characteristics were as follows:

- Task-focused
- Social

- Intellectual
- Participative
- Action-focused
- Flexible
- Complex
- Creative
- Ambiguity-tolerant
- Composed
- Empathic
- Energetic
- Humble
- Confident

Among the extremely small group of HR elites whom they studied, Filler and Ulrich discovered that their characteristics most closely matched the demands that would be made of their CEO counterpart—more closely than their C-suite counterparts in Finance, Operations, Marketing, IT, for instance. Their "bold prediction" (their words, not mine) was that CHROs will step up as significantly viable candidates for the CEO position. And boards would do well to consider their candidacy seriously.

"If future CEOs must manage organizational challenges as much as customers, products, and financial difficulties, then CHROs may uniquely have the skills to move into this role," they wrote. "...Today's CHRO already resembles the CEO on leadership traits as much or more than does any other functional executive."

The authors took great pains to reassert the fact that the CHRO population they studied was the *crème de la crème* indeed. But when you consider the list of characteristics and its implications on the way any high-potential HR executive performs, it's not a huge stretch to draw the inference that a solid grounding in HR leadership characteristics prepares professionals for CEO responsibilities. And those characteristics can be found in high-potential HR professionals throughout the world—not simply in the downy feathered nests of the extreme elite.

But that's only half the story. There is also the matter of experiences—and the actual behaviors that are demanded from CHROs and CEOs alike in their respective roles. This is where sensible, visionary CHROs discover that they are already functioning in the role of CEOs in their own discreet departments. When you stop to think about it, you will see that the HR department most closely replicates the entire corporation. While other departments such as Finance or Public Relations borrow bits and pieces of other departments' functionalities, the HR department encompasses the essential elements of every single other department.

CHROs need a thorough grounding of the cross-functional considerations of their entire company in every aspect of their own initiatives within HR. Consequently, they must perform as CEOs of a full-fledged enterprise within the larger organization. I submit that in addition to cultivating the *characteristics* that best position CHROs for advancement as Filler and Ulrich have indicated, CHROs will benefit by regarding their *experiences, behaviors,* and *accomplishments* as examples of CEO perspectives.

CEO/CHRO corollaries can be found throughout the company. For the purposes of illustration in the limited space allowed in this chapter, I will focus on five different functions and how the CEO posture in addressing these functions equips CHROs for a more substantive, comprehensive career path.

Legal

As this chapter was under development during the summer of 2015, there was a rash of shootings across the country. Each one had its own backstory and tales of the victims and various motivations. But one had a direct tie to HR practices, and how as a profession we owe it to ourselves, each other, and our communities to be more active partners in our companies' legal interests. You may remember it: It was in a small Virginia city where a former employee shot and killed two of his colleagues on live television. The chain of events that led to this horrible moment quickly pointed to a troubled history of past employers. He had left a wake of conflicts, litigation, and EAP referrals. But no former employer told any future employer, "This guy is trouble. Don't hire him."

All across the nation, as the details unfolded on the news and TV footage began to replay over and over again, a handful of employers saw his picture and thought to, "I know that guy." And then, "Could I have done something to prevent this?" The answer is frustratingly ambiguous: Maybe so. Certainly HR isn't to blame for this man's actions, any more than the victims were themselves. And, based on his history, it's safe to assume that he probably would have done something similarly horrible elsewhere—maybe at another workplace. But this one particular set of circumstances with these particular two victims? A well-chosen word along the very lengthy chain of former-employer-to-future-employer recommendations might have sent his life story on a different trajectory, saving a couple of lives in the process.

As with so many business- or workplace-related headlines over the last fifteen years, the question comes up: "Where was HR when the earliest signs were unfolding?" In most recent history, a military version of this question surfaced during the investigation of the 2009 Ft. Hood mass shootings when thirteen army personnel were killed and thirty-three were wounded by an Army major and psychiatrist. In both the Ft. Hood murders and this past summer's tragedy, there had been unmistakable signs for years that the employee was dangerously unstable. And yet, for fear of adverse legal actions, each team of employers or coworkers passed the eventual murderer on to the next workplace. Without a word of warning to each unlucky recipient.

Why? Because as a profession we have collectively agreed that giving the next prospective employer the heads up could get us in legal trouble. You, yourself, probably have received instructions from the Legal department that when a prospective new employer calls, just play it safe and only confirm dates of employment. That keeps any potential legal trouble from setting up shop at your doorstep. Probably nothing bad will happen anyway. The Legal department has given you its blessing. Carry on with your day. Focus on HR areas of concentration that you can better understand and control. Let the experts consider, advise, and consent. Isn't that what wise delegation is all about?

As HR leaders we're expected to delegate—obviously—to the experts. That's the most efficient use of our time and influence. And who is the most irreplaceable expert (certainly no one whose expertise you can duplicate, unless you are an attorney yourself) than your corporate legal counsel?

Given all the potential legal hazards of your company's relationships with your employees, can you really be blamed if you simply assigned your Legal department the burden of fully understanding all the legal ramifications of every single employment situation? You stand to save yourself the trouble of a myriad of missteps from the local levels all the way, quite literally, to the United Nations, if you simply handed this work over to the people who actually enjoy staying on top of the ever-growing tower of rules and regs. This is what they do best. And more likely than not, they are glad to take the legal aspects of HR off your plate. They're unlikely to say no to your request for help because the more control they have from the very beginning, the more they can control the entire company's risk profile.

But there is a difference between *delegate* and *abdicate*. And HR needs to guard against the temptation to hand over the legal functions altogether. As the CHRO, it's still your prerogative to play the last legal decision card—equipped, of course, with the very best legal advice available to you. The final decision is yours.

We're presuming here that the question "What is the right thing to do?" is the shared question for everyone in your corporate culture, with everyone committed equally to doing the *right thing*. But can you be sure that the *right thing* for HR is the same *right thing* for the Legal department? Are you two pursuing the same ends with this question? For the HR department, the *right thing* may be to have a full cadre of top quality talent who can work safely with each other in a mutually supportive culture. For you, the *right thing* could be any initiative that you can take legally to advance the people side of your corporate strategy.

But for Legal, the *right thing* might be any and every prudent action that can be taken to protect the company from the complications and expense of any potential litigation. When you were out of hearing range, the CEO might have once said to General Counsel: "Whatever you do, just keep us out of trouble." That is certainly a reasonable request, and one that Legal can understand. So when you bring an HR question to Legal, the answer you receive might be easily measured against the trouble-reduction yardstick. It won't do you any good if your advisor is mainly thinking about the adverse impact of negative word-of-mouth about an otherwise qualified and very desirable candidate. But *your* mission involves creating a collegial culture of contented coworkers, and a safe community that can sleep at night without worry that a silent former employer just made it easy for a shooter to come to town.

Happily, the daily intersections between HR and Legal are rarely so dramatic in their implications. And frankly no one expects any seemingly insignificant HR/Legal policy such as "don't provide details when a future employer calls about a past employee" to have tragic consequences. So it truly is the smallest daily collaborations between HR and Legal that will have the longest-term impacts.

As the CEO of your HR department, you have the responsibility of getting the legal advice that you need to serve that strategic objectives of both your department and the larger company. No one is expecting you to be an expert in case law, and to know the smallest details of labor laws in every state or country you do business in. Keeping up with the new regulations handed down by the National Labor Relations Board—and avoiding becoming an NLRB test case yourself—can take up almost all of your time. So you need Legal. No doubt about it.

It's up to you to have at your disposal the best expert advice available. Your legal support should be collaborative team of experts, working *with* you to deliver the answers to the questions you ask to serve your needs and the corporate values, not simply the legal discipline of reducing risk exposure. You may actually choose to take on that risk, if the benefits of the positive outcome outweigh the benefits of the risk avoided.

Each legal decision should be ultimately your own—made with the full knowledge of everything that's at stake. The ripple effects of that decision will be yours too. Legal is your friend, but not the boss of you (unless, of course, HR is embedded in the Legal department of your org structure). Wise counsel is just that, wise *counsel.*

Innovation

A key component of every employment brand in today's business world is how safe and inspired employees feel to contribute breakthrough thinking to their daily work. Even though innovation is commonly considered strictly the province of research and development, or the "creative" department, HR owns the *culture* of innovation. Are your employees confident that their ideas will be treated with respect? They won't be shut down with, "It's been tried before?" Their ideas—and the credit—won't be stolen by their peers or managers? That they will be rewarded for venturing out on the innovation limb with weak or half-formed notions that still need cultivating by a larger team? This is where innovation becomes a matter of workplace culture, not simply discreet job descriptions. And, therefore, this is where and why HR owns innovation. Create a culture that fosters innovation and you will add one more cultural component to the workplace that enables individuals to do their best work.

Given the fact that the HR function is so bound by processes and procedures—even among the most free-flowing creative environments—it might seem counterintuitive to assign the CEO of the HR department the added burden of breaking down the walls that constrain revolutionary, break-through thinking. But only HR has the ability to influence the entire community of employees—through the corporate culture that *you* engineer and cultivate with intention and purpose.

A culture of innovation depends on its people trusting each other and creating a safe place for each other to take idea risks. Therefore, as the leader of the human capital side of your business, you are the driver of creating a workplace where deep, meaningful human interaction is possible, hazard-free, and encouraged. You are the person who lays the foundation of a culture where it's universally understood that it's safe to connect, to collaborate, to share, to transform, even, when necessary. Not only is it safe, but it's also expected.

To be responsible for a sustained environment of ground-breaking, original outcomes without any kind of authority to enforce it is the main challenge for HR. Notice I used the word *influence* above. As much as it is inarguably your purview to promote active innovation within your company, innovation is not a lever that you can simply pull on demand. You can't start a stop-watch, ring a bell, set a timer, and announce, "Okay for the next 55 minutes, we shall all ideate. I want to see only good ideas here, people. And...go." (Unless, of course, that's part of a workshop activity in an already innovation-friendly culture, in which case it can actually be fun.)

You already have multiple resources at hand, starting with the currently established innovation pipeline that you can tap at will. Recruit the expertise of your in-house innovation experts and brainstorm ways they can lend their skills and techniques to the rest of the organization. Start by inviting them to partner with you to develop, incubate, test pilot HR offerings, either business unit by business unit, throughout a division or region, or within HR exclusively. It's their job to develop and activate break-through ideas to further corporate interests. Borrow their unique skill sets to benefit the people side of the business.

Boost innovation by consciously looking for ways and methods to maximize the effectiveness of these networks and communities. Design structures and processes to allow people with different ideas, backgrounds, and areas of expertise to interact with each other. Provide opportunities for employees to communicate and collaborate with each other in ways that are outside their normal job functions. Redesign your work station layouts, for instance, to position non-related departments next to each other. If your company has break rooms or cafeterias, lay out the tables in such a way that you can foster happenstance communication and conversation among people who wouldn't otherwise know each other. Remove individually assigned permanent workstations altogether, for that matter. And design common worktables and benches where people simply sit and plug their laptops into outlets to do their work. Every day results in new collaborative pods of coworkers that begin with the question, "Is this seat taken? Mind if I sit here?"

Whether the opportunities are physical space or projects where a diverse group of employees can come together and work collaboratively, these are what London Business School professor Lynda Gratton calls *hot spots of innovation*. HR is in the best position to identify and leverage these "magnets of creativity," where employees of all levels, ages, area expertise, and interests can come together to create new, innovative advances that will benefit the company overall.

Finally, don't overlook the traditional ways that HR can activate cultural transformation—in this case a culture of enhanced innovation.

Identify the competencies most likely to foster a community of trust and breakthrough thinking in your particular company. Work with a cross-functional team (modeling the innovative practices you want to promote within the company culture) to build out the characteristics, accomplishments, and measurements that would support each competency that you have identified as a team.

Set up a recognition and rewards system that continues to promote innovation within a safe, receptive culture. Identify what organizational roles you want to especially promote innovative work styles and to what extent. Establish systems that track and measure behaviors that promote innovation, especially from a management perspective. And then design a recognition and rewards system that promotes those behaviors at the level you want them supported in your culture.

Use the HR department itself as an internal lab to promulgate an innovative culture. Design interview questions specifically to elicit from the HR candidates examples of how they exercised innovation in their last positions. Create cross-functional teams, pulling people from across HR (some of whom don't normally work together), and give them a defined charter to work on. When that project is completed, dismantle that particular team and assemble a new one for a new initiative. Frame these projects as high-prestige opportunities that will bring exposure to the participants.

Customer Service

As we discussed in the introduction of this chapter, our job as the HR leader in the organization is to nurture an environment that makes the greatest use of our most expensive asset—which would be our employees. This single mandate boils down to one thing: Removing the barriers that keep our people from doing their best work. This, in turn, inevitably puts us in the role of customer service. Our people are our customers. And it's our job to serve their needs.

Everyone is someone's customer. We all depend on a mutually beneficial relationship with businesses that will result in relatively predictable, reliable customer service that keeps all partners happy and committed to sustaining a continued relationship. The minute the quality of that customer service trips and stumbles, faith is broken, trust is strained, and customers begin to look for alternatives. So, naturally, the wise companies have a customer service function in place to address those needs and opportunities. But does that mean they are committed to being all things to all people? Absolutely not.

The kind of customer service that you want to offer your entire employee population is based on a defined set of deliverables that can be delivered consistently and dependably. In return, you will attract the right customers and keep the relationships intact.

What do customers want? Universally we all want to know that our purchase decision (in this case: our career decision) will satisfy our need, relieve our pain point, help us achieve our goals, give us what we paid for. We want to know that our investment in the relationship is one that we don't have to make again for the reasonable shelf-life of this decision. We want to know that we will like and identify with the other customers to a reasonable degree—that they make up a community we can be proud to belong to. We want to know that our decision to enter into this relationship won't make us look stupid in front of our friends and family—or potential employers into the future.

The same principles of customer service can and should be applied to the value proposition that HR extends to all your internal customers—in other words, your employees. Decide in advance what kinds of employees/customers you want to attract, what set of promises you can dependably offer them, and what actions would bring those promises to life. For instance, how quickly can your employees expect a response from HR? How many times is your department's phone allowed to ring before someone picks up? Are email or voice mail acceptable to your customer service value proposition? How much self-service is expected of your employees? How much would they tolerate? How many clicks must the employees make online in order to access their employment records? How cheerfully will your HR staff help a baffled employee navigate the dark alleys of your intranet subfolders?

Within reason, of course, your customer service profile is completely up to you. It's driven by the culture and working environment that you want your company to offer your *internal* customers, the kinds of employees (your customers) who are best suited for extending your value proposition to your *external* customers. And what exactly they need in order to do their best work.

You can't make these decisions in a vacuum. You are best served by simply following the basic principles of your customer service department as they practice them every day:

Understand who your customers/employees are in granular detail. While high-value employees want to be "surprised and delighted" by their relationship with their employers at least to some degree, what they need and how they need it delivered varies from population to population. You can choose to deliver those services to them, if you can draw a distinct connection between that service and their performance. Or not. It's your choice. Just be consistent and reliable with the choice you make and how you deliver on that choice.

For instance, while on a tour of the backstage of a Disney theme park once, I was impressed to see that Disney provided additional services to help their "cast members" prepare for their shifts—even to the point of having hair salon services available to them. Do they need shoelaces? The right socks? Did they come without their uniform-specific shirt? Or, did they take a dare at a party last night and shave half their head, while dying the other half purple? Understandably, that is not a Disney-approved look, and corrections must be made.

The management could send these kids home with stern instructions not to come back until they shape up—with their pay docked for the day, and maybe progressive discipline that would lead to their eventual termination. But in the case of this particular property, management recognizes the "profile" of its internal customers, who are barely out their teens, if that. This demographic tends to forget things like socks. And, at this age, it can be awfully hard to resist an appearance-altering dare.

Kids will be kids. And they're learning how to be adults—not always successfully. So, instead of taking on the expense of dismissing them for the day, or forever, Disney chooses to simply make it easier for them to do their work. Disney has self-imposed barriers—appearance standards being chief among them. But in the interest of helping these kids do what they do best, accommodations are anticipated and offered. That's customer service.

Segment out your preferred customers; know what they want; and give it to them. Companies aren't reticent to identify high-value customers and go out of their way to provide a higher standard of service to those individuals. When you're a preferred customer, they make sure you know it. You're given extra points on your credit card. Fewer black-out dates on frequent flyer tickets. Exclusive sales on in-demand merchandise. Lower interest rates. Really great seats at the stadium. Companies extend themselves a little bit further for these customers because they're valuable to stay in relationship with, difficult to acquire, and very expensive to lose and then replace.

The same can be said of your high-potential, most desirable employees. There are categories of talent who are especially difficult to recruit and too valuable to lose. You want to be able to identify them in measurable ways. And you then want to have in place programs, perks, and compensation plans designed specifically to retain them—and to sustain their passion for an ongoing business relationship with you.

Just as customers fit differing profiles, not all high-value, high-potential employees are the same. If they're Millennials, perhaps they'll be attracted to ongoing developmental opportunities, chances to sit in on executive meetings, or assignments with especially valuable mentors. If you want to retain them for the long-term, give them faith that their own long-term investment in their careers with you will pay off.

If they are late-career Baby Boomers, they're still extremely valuable to you. Especially if they carry in their heads essential institutional knowledge that will deplete your company of competitive advantage the minute they walk out the door for the last time. These people probably don't need mentoring, but they might enjoy the opportunity to influence future generations by being the mentor themselves. Or maybe they would appreciate a long, protracted wind-down of their careers, with specifically defined deliverables that will allow them to walk out for the last time satisfied that their job is complete.

Or maybe they don't want to sever ties at all on the last day. In that case, perhaps you can work with your preferred customers in one of those innovation team settings I described above, to create a kind of emeritus program that keeps your retired, but still preferred, customers within easy contact for additional training and development.

The behaviors, solutions, standards, and metrics that you choose should be driven by what is meaningful to your customers and what you reliably commit to sustaining over time.

People will be watching. And they will be talking. Which is always the case when it comes to customer service. When it comes to customer service, you want your word-of-mouth to be positive, with an employee promise that is in alignment with the value proposition of your external consumers—the customers themselves.

Marketing

Customer service is your main relationship-building set of tools to keep your people engaged once they're onboard (after the sale, so to speak). However, your role as CEO of your company's HR function requires you to help establish relationships with your target markets long *before* the sales conversation even begins—in this case, the interview. This is the function that helps you set the tone between your company and your industry, your community, even the future as you introduce your company to your target markets as a possible, eventual employer. HR is an essential brand channel for your entire company; likewise, the skills and techniques that reside within the company's Marketing department are essential for building your company's brand as a desirable place to work. Borrow them freely.

Use the variety of marketing levers already at hand within your company to move your constituents from loyal customers to potential talent. These techniques will help you penetrate markets that might have otherwise been closed to you; create an army of ambassadors who will eventually help you expand the pool of quality candidates likely to apply for positions in your organization; even minimize their time-to-productivity because they begin their first day of work ready to find their way into the company culture since they already know it so well from the outside. They will also help you spot disconnects and discrepancies between the stated brand promise and what is actually delivered. Disconnects between the external brand promise and the internal brand delivery can be devastating to both customer and employee alike. Closing these gaps will serve you well in improving delivery on both the employee value proposition and customer value proposition.

You have most likely had this experience: You are attending a business luncheon at a lavishly appointed hotel ballroom. Appointments and lighting sparkle and gleam. The acoustics are softly cushioned and muffled by thick napery and carpeting. But then the illusion is abruptly destroyed with the opening of a door leading to the service areas. At a glimpse you see blaring light, scuffed white cinderblock walls, stacks of those aluminum lids that two minutes ago kept your salmon over asparagus fresh-out-of-the-oven warm. That discrepancy shocks the senses, but you're not surprised. Of all people, you know all too well that the "back of the house" is always different from the "front of the house."

True, there are practical, safety, and cost reasons to have a staging area for the industrial side of delivering on the customer promise. It's unrealistic to expect otherwise. Still, does the discrepancy have to be that stark? As the HR professional, you see the disconnect and wonder how it disengages the wait staff. Or have they stopped caring altogether? But you're also the customer at this particular moment. And that disconnect also serves to show you what an illusion—what a *lie*—the customer-facing world can be. Consequently, your experience as the hotel's customer is also compromised.

Employees experience that same discrepancy between their knowledge of the company as customers and that first moment when they are experiencing the proverbial back of the house. The illusion is shattered, and they start looking for the other lies. As the HR CEO, you can reduce that experiential gap—even to the point of almost eliminating it altogether:

Conduct a gap analysis of the two value propositions: In recent years experiential marketing has become the favored method for differentiating one company from another company in the similar space. To draw an immediately obvious example: Ritz-Carlton hotels, as compared with, say, Motel 6s. The deliverable is fundamentally the same: A decent night's rest in a safe, comfortable environment. That's the bottom line. But what sets them apart, and legitimizes the difference in their companies' price points, is the nature of the experience each one promises their guests. Guests know what to expect when they book their room. A switching of one set of experiences for the other would come as a horrible shock to some, and a very pleasant surprise to others. That would be the gap.

Where are the gaps between your promised set of experiences to your customers and the delivered set of experiences to your employees? An organization that stands on its values as its main set of deliverables on the customer experience should be able to translate that same set of values for the employee experience. At the Ritz-Carlton, for instance, where the service motto is "ladies and gentlemen serving ladies and gentlemen," the employees have every reason to expect that same high level of interaction between themselves and the HR department. If they don't, the promise is broken, and it won't be long before the service value chain is disrupted and the paying customers feel the disconnect themselves.

Align your internal deliverables with external facing offerings: The transition between external and internal service should be practically seamless. Going back to our example of the hotel ballroom versus the glimpse of the service hallways, true the service hallways must be fitted out to facilitate the free and safe passage of people transporting hot food and sharp objects. And expensive wallpaper will get torn and scuffed if it is lining the industrial hallways. But why not paint the walls a utilitarian version of the color scheme that is in the ballroom? Take the scuffs marks off the paint. Provide receptacles and shelving to keep the passageways clear, safe, and pleasant.

This is a metaphor, of course. The main thing is to show your employees the same philosophies and values in action that you are extending to your external customers.

Remember that job candidates are still your external customers: All transitions carry with them some awkwardness. That transition from outside customer to candidate to employee presents multiple opportunities for your company to fail on its brand promise. Somehow, somewhere, when individuals move from being external customers to candidates, in many companies they lose their prestige that is naturally afforded the outside customer. They somehow become supplicants, needy aspirants for that cherished plum that your recruiters can decide to bestow or withhold. And they are treated accordingly. "Don't call us, we'll call you," sound familiar?

The vast majority of individuals who present themselves as candidates will return to the larger pool of customers. And as the head of your department's marketing function you want to ensure they will stay loyal customers. Does your recruiting department treat them as valued guests while their application is in process? Do they extend the basic common courtesies of providing some kind of status reporting along the way? Granted, your recruiters are dealing with perhaps hundreds of applications. And the experience of one individual—especially one who will eventually end up on the "no" pile—may not command the same valued-guest treatment when the recruiters are faced with a tsunami of eager applicants, all vying for the same position.

The temptation is to treat these candidates as faceless commodities, as opposed to unique human beings. But remind your recruiters that all those people will be customers again. And they deserve the treatment that any customer would reasonably expect based on your company's brand promise.

Close that experiential gap and both your customer service (especially customer retention) and your marketing departments will thank you.

Information Technology

Think IT and HR, and information systems might come to mind. Very tactical. Very nuts and bolts. Reports. Data. Statistics. However, let's look at HR and IT through the lens of your role as the CEO of the HR department, specifically with your mandate of lowering the barriers to peak performance for all your employees. Then IT becomes very exciting indeed. Primarily because, when you do it right, you can remove the last barrier entirely—which is the HR department itself.

In a nutshell, the role of IT inside the HR world is to enable HR to empower employees to get along without you. As this chapter was being written there was a video in circulation that showed how a messy desk of the 1980s—complete with all the clutter of that time: original Macintosh, files, pictures, fax machine, tape recorder, Rolodex, camera, desk drawers, calendar, dictionary, calculator, even framed photo of the family dog—gradually by 2015 on the timeline, the desk transformed into a single surface with one very sleek laptop. Everything else had disappeared. It was either replaced by an app, or an app made the accessory irrelevant. There may not be an app for the stapler, or instance, but why would you need one if you don't work with paper documents anymore?

This is the goal HR should hold for its IT function. IT can clear the decks and remove the clutter and noise that HR by necessity—or by proclivity—still clutters up the daily working life of our people. HR is infamous for getting in the way. It's not that we want to. It's just that in many ways we've had to over the decades. And it's time to take IT beyond record keeping and use it to drive solutions that will streamline our peoples' working days. Even if that makes us disappear like an old unused bottle of mucilage.

Let's look at IT from the perspective that a CEO might. IT facilitates the rapid, timely, accurate exchange of essential information throughout the organization, among all stakeholders, internal outward, and external inward. It's not data for data's sake. It's information that is specifically identified and exchanged to enhance the experience of all the stakeholders in relationship with the company. It improves the relationship today, and it provides the essential insights necessary to predict how to cultivate quality relationships in the future.

As you consider all your technology positioning through the perspective of the CEO department, your driving questions should be beyond cost and address how the technology supports the kind of relationship your customers—in this case your employees—will have with your organization. It's about more than just acquiring the latest whiz-bang, speedy data crunching capability. It's about how the tools at your disposal will enhance customer loyalty and engagement by helping them do their work better, and perhaps, even more enjoyably.

So you have to ask yourself and your IT providers the questions that CEOs would ask—beyond how much the IT system may cost and what its shelf-life may be.

Privacy: What will be our employees' expectations for their privacy, even during their off-hours, if their devices are still in their possession? Does the company have the right to monitor what they say and do at the local bar, for instance, or even as they stand next to their backyard barbeque? Can the employees disable any kind of tracking capability on their devices during their off-hours, assuming that disabling won't harm company property? Can or should the company install similar capability on employees' personal property as a condition of employment?

Customer service: What do you want your IT support systems to say about your customer service philosophy regarding your employees? If you have decided that you want your workplace experience to be a luxurious, high-service environment (like, say, a Nordstrom), do you have human beings in place to act as a sort of concierge for your employees? Are they guided every step of the way so they don't waste precious company or personal time futilely clicking their way through confusing web pages? Or do you want your workplace environment to be more self-service, like, say, Amazon? Is your online portal into the back-office of your company set up automatically to guide the employee through the various steps without the need for human assistance? There is no right or wrong answer here. It's only about what's right and appropriate for the experience that you want the company to offer your people.

Freedom: Remember that old Southwest Airlines tag line, "You are now free to move about the country." Well, as it turns out freedom is never free. It does demand its own set of trade-offs. Can you commit to a company culture that encourages teleworking or some kind of mobile workforce in unspecified geographic locations? Are your company culture and your industry conducive to unleashing your people to work whenever and wherever? Are you able to extend that offer and have the courage to sustain it, even when incidents occur episodically to challenge the wisdom of the idea? Do you have the budget and the will to redesign your physical workspace to support this plan?

As the CEO of your HR department, this level of decision-making and the commitment you must extend to your people involve more complex, higher-altitude envisioning of what value your IT activities can truly bring to your workplace environment. That is the privilege and that is the reward of holding the CEO posture as you make HR decisions that may be dismissed by less visionary colleagues as "just another day at the office."

Conclusion

"What is the future of HR?" This is a question that never seems to settle on a single, once-and-for-all answer. Even such luminaries as Dave Ulrich have built their careers on asking that question, answering it, waiting for a few years, and starting the cycle all over again.

With this new correlation between the two sets of characteristics that are found to be common among both top flight CEOs and CHROs, the dots are connected between the hopes of CHROs who aspire to more and the desires of boards to attract and retain CEOs with the wisdom and emotional intelligence that CHROs bring to the table.

And yet there is plenty of room for growth among the CHROs who don't necessarily aspire to the senior-most ranks of the company. And these correlations are significant to them as well.

As you move up through your career, develop the discipline of reviewing your experiences and gathered wisdom through the lens of the CEO perspective. When you describe your experiences to future recruiters and selection committees, speak to them as a CEO might—not only in terms of financials and outcomes achieved, but also in terms of the holistic dovetailing of all the moving pieces of your organization.

Present yourself as CEO material, even as you develop your HR career and reach for the highest levels of your career. You will be putting the HR profession in an entirely fresh and elevated light. Share the vision with those who will look to you as the one who will lead their company into the future.

John Sigmon is a visionary strategist with nearly twenty years of human resources and business innovation successes across for profit, not for profit, and public sector organizations.

He began his tenure at AARP as an HR business Partner, was later promoted to the VP for HR Consulting Services, and currently is the Chief Human Resources Officer. Prior to his career at AARP, John served as the Director for HR Strategy at both the Library of Congress and the Government Accountability Office, and as the Chief Human Capital Officer at the Federal Election Commission.

John is a frequent contributor and speaker on a variety of topics including, "The Modern HR Environment," "Employer Branding and HR," "Workforce Engagement," *and* "Navigating C-Suite Relationships."

Follow John on Twitter @YourHRIdeas or on LinkedIn www.linkedin.com/in/johnwsigmon

Chapter 10

The Ten Inflection Points of Coaching: Navigating the Successful Leadership Coaching Journey

Ian Ziskin
President
ExecExcel Group

Several years ago, I was sitting in the office of a new coaching client, a CEO who had been hired from outside the company only a few months before. He was telling me about his mission: To transform a highly successful organization with a strong engineering and technology heritage into an even more successful global enterprise. I listened to him describe how flattered and excited he was to be sought after and recruited for this role, his first CEO-level opportunity. He shared how energized he was by the challenges he had encountered early in his tenure, and the ideas he had for leading the large-scale changes required to address the challenges he was anticipating.

It didn't take long, however, for his voice to change and his demeanor to shift from an air of self-confidence and enthusiasm to one of self-doubt and uncertainty. He had received feedback that his leadership style was getting in the way of achieving the mission the Board hired him to execute. That's why the Board asked me to begin working with him, and he knew it. As we talked, he acknowledged that he was becoming increasingly concerned that this CEO role might not really be what he thought it was, and that perhaps he might not be the leader he thought he was either.

Fortunately, the fourteen months we spent together during our coaching engagement yielded positive outcomes—the business strategy and transformation well underway, with this new CEO well regarded and embraced. This experience, as with so many others like it before and since, is characterized by a series of ten critical inflection points during the coaching journey. There is a pattern to the coaching process, a way of seeing around corners to anticipate what key coaching decision makers, purchasers, and clients should expect from their coaching experience. This chapter is intended to help the key decision makers, particularly the first points of contact, such as operating or HR leaders who are buyers of coaching services, think through what they might expect from an effective coaching engagement.

1. Setting the Tone (Expectations)

The first step in the coaching process is where you, the operating or HR leader who purchases coaching services, can add significant value to the coaching engagement. This is the time for you to ask essential questions:

- What are the business and leadership effectiveness challenges that we are trying to address?
- Is coaching the best solution relative to other alternatives?
- What is realistic to achieve and in what timeframe?
- What does success look like? What does failure look like?
- Who should be involved, and what do they need to do to contribute to the coaching client's success?

- What information will be kept confidential between client and coach; what will be shared with others?
- Does the coaching client need remedial help to improve effectiveness and/or developmental support to be prepared for the current role, or bigger, more complex roles?

Any good coach should be setting the tone for the coaching engagement by establishing shared expectations among themselves, the purchasers, and clients of coaching services. Likewise, as the purchaser of, and key point of contact for, coaching services, the ultimate power and responsibility are yours for setting expectations and helping your coaching clients get the most out of their coaching engagements. Ask the right questions and help set the tone up front.

2. Seeing the Wind (Feedback)

Feedback is like the wind. It's there, even when we can't see or hear it. No matter how committed a company is to providing candid, quality feedback to their talent, virtually every coaching client I have worked with wonders whether they are really getting the straight story from their bosses, peers, and direct reports. Likewise, these coaching clients can be confident that they are being talked about.

Not surprisingly, candid and meaningful feedback becomes increasingly rare the higher up the organization leaders rise. Everything is busier, tougher, and more complex. Time and emotional bandwidth for this kind of conversation at senior levels are scarce. Still, it is so needed.

Coaching is about seeking the truth through focused, intentional, and active gathering of feedback, and then, helping the client deal with it constructively. Qualified coaches are skilled at bringing out relevant and often unspoken feedback that most benefits the client and their colleagues, in a confidential and safe manner.

Your job, as the main point of contact and the buyer of coaching services, is to ensure that this process happens.

3. Finding Buried Treasure (Strengths)

In the spirit of gathering constructive feedback, coaches often overlook client strengths because they find it easier to focus on what needs to be improved. Ironically, strengths are what have helped successful clients be successful in the first place. Therefore, understanding and capitalizing on strengths are often more important than understanding development needs. Strengths represent not only what coaching clients are good at now, but also what they *could* be good at later based on passion, priorities, learning, development, resources, time, and even the chance to go back into the past to reclaim forgotten or underused talents. Sometimes, strengths do not jump out at us. We need to find them and nurture them.

Clarifying and developing strengths will position clients for continued upward trajectory in their careers. As long as their strengths outweigh their weaknesses, the clients' chances of success remain excellent. But if their weaknesses start to overshadow their strengths, that's when they face the potential to derail.

Your role as the buyer of coaching services is to make certain that potential coaches use a strengths-based approach to working with clients.

4. Polishing the Lens (Development)

Despite their towering strengths, coaching clients usually have a few developmental needs that get in the way of their maximum effectiveness. Often these needs are blind spots they're not even aware of. Sometimes, they are painfully aware of their developmental needs, but they don't know what to do about them. Or they may simply not be convinced that they should care about these areas that need improvement.

Developmental needs may or may not be weaknesses. They may instead be considerations that leaders need to focus on to best position themselves for greater success in their current or anticipated new positions. The key questions to address at this inflection point are:

- Which few development needs matter most to achieve success?

- What can the client do to improve or develop?
- Are they willing and able to try?

There are various tools available to help the coach and client gain clarity, to polish the lenses through which client capabilities can be seen. These tools may include 360 degree feedback reports and other assessments that the organization already has in place or expects the coach to use. Personally, I prefer to interview clients and their key constituents using three very basic questions:

- What are the clients' top few strengths that make them particularly successful?
- What are the clients' one to two biggest development needs that, if addressed, would make them even more successful?
- What advice do you have for the clients that would give them the best chance possible of being successful in their current and future leadership roles?

I also like to use a tool called the *personal leadership profile* to help clients envision the kind of leaders they ultimately want to be, and what they want to be known for as a leader. This profile helps clients think about issues, such as:

- Their personal leadership philosophy or brand.
- Situations when they have been at their very best as a leader, when they felt really great about the role they played.
- What key leadership lessons they drew from that experience.
- Their hot buttons and strongly held beliefs that influence how they behave as a leader.

One unexpected discovery from using a personal leadership profile is that clients are often uncomfortable talking about themselves. The personal leadership profile, therefore, serves multiple functions. It:

- Helps clients envision and define what they want to be by the end of the coaching process, and become more comfortable in expressing those aspirations.
- Informs the design of the coaching engagement from beginning to end.

- Establishes a foundation through which clients consider their own life's experiences via their own set of lenses.
- Builds client storytelling skills that will ultimately help them lead by inspiration and example.

No matter what tools a coach chooses to use to support a client's development, your comprehensive role as the buyer of coaching services is to ensure that the coaching client will receive a well-informed set of lenses through which they can see themselves in the eyes of other key stakeholders—and then learn what to do about the things that matter most to success.

5. Building Self-Confidence (Belief)

Self-confidence is created when belief and hope are accompanied by reason. Self-confidence is essential to effective leadership. But counter-intuitively, coaches often discover there is a lot of work to be done to help their clients close the gap between who they believe themselves to be today—and how they need to be to perform effectively in current and future roles.

One of the most valuable outcomes of any coaching engagement is helping the clients walk away with higher self-confidence about their fundamental value and ability to do good work, as well as clarity about obstacles and developmental needs.

Trust in the coach, of course, is a key component to fostering self-confidence in clients. To that end, it's essential for the purchaser of coaching services to understand the coach's operating philosophy (some coaches believe in tearing down their clients, to build them back up again—an approach I personally do not agree with). Self-confidence in clients largely comes from being surrounded by others who believe in them—not blindly or abjectly, but enough to make the clients feel good about themselves.

There is a fine line between self-confidence and arrogance. That's why cultivating self-confidence is an essential inflection point for success in any effective coaching relationship. As a buyer of coaching services, look for coaches who have the ability to build confidence while unmasking arrogance.

6. Raising the Bar (Aspiration)

Self-confidence breeds belief in one's ability to accomplish more, and to aspire to bigger and greater things. Once a solid foundation of confidence is established, coaching clients are ready to start considering how they can raise the bar on their performance and dreams—what they want out of life, their careers, and their relationships with other people and with their companies.

This is the time when coaches help clients sort through all the aspects of the question, "Is this the path I want to be on after all, and am I prepared to do what it takes to get to where I want to go?" Circumstances change, dreams change, self-direction can change. This inflection point in the coaching process is therefore an excellent time to double-check to ensure that the clients' aspirations are well-aligned, not only with their own expectations, but with their companies' expectations for them.

As I like to tell clients, "The closer you get to the sun, the hotter it gets." More senior-level jobs often have complexity, politics, scrutiny, risks, and consequences that are not fully anticipated by leaders until they actually get into those jobs. By then, it's too late to learn how to navigate these conditions. It's therefore imperative that, as a key decision maker in the coaching process, you understand the coach's approach to helping clients define, understand, and prepare for raising the bar.

7. Making Practice Perfect (Preparation)

As coaching clients lift the bar on their aspirations with a coach's help, they soon come to realize that reaching for broader, more complex leadership roles will require radical preparation for new, unfamiliar, and often uncomfortable responsibilities. This process requires understanding and then practicing to handle the scenarios that clients are likely to face on the job—much like an athlete or musician would practice to prepare for a game or performance. Key questions that an effective coach might lead a client through include:

- What does the current or anticipated job entail—including the fun, and not-so-much-fun elements?
- What might a typical day, week, month, or year look and feel like—and how should you best spend your time?
- What would an effective game plan be—what would the clients actually do if they got the job? What would they change? What would they preserve? Who would they rely on? And who might they need to replace?

Preparing to address key decisions and situations that coaching clients might face, before they actually have to face them, helps them develop the mindset and "leadership muscle memory" they will eventually need under real life conditions.

Making practice perfect is often best done by coaches who have direct experience making that leadership transition themselves. While I believe that effective coaches come in all shapes and sizes, with varied backgrounds that range from I/O psychology to former executive roles and everything in between, the preparation inflection point is best handled by coaches who have "been there and done that."

The coach who has had first-hand experience in leadership roles can best take clients through a process of imagining, preparing for, and executing on the game plan required for success before the clients even step into the role—because the coach has been there before. If you are making a purchasing decision to bring in a coach on behalf of an executive client, and believe that a major component of the coaching engagement will need to focus on preparing the client for bigger, more complex, or more senior roles, give special attention to whether the coaches you are considering have the personal experience base to address this critical inflection point.

8. Visualizing Success (Optimism)

As clients imagine what their future roles will demand from them, they have to answer the question, "Can I actually see myself in that role, meeting those demands, and am I excited or scared by that possibility?" Even if others see potential in the client leaders, the clients must see it in themselves, and develop the optimism that makes for success.

Are perfection or complete readiness for a job prerequisites for optimism? Of course not. But, with optimism, clients can more easily visualize the success that is within their reach, and they can see themselves achieving it. Coaches can help clients develop an appropriate level of optimism by teaching them to imagine scenarios and how to master the self-talk that accompanies successful visualization.

They can also teach coaching clients to mentally draw circles of isolation around challenges, to compartmentalize problems in a way that helps clients see that the rest of their universe is basically okay, or will soon be okay. These coping mechanisms to build optimism can be further enhanced based on past experiences that coaching clients can readily call to mind, situations in which they have demonstrated the capability to drive desired outcomes from difficult challenges.

It is the coach's role to help clients develop what I call *brutal optimism*—the ability to see things for what they really are, while seeing the possibilities of what could be, what will be, as a result of their influence. Similarly, it is the role of the purchaser of coaching services to test for and ensure that coaches and their clients will have the chemistry required to strike the right balance between optimism and hallucination.

9. Staying in the Moment (Realism)

It's essential for both coaches and their clients to know where the line is drawn between optimism and realism. As coaches encourage their clients to achieve the appropriate level of optimism, they also must help clients come to grips with what's truly realistic. Can they tell the difference between a stretch goal that is tough but achievable, and a grandiose aspiration or misinformed belief about themselves that might be holding them back or damaging their credibility?

Most coaching clients come into engagements with a long track record of success. And, past performance is usually the best predictor of future success. But, potential is still anticipatory and somewhat imaginary.

It involves future expectations based on a trajectory that the person has already achieved to date. However, potential is also influenced by factors that are not entirely within the control of the coaching client, such as strategic changes in direction or a change in boss, coupled with factors they do control, such as their leadership behavior or willingness to learn from mistakes.

Therefore, coaches are expected to help clients understand the difference between their performance and their potential, and to maintain a realistic and balanced view about both dimensions. As a buyer of coaching services, make sure the coaches under your consideration understand these differences, and that they know how to build an appreciation for this dichotomy in their clients.

10. Deserving to Win (Inevitability)

The pursuit of personal growth and career success is a competitive endeavor, even if clients are competing only with the aspirations they have for themselves. And, as any athlete would advise us, the belief that they *deserve* to win is crucial to actually winning. Therefore, winning is first a state of mind before it can become a reality for highly successful talent. A belief in the inevitability of winning stems from devoted preparation, good decision making, strong execution, and hard work. Winners believe that success is inevitable because they have the wherewithal to make it happen—and they deserve for it to happen.

At this final inflection point in the coaching process, the big value a coach can provide is helping clients reach the point where they identify with being a winner who deserves to win, who deserves to successfully deliver on current commitments, who deserves the promotion, who deserves the tough assignments, who deserves the respect of their colleagues, who deserves the self-satisfaction that comes from working very hard and competing.

It's not about the trophy. It's about enjoying the development journey as much as the destination. And appreciating the ride. Athletes and musicians learn to love playing before they learn to love winning. So do the best coaches and the best coaching clients. As a key decision-maker in the buying decision, make sure your coaches and their potential clients likewise enjoy all the elements and actions that go into the "game."

~~~~

With these ten inflection points in mind as a foundation for successful coaching engagements, it's important to note that coaching is a continuously evolving process—just as leadership is a continuously evolving capability. Issues change. Organizations change. People change.

This evolution underscores the need to think of coaching as a cyclical, non-linear experience, rather than an episodic, linear one. First, the ten inflection points described in this chapter all need to happen. But they rarely occur sequentially. Think of them as a recipe for effective coaching rather than a checklist that must be followed in precise order.

Second, consider coaching as an organic process to help clients reflect, refresh, retool, and revitalize their effectiveness—much the way athletes and musicians work with coaches to rebuild their swing or refine their technique. Coaching may not always have a defined beginning and end. Rather, it may ebb and flow, begin and begin again, as circumstances warrant.

Third, bear in mind that coaching is only as good as the people involved in the process—the buyer, the boss, the peers, the direct reports, the client, and the coach. The work environment in which the coaching engagement takes place actually does matter.

In light of the above conditions, the nature and scope of coaching will inevitably transform over time. I see five trends on the horizon that will most significantly drive changes in coaching.

Episodic to career-long relationships: We will move from six- to twelve-month coaching engagements that address specific needs within specific timeframes to more career-long coaching relationships that mirror those athletes or musicians who rely on constant challenges and performance tune-ups from their coaches.

In-person to virtual engagements: As the economy is going global, so is coaching. Thanks to technology, purchasers and clients have
~~~~

more power over securing the right coach for the right assignment, independent of where that coach is physically located in the world.

Coach to coaching staff: As coaching becomes more career-long and virtual, it will also lend itself to being more customized to specific needs at critical inflection points in the client's career—therefore supported by members of a coaching team who can be brought into the coaching process where appropriate.

Executive to high-potential: Company-sponsored coaching has largely been reserved for select individuals at the executive levels. But this approach is counter-intuitive. This is like reserving coaching for budding athletes until after they reach world-class status. We should expect to see a shift toward using coaching as a development tool for promising talent much earlier in their careers when it can make an even more significant difference to career success.

Individual to team: Clients don't operate in a vacuum and their effectiveness is highly dependent on the performance and interactions of others. Individual coaching is like working only with the quarterback, and then letting the rest of the football team figure out the plays on their own. Individual coaching will be augmented with team coaching to keep organizational performance at a high level at all times, with coaching processes coordinated to enhance the strengths of the entire team.

Conclusion

Coaching has been held in increasingly high regard now for about fifteen years. But, that sentiment is anything but universal. An important part of enhancing the credibility and effectiveness of coaching involves the process of assigning the right coach to the right coaching client in a way where all participants can reasonably expect a productive outcome.

Even though coaching has become an increasingly accepted, and sought after, leadership development tool, there is still likely to be a stigma associated with it. Coaching clients might ask, "Am I getting a coach because I need to be fixed? Is my own leadership criticizing me behind my back? Am I falling short of expectations in some way?" Purchasers of coaching services may ask, "Is this investment really worth it? Will it make any difference at all to an individual's success? How will we really know whether the time and money involved produce any tangible results?"

So it's essential that the entire process of matching coach with client start off on the right foot—possibly even before the coaching clients even know that a coach is about to enter their lives. As we have seen through the ten inflection points addressed in this chapter, they are not only essential for helping to keep the coaching engagement focused and productive, they are also valuable for you the purchaser to use as a guide for identifying and matching the appropriate coach to the coaching client.

You can use these ten inflection points as a set of guidelines for finding the right coach for your leaders who will receive coaching. And you can use them as a set of talking points to guide your conversations with the coaching clients' bosses and their bosses.

While you might be interested in a coach who has a track record of success—and who may even have all the right credentials and certifications—they may not necessarily be the coach with the best approach, philosophy, and process for the particular coaching client at hand.

This set of ten inflection points will provide you a framework to establish confidence in the entire process—from selection to outcome. You deserve to know that coaching engagements will be worth it, and so do the leaders in your organization.

Ian Ziskin is President of EXec EXcel Group LLC, a human capital coaching and consulting firm he founded in 2010, following a highly successful 28-year career that included serving in Chief Human Resources Officer and other senior leadership roles with three Fortune 100 corporations–Northrop Grumman, Qwest Communications, and TRW.

Ian delivers services to clients as a board advisor, coach, consultant, teacher, speaker, and author. Ian also serves on the Board of Directors of Axion Health and on the Advisory Boards of Humantelligence, and RiseSmart. He is an Executive in Residence with the Center for Effective

Organizations at USC's Marshall School of Business (Los Angeles) and an Executive Advisor to Executive Networks, Inc. (San Francisco).

Ian's first book was WillBe: 13 Reasons WillBe's are Luckier than WannaBe's (2011). *He is also a contributing author to* The Chief HR Officer: Defining the New Role of Human Resource Leaders (2011).

Contact Ian at IZiskin@exexgroup.com or call 631.828.2722.

Chapter 11

Building Belief: The Five Keys to Lasting Cultural Transformation

Joseph M. Patrnchak
Principal
Green Summit Partners

As we mature in our HR careers, our reasons for selecting our next professional opportunity also change. At first, of course, it's about getting your foot in the door, building the necessary experience, and being able to make the rent on your first apartment. Then as you advance, it's about taking on the necessary experience blocks to transition yourself from being a limited generalist to a specialist to a more advanced generalist with line experience, and back and forth until you reach the C-Suite, assuming that's your ambition.

Finally, with every other aspect of your career and financial foundation squared away, *significance* takes on a more prominent value in your choices. While you always want to work for companies whose mission you believe in, of course, when you have all the other career components in place, you get to focus on the answer to the question, "What kind of difference can I really make here?" That answer can be either an inspiring question or a troubling one.

When I was being considered for the CHRO role at Cleveland Clinic, I was troubled. Was I the right person for the job with my background in technology and insurance industries? Was this the right next step for me? But two incidents that occurred during my earliest moments there told me that this was the place where I was meant to be to offer significance that would also be meaningful to me.

On the day I expected to be offered the CHRO position, I still wasn't sure I wanted it. It would require a move to Cleveland from Boston, where my roots and professional network were. While I had just been with Blue Cross Blue Shield of Massachusetts as senior vice president, I had no experience in the direct health care delivery environment. All my previous companies were in the tech industry: Digital Equipment Corporation, Compaq Computer, and Hewlett Packard. What could I possibly offer Cleveland Clinic? And did I even want the opportunity? The prospect of learning an entirely new industry at this point in my career was a big question for me.

I arrived well before my 7:30 appointment with the CEO because I wanted to catch a glimpse of what it would be like coming to work in the morning if I took the job. There's lots of energy at this hour at Cleveland Clinic. People coming in from all over the world. All ages, professions, and ethnic backgrounds. I then decided to settle my mind in the hospital's chapel with a little quiet reflection. My conflicted feelings must have shown on my face, because before long an environmental services worker approached me, gently put his hand on my shoulder, and asked, "Sir, are you okay?" "Yes," I said, "I'm fine," humbly realizing that I probably looked like someone who was wrestling with anxiety because of a loved one who might be a patient.

He left me alone for a while longer. But before he left the room, he returned to me and quietly said, "I just want you to know that you will be in my family's prayers tonight." I nodded my thanks.

I never saw him again.

That moment of humanity solidified my decision to accept the position. This was a place where caring people can find significance in their work, no matter where they are in the org chart. And I wanted to help them do so.

Then a few days before I officially started, I decided to slip into an all-hands meeting where the CEO was making a presentation to the staff. Since I was still officially an outsider, I discreetly chose a seat in the back row. I asked one of the doctors if the seat next to him was available.

He said, "Yes! Please! By all means!"

I jokingly replied, "Well, it looks like there are no assigned seats here because every other seat in the auditorium is open."

He responded, "We should have assigned seats here, because they treat us all like children around here anyway." Data point noted.

At the end of the presentation, the CEO wrapped up by saying, "And now, I'd like to introduce our new CHRO, Joe Patrnchak, who will be joining us in a few days. I see him sitting back there in the back row. Please stand up, Joe, so the team can welcome you."

After I sat back down, I could feel the doctor's eyes cutting in my direction. And then he said, "So, did I give you my name?" "No," I said, fully expecting a more complete self-introduction.

"Good. See you around. Have a nice day." And with that, he stood up and left.

I never saw him again either.

These two incidents told me the two different stories about the same thing: The essential power of caring at Cleveland Clinic. In the case of the environmental services worker, his daily experience of his job allowed him to safely keep his caring vibrant and close to the surface. While his own job may not be as celebrated as that of the surgeons and other healthcare providers, he knew the significance of his presence there in the chapel to heal and provide comfort. And I felt it!

In the case of the physician, I would say that his caring was just as alive but somewhere along the line—either suddenly or gradually—there was a breach of faith between himself and the sense of calling from his profession. And it would be my job to restore that faith to the hospital throughout the entire organization. It was my new calling to enliven a culture of caring in an environment already renowned for its world-class excellence—to help build an engaged workforce to build off its clinical excellence; to also develop a great service environment to deliver a great patient experience.

This chapter is about how we at Cleveland Clinic made that happen.

"Respected But Not Liked" No Longer Works in Healthcare

When I first began at Cleveland Clinic, its worldwide reputation for clinical excellence and saving people's lives was solidly indisputable. Cleveland Clinic has the highest acuity level of any hospital in the United States, which means that the sickest people in the world come there, and 99 percent of them go home. However, it was also commonly, but privately, said, "The patients here are always grateful to be taken care of by us, but they don't also like us very much." This gap in the clinic's connection with the patients and their experience of our caregiving was at direct odds with our global brand for excellence.

The Cleveland Clinic is without question one of the most highly respected health care institutions in the country, if not the world. Patients who turn to this hospital have every reasonable expectation that they are receiving the best possible care available anywhere. Likewise, the physicians and other healthcare providers know that to be associated with Cleveland Clinic is a career-making professional accomplishment.

The Cleveland Clinic's longstanding reputation for health care and pioneering research dates back to its founding in 1921. And it has been ranked #1 in cardiac care since 1994. For the years 2014-2015, *U.S. News and World Report* ranked the Cleveland Clinic #1 in Cardiology and Heart Surgery; Pulmonology; and Urology. The hospital was ranked #2 in Diabetes and Endocrinology; Gastroenterology and GI Surgery; Nephrology; and Rheumatology. And it came in at #3 for Gynecology and Orthopedics. So naturally it would follow, at least intuitively, that excellence in healthcare and the *experience* of caring itself would go hand in hand. For both the patients and Cleveland Clinic employees alike.

But, while the expectations of outcomes might be reasonably positive, the *experience* of being either patient or provider at the Cleveland Clinic did not track with quality of care rankings back in 2008 when I began my own tenure there. Patients and employees alike reported the disconnect between the excellence of care and the actual caring itself that would be expected to go along with it. In March of 2008 the first Federal Hospital Consumer Assessment of Healthcare Providers and Systems (HCAHPS) survey placed the clinic at just at or below the national average ranking for patient satisfaction for most categories, except the "would recommend" category—which would reasonably speak to the quality of patient outcome that they could always expect to receive from Cleveland Clinic. Likewise, a Gallup, Inc., survey of employee engagement placed the clinic only in the 44th percentile of health care systems in its global database.

Industries such as hospitality and retail that depend on the enduring good-will of their customers for their long-term successes based on repeat business understand full-well the service profit chain and the great employee experience/client experience correlation. Healthcare has been late to that particular party. Healthcare hasn't had to worry about repeat business (in fact, on a per-customer basis, repeat business is not a good thing). And so, until recently, the service-profit chain hasn't been high on the field's list of concerns.

The traditional discipline required in the healthcare setting has elevated the doctors and surgeons above the rest of the hospital community. And, let's face it, anyone who benefits from the life-saving skills and knowledge of the entire hospital staff is going to feel rather churlish to complain that he or she wasn't coddled like they might if they were at a St. Regis or Ritz-Carlton. If their feelings were hurt or if they were treated abruptly by a surgeon who clearly saw them as merely the isolated body part that was being worked on, who cares in the long run? They're just grateful to be able to look forward to an extended life with their deeply relieved family.

But they still didn't like us very much.

Naturally, most of us want to be liked, at least to some degree. Up until 2008 being liked wasn't an actual financial imperative. But with the introduction of the HCAHPS survey, the extent to which patients were satisfied with their experience while in our care had a direct impact on our financial interests. "Patient Experience of Care" would make up 30 percent of our total score, which would then determine our eligibility for Federal reimbursement. (To illustrate how important patient experience is, actual "Outcome" is only 25 percent.)

It had become imperative to be more than just liked. We needed—and wanted—to extend to our entire community of employees, patients, and neighbors the spirit of authentic caring and deep respect for everyone who engages with us.

So in 2008 we committed to transform Cleveland Clinic into "a great place to work and grow." This was an essential objective to deliver on the Clinic's promise based on its value statements: "Patients first" and "Every life deserves world-class care." That meant not only world-class clinical care but also world-class service. Consumerism and transparency have finally hit healthcare. Patients could be directed by health plans and other services to where both existed. And hospital rankings, such as the one by *US News and World Report,* now included patient experience scores, which naturally impacts reputation.

"We Are All Caregivers"

Anyone who has either given or received customer service training courses knows that it's unrealistic (not to mention unreasonable) to expect high-level customer service to be authentic and sustainable unless the employees feel that same kind of service value proposition extended to them as well. Consequently, we knew that our employee engagement scores and our patient satisfaction reports were interwoven. (For instance, in a study of ninety-four hospitals with more than 130,000 employees, Gallup discovered a correlation between employee engagement and higher HCAHPS scores.) We had to address both simultaneously, in an integrally designed fashion—starting with our culture. Which was really the only place to start if we wanted the improvements to stick.

We started with the most basic of all foundations—what we called ourselves.

In any traditional hospital setting, a sense of dualism pervades the culture. You have your surgeons, doctors, nurses, nurses' aides, etc. These are the highly trained professionals who are directly responsible for the patients, their care, and their outcomes. Then you have the supporting staff, from the executives in the administrative offices, to the HR department, to the medical transcriptionists, to the guy in the garage who helps visitors park their cars.

In the case of Cleveland Clinic, the dichotomy was even more pronounced. We had two major designations for everyone who worked there. They were referred to as "staff" (the doctors) and "non- staff" (everyone else). This detail—as insignificant as it might appear to be—had to have a negative impact on anyone's sense of commitment to the Clinic's mission. It's hard to come to work every day and feel important if you are a "non" anything.

As my own experience with the chapel environmental services worker shows, each of these roles is a caregiving role. If they're not engaging with patients and their visitors directly, they're providing care for the employees themselves. This understanding came out of my previous industry experience in services businesses, where there is no such thing as a back office or back office person. Everyone needs to see his or her role as important in the value chain of delivering great service. Either you are in front of a customer providing service or you are in support of someone who is. Thus you create a holistic services environment; a culture of service where everyone sees themselves in the full mission of the community.

People who come to work at a hospital don't come to work as *employees*. They come to work as *Caregivers*. That is where their elevated sense of mission and fulfillment lies. So that is where we began the process of transforming our culture into one where everyone can be expected to deliver *care* with the same level of regard, regardless of their title or position in the hospital. Likewise, by bearing the title *Caregiver*, they also carry the constant reminder that caring comes first—no matter whether they are a surgeon, scrub nurse, radiologist, payroll specialist, or groundskeeper.

So, reinforcing our leading message that everyone had a role to create a great patient experience, we designated everyone who worked at the Clinic as a *Caregiver*. This would be the person at the patient's bedside delivering food, cleaning the rooms, taking a parking ticket, simply helping someone in the hall way who looks lost, or collecting a payment a couple of weeks after the patient has gone home. *Caregiver* is a title that reinforced the cultural belief that all work has dignity, and all those who do the work have dignity. By adopting the moniker of *Caregiver*, we all became an important part of the mission, "Putting patients first" and "Every life deserves world class care."

The Cleveland Clinic Experience

So far we've established that every Caregiver at Cleveland Clinic plays a critical role in the way everyone *experiences* their relationship with us. To embed that belief into the culture, in a way more meaningful than a simple slogan, one of our first initiatives was to develop the half-day program, which we named the "Cleveland Clinic Experience," in which every Caregiver would participate.

We needed to reset our language and service expectations with our current Caregivers before we started onboarding new hires. The session sizes were intentionally small—only eight to ten participants—and they would be made up of Caregivers from throughout the hospital, all there as equals, regardless of their position in the organization. All 43,000 Caregivers, including the doctors, went through the experience training over a nine-month period. We had over 400 facilitators volunteer to work the sessions. They came from all roles within the system. One was a painter, who facilitated over twenty-five of the sessions. He said that the experience of leading the sessions changed his life. No doubt he changed a lot of people's lives in return.

Servant Leadership Culture

Just as they are Caregivers externally to their patients, they are also Caregivers internally to each other. With that in mind, we focused on transforming our conventional command-and-control leadership culture into one that is commonly recognized as *servant leadership*, a concept introduced by Robert K. Greenleaf. According to Greenleaf, the role of a leader is servant first, sharing power, and placing the needs of others and the organization above his or her own. At Cleveland Clinic, we needed a "new teachable point of view" when it came to our leadership culture, if we were going to create a services environment. Servant leadership was the obvious choice.

Referring back to our goal of creating "a great place to work and grow," we provided all of our more than 3,100 leaders with the training that reinforced each leader's obligation to nurture their direct reports. Additionally, more than 120 servant leader champions had further training to allow them to perform as servant leader mentors, to support the rest of the leadership levels, and to keep the serving leader principles alive and relevant in their respective departments.

Caregiver Celebrations

Leading employee engagement studies have proven that engagement spikes when individuals feel acknowledged and appreciated by their supervisors. While this would appear to be a self-evident truism to most of us, cultures that have emerged over decades of command-and-control leadership styles (such as the rigidly hierarchical conventional hospital setting) also send the message, "I'll let you know when I'm unhappy with your performance. If you don't hear from me, just assume everything is fine."

Clearly that is an insupportable management style in these times. And by 2010, Cleveland Clinic replaced it with a more proactive and strategic recognition system designed to encourage leaders to acknowledge their high performers often and in relevant ways. We designed our Caregiver Celebrations program specifically to support and reinforce the clinic's values:

Quality: Maintains the highest standards and achieves them by continually measuring and improving outcomes.

Innovation: Welcomes change, encouraging invention, and continually seeks better, more efficient ways to achieve goals.

Teamwork: Collaborates and shares knowledge to benefit patients and/or fellow caregivers for the advancement of our mission.

Service: Strives to exceed patients' and/or fellow caregivers' expectations.

Integrity: Adheres to high moral principles and professional standards by a commitment to honesty, confidentiality, trust, respect, and transparency.

Compassion: Demonstrates a commitment to world-class care by providing a caring, supportive, environment for patients, patients' families, and fellow caregivers.

The rewards ranged from nonmonetary acknowledgments from managers, peers, and patients to on-the-spot financial acknowledgments (budgeted at $25 per direct report) to $250 quarterly awards to $2,000 annual awards given to fifty Caregivers, all the way to an individual and team award of $10,000 given by the CEO himself. As special as the annual award is, of course, the main emphasis of the Caregivers Celebration program has been to make acknowledgements quick, easy to use, and everyday.

In 2010, the first year the Caregiver Celebrations program was implemented, an average of 7,515 awards were given per month. By 2013, over 19,280 awards were given per month. We tracked by organization how many of these awards were given monthly and were able to correlate higher levels of engagement in those who used the program more frequently.

Caring for Our Caregivers' Well-Being

Caregivers can't help their patients achieve wellness unless they are well themselves. In 2008, the same year we launched the "We're All Caregivers" campaign, we also rolled out a proactive Caregiver wellness strategy. We started the program with free Weight Watchers memberships and a $100 participation incentive, but eventually transitioned into a program where we offered up to 30 percent savings on their health plan premiums.

By the end of 2012, almost 70 percent of our caregivers lost over 300,000 pounds as a result of our partnership with Weight Watchers and Curves, as well as other fitness support services. Additionally, we were able to track significant reductions in hospital admissions and emergency room visits by Caregivers who were participating in the Chronic Disease Management Program. These programs resulted in annual savings of about $14 million.

More than half of the Caregivers have participated in our wellness programs. Participation in the chronic disease management program (obesity, asthma, diabetes, hypertension, and hyperlipidemia) specifically increased 825 percent, four times the national average. Wellness initiatives have produced a savings of $78 million since 2010.

Diversity and Inclusion

While all the Caregiver engagement programs embraced the entire Cleveland Clinic population, we also made a special effort to engage women and minority/special interest groups, such as African-Americans; Hispanics; Pan-Asian; LGBT; military vets returning to civilian life. We founded employee resource groups (ERGs) specifically tasked to provide mentoring and help for these populations to assimilate into the ever-evolving Cleveland Clinic culture.

Where these groups started out as social and support groups, as the years progressed, they matured into being essential to strengthening the connection between their members and the clinic's mission. This has become especially valuable as Cleveland Clinic seeks to reach out into the community to support the wellness of these populations.

The Five Keys for Sustainable Culture Change

Fresh starts are always attractive. And you can probably use all ten fingers to tick off what's wrong with your current culture and how you'd like it to change. You want people to be nicer to each other. You want people to be nicer to your clients and customers. You want your clients, customers, and employees to come back tomorrow. You want them to refer their friends.

You definitely want the culture change to endure, with or without you there to serve as its persistent evangelist. You may not have any plans to leave your position, but that doesn't mean that you're there permanently. So whatever you put in place must be able to thrive without you.

Endurance is one consideration. The other is intentional design. Without intentionality and specificity going into the transformation process, you risk your organization simply reverting to its old ways just as naturally as muscle memory. Or you risk having an even worse culture, one that is even more cynical and demoralized because all those glorious promises that were made at the outset turned out to be just another distracting sideshow of good intentions without substance to support them over the long run.

As you are engineering your intentional culture transformation, keep these five essential keys in mind for that sustainable change that you are striving to achieve:

1. Acknowledge the dissatisfaction. No real significant change happens without some high-level, pressing degree of dissatisfaction about what the current condition is. Anyone who has tried to lose weight, quit smoking, or start an exercise program, will tell you that true motivation to change must come from a moment of revelation where there's just no getting around the pain anymore. You have to feel it fully in order to really know it. Then you can do something about it. Because you're finally motivated.

2. Catch the vision and turn it into a cause. To transform our culture into "a great place to work and grow," we had to extend that vision to all the people who worked at Cleveland Clinic on an equal basis. All Caregivers are healers. And our vision and cause was to extend that belief beyond those providing direct medical care. Healing is spiritual, physical, environmental, and emotional. In this way, the payroll accountant managing our Caregivers' paychecks is just as much a Caregiver as a floor nurse. No matter what they do, they play a role in helping to create a more calming environment for patients and their families.

What is the vision of your organization? And what is the shared cause that would rally all your employees?

3. Care for your people so they will care for your customers. You can experience a great deal of improvement in both customer satisfaction and employee experience when you focus your attention on making sure your people feel cared for—not from the very top of the organization—but from their immediate work group, supervisors, even the customers themselves.

Release any command-and-control elements that might remain in your culture. Be sure that engagement is a "local" phenomenon—that the supervisors are equipped with the freedom they need to unleash their employees' self-direction and initiative.

4. Hardwire the change into every aspect of your leadership development. Servant leadership is all about working with high levels of emotional intelligence to demonstrate that our job as leaders is to serve and support our people and bring out the best in them. In turn, they become better servant leaders themselves—wiser, more caring, healthier, and more effective for the organization over all. Not coincidentally, we found that units with top engagement scores consistently had the best quality and safety scores as well.

5. Commit yourself to a long journey of transformation. You want to build a pyramid, not a sandcastle. For such a change to endure the tests of time, you have to take the time necessary to build it solidly. There may not be the rapid returns on your risk and investment that you might be looking for. But when the transformation is built to withstand whatever the future might throw at it, you will be glad that you invested the upfront effort to make this a rock solid change.

Set reasonable, achievable goals at the outset, so your people can meet them at their local, departmental, unit levels. Reinforce your vision in them by demonstrating that the transformation is within reach. Build up their strengths; don't just focus on their weaknesses. That way you are also building up their trust in you, and their direct reports' trust in them. You are modeling the coaching, support, and resources to them that you want them to pass on to their own people.

Identify and celebrate best practices leaders. Look for opportunities for them to share their experiences and outcomes with others. Put your CEO out front at every opportunity, repeatedly reinforcing the message of commitment to this transformation as a permanent shift.

Conclusion

This journey toward a cultural transformation with staying power has really been about one thing: Build belief. Belief that everyone will be treated with caring, as well as the belief that their workplace is a good place to entrust their career, their profession, their peace of mind, and their health.

Building belief—especially from the position where we started—takes time. And so we approached the conversion as a campaign—a campaign that required high-level investment, strategic thinking, and faithfulness during the uncertain initial years.

Over that time, we saw more than mere leaps in our engagement scores. Engaged to non-engaged ratios went from 2.58:1 in 2008 to 10.1:1 in 2010. (According to Gallup it takes a ratio of 4:1 just to reach a neutral point.) Additionally the clinic went from the 44th percentile to the 87th during that period in employee engagement, as measured against all other health care systems in their extensive data base. We also experienced a 47 percent in our "grateful patient" contributions—these are voluntary philanthropic funds that are so essential to the sustenance of any hospital.

It's not enough to do the right thing. You have to do the right thing with persistence, repetition, patience, and consistency. You have to overtly proclaim the new intention, and then honor it. Most organizations have very short time frames with which to activate changes and transform perceptions. But when you are undergoing a radical culture shift such as this one, be prepared to invest years to the cause of transforming people's perceptions from fear toward trust.

What happened for us at Cleveland Clinic can happen for your organization.

Joseph M. Patrnchak is head of Green Summit Partners, a consulting practice dedicated to helping organizations bring out the best in their people. Prior to establishing Green Summit, Joe served as Chief Human Resources Officer at Cleveland Clinic. Before joining Cleveland Clinic in 2007, Joe served as Chief HR Officer and Senior Vice President at Blue Cross Blue Shield of Massachusetts (BCBSMA). At BCBSMA, he played a key role in reenergizing this mature organization through new strategic planning, performance management, and leadership development processes, and through innovative work-life, career development, and employee health programs that improved engagement to benchmark levels.

Previously, Joe served as Vice President of Human Resources for HP/Compaq/Digital, including leading HR for the $4.5B Global Customer Services Division, which was cited for five years by IDC, Gartner, and Forrester as the technology industry's #1 or #2 service business.

A co-founder of the Healthcare Human Resources Forum, and a frequent conference speaker, he is the author of "Building an Engaged Workforce at Cleveland Clinic" (Journal of Healthcare Leadership, 2013) *and "Implementing Servant Leadership at Cleveland Clinic: A Case Study in Organizational Change"* (Journal of Servant Leadership, 2015), *and co-author of "Rewards, Recognition & Employee Engagement at Cleveland Clinic"* (Journal of Healthcare Leadership, 2014).

Joe can be contacted via joe@gsummit.co or call him at 216.970.9260.

Chapter 12

Blending Cultures: Success Factors in Merging Knowledge-Based Companies

Mark Walztoni
Human Capital Advisory Services Practice
Crowe Horwath LLP

The strategic combining of assets has been used as a tool for expansion and market positioning since long before the written record. Setting aside, for the moment, the sacking of villages and the forceful, violent annexing of entire nations, mergers and acquisitions (M&A) are traditionally a bloodless affair, with all parties more or less agreeable to the arrangement. Marriage contracts, for instance, have for centuries combined the assets and liabilities of strong families to make the combined new entity even stronger. Land deeds have passed hands to expand the power base of landowners. While it can certainly be argued that not all participants have been 100 percent on board with these arrangements, over time humanity has found a way to work these things out with minimum damage to lives and landscape.

In the business world, companies, of course, have reconfigured themselves with the objective of diversifying their market presence; expanding into new markets; taking on new product offerings; absorbing the competition rather than fighting it, etc. These mergers could also be regarded generally as rather bloodless. From the perspective of the captains and kings of the transaction, it is a good day if there is a relatively smooth exchange of the keys to the warehouse (with all contents accounted for), or the passing of the combination to the vault where the critical formulas, code, and patents are kept, or a glitch-free activation of the magnetic cards that provide access to the reserved parking spaces.

But with the rise of knowledge-based companies that are merging now (professional services firms, management consulting firms, even high-end design companies, any enterprise that depends on the knowledge and creativity of its staff), there's a new consideration. Merging companies aren't just acquiring client lists, real estate, or intellectual property. They are acquiring the talent itself—the very people who make the firms competitive. When the deal is struck and contracts are signed, the assumption is that the people themselves are part of the bargain. But unlike warehoused inventory sitting safely on pallets, people have feet. And people are free to walk.

In the M&A process of knowledge companies, the HR role carries a vital responsibility that has been overlooked by leaders who are using the old models of transferring company assets. When the intrinsic value of the merging companies is the talent itself, the time has come to revisit your people strategies. Your role as the HR leader in an M&A process is to help the merging companies retain their critical talent—and therefore value—through this unstable transition period.

Your job has many moving parts:

- To help keep the best talent engaged in the newly formed entity.
- To help the new company emerge in a way that fulfills the vision of all the key players.
- To help all the key stakeholders (including those individuals who will be looking for new employment once the merger is complete) move through the changes with the maximum

amount of grace and a minimum amount of damage to careers, reputations, and lives.

- To do all these things in the least amount of time without compromising quality and effectiveness of the new company's performance in its marketplace.

Why So Many Mergers & Acquisitions Fail

According to Christian Clayton in the 2011 *Harvard Business Review* article, "The Big Idea: The New M&A Playbook," studies show that between 70 and 90 percent of mergers and acquisitions fail. They either fail to achieve their objectives or they suffer an overall drop in productivity in the first four to eight months. People issues and cultural compatibility are cited as the top integration failure factors. So if you don't address the people and culture problems that naturally emerge during this high-stress circumstance, you risk falling into this group that suffers failure or a drop in productivity (which, in the knowledge economy, results in severe negative outcomes deep into the future; it's not just a matter of a disappointing quarter of widget manufacture).

When the value of the transaction is the quality of the talent itself—otherwise known as *people*—companies would do well to recognize that the transition period itself puts the engagement of their most valued asset at greatest risk for all the hazards associated with damaging disengagement. If the C-suite is handling the M&A process like a typical transaction of tangible assets, the true assets are at risk of the typical consequences of disengagement: Leaving, quitting in place, or even actively sabotaging the enterprise.

The result: Competition acquires the talent you wanted to keep. The quality of services your new firm offers diminish significantly. And your firm's reputation is in peril.

This may be a time when senior leaders are least focused on the health of the workplace culture. But it is definitely the time when it should be the most focused on the interests and needs of their A Players and A Teams, and their engagement levels. Otherwise, the final merger may be the acquisition of B Players at A Player valuation.

You risk losing critical differentiating talent, innovators, people who are out billing high-value contracts, keeping existing customer relationships healthy and intact. When that happens, not only do you lose your talent, but your competitor also swoops in to snag those customers—who are now in transition themselves. Both parties of the M&A end up worse off than they were before the merger began.

This is what I call the *triple bump* in this scenario. You first lose your A Players. And then you can't recruit replacements because word has gotten out that your new enterprise is not the place where high-value talent would want to risk their careers. The remaining employees do what typically happens in a disengaged culture—they "quit in place," not offering their best brain power to the enterprise, holding back until they see what eventually happens to the company.

If people don't feel that their interests are aligned with the company's interests anymore, they simply aren't going to put forward their best effort. Add potential culture mismatches as two very different enterprises merge and struggle to find common ground, and you stand to lose both your best talent and your most cherished customers.

Let's take a moment to consider some of the standard engagement markers and how they are affected by the high-stress conditions of an M&A process:

Do employees know what is expected of them? In an M&A situation, individual job descriptions and expectations can change overnight. Professionals and knowledge workers identify strongly with their work. And they expect to have control over their careers. To have their job descriptions, expectations, productivity goals radically modified without previous warning or consultation with their managers sends them the signal that they are regarded as mere talent widgets. No A Player wants to be a talent widget.

Additionally, compensation and incentive structures that change radically with short or no notice alienate individuals who take personal pride in their work. When knowledge workers agree to accept a position, they have thought about it and concluded that the expectations are in line with their abilities, and the compensation is in line with their efforts. To change the mix of deliverables and rewards without involving their input will invite confusion, frustration, and resentment. Three unengaging emotions.

Do employees have the materials and equipment they need to do their work? In a merged company scenario, employees will be coping with new, unfamiliar products, specs, pricing strategies, methodologies, and policies. Even the new company culture itself might get in the way of engaged, enthusiastic performance. In one newly formed merger, for example, departments were inexplicably pitted against each other in client acquisition activities. Internal competitiveness that impacts external relationships to the point that it's a zero-sum game does not engage A Player talent.

Do employees feel that their supervisors care about their performance and development? Probably not. The senior leadership is most likely focused on their own careers during the initial M&A planning phases. They know more about what's happening than the individual contributors. And they'll know it sooner. They have their own self-interests top of mind. Encouraging the development of rank-and-file has most likely been back-burnered—especially if it's not clear which ones of those individuals will eventually be let go.

In the earliest stages of M&A activity, the culture changes are subtle and disturbing. There are now closed doors that were once routinely open. There are distracted supervisors who don't have the emotional bandwidth to care about their departments when they're thinking about how quickly they might be able to find a new job themselves. There are an increasing number of vacant workspaces. There are abandoned projects.

Additionally, high-value talent is seeing that their competencies might not be what the newly formed enterprise needs. All that hard work they invested in preparing for their next role has come to nothing because that opportunity no longer exists, or that role is assumed by someone from the other company.

Do employees feel that their opinions count? High-value knowledge workers have ideas, innovations, and opinions. And they want to contribute their perspective to their organization at the highest possible level.

But in a merger situation, their opinions might be based on a set of variables that were relevant yesterday, but not today. Or they may discover that in the reorganization, their reshuffled position has found its way to the bottom of the deck. And their access to the essential decision maker is blocked by levels of people they don't know.

Or perhaps there is a culture clash, where one company nurtured a collegial, egalitarian, innovative culture where all voices were welcome. But the other company in the merger was a more command-control culture where the underlying message was, "When I want your opinion, I'll ask for it." Employees at home in either culture will clash with the combined entity. The culture that prevails will alienate the top talent from the culture that must now defer.

A Three-Part Culture-Based Solution for Successful M&A Integration

HR leaders have heard the hackneyed expression, "People are our most valuable assets," so much that the truth of the principle has lost its resonance. But it is never more relevant than it is in the M&A of knowledge-service companies. People really are their most valuable assets. Warehouses don't walk. Real estate doesn't rethink its career path. Widgets don't post snarky commentary on public Internet forums and then find a better offer elsewhere. But people can. And they do.

In a knowledge-based company, where the differentiating competitive factor is the knowledge and talent of the people, the value that is placed on the company is significantly dependent on the quality of its people. But you can't force your people to stay. And the best ones—the ones who contribute the most to a company's value—can leave at any time. So, in an M&A situation where you are combining companies that rely heavily on their talent, you are actually trading in volunteers.

As the people leader most responsible for creating a culture that offers your best talent all the reasons why they should want to stay, it's up to you to be the one to make sure all the essential retention and engagement components are in place. Without your concerted attention to this mandate, you will have a clash of cultures and the chaos that results.

Here is a three-part methodology you can follow that will help you see your organization through the transition adventure and stay focused on successful people organization and deployment, even as you face the potential of your own personal career upheaval. You may end up circulating your own resume within a year's time yourself. But, in the meantime, follow this program of high-value talent integration, and you will have a powerful story to tell that demonstrates your proactive effectiveness in helping any employer you're associated with attract and retain its most competitive talent.

Step 1: Conduct Cultural and Talent Due Diligence

You probably won't be the first to know that a merger is in the offing. But let's hope that you find out early enough to help pilot the process to the benefit of both the new company and its employees. The due diligence phase is your opportunity to capture the earliest possible understanding of the gap between the current iteration of the two still distinct companies and the ultimate iteration, once the merger is complete.

Clearly understand what the ultimate outcome will be. Before you can help your new entity achieve its goal, you have to see the vision for the endgame as clearly as the senior leadership sees it. Will it be a merger of equals? Will one absorb the other? Will the acquiring company honor the culture and values of the new acquisition, for instance, the Amazon acquisition of Zappos, where personal service is preeminent? Will there be two different sets of employee value propositions that must somehow find common ground that inspires and engages all? Or does the prevailing company intend to wipe out the culture of the other company, with every expectation that the employees will simply fall in line with the new way?

Connect with your direct counterpart in the other company as early as appropriate. In previous decades, this relationship might have been more competitive than cooperative. But now that careers are so mobile, you will both benefit from having a collaborative partnership. This way you can both fulfill your mandate to see the companies through the merger process, while supporting each other in your respective career goals. Do you completely duplicate each other in terms of skill sets, interests, and ambitions? Or do your strengths dovetail? Is it immediately obvious that one will be better suited for the new company? If so, how can you coordinate your work together over the transition process so that you are each best positioned for your immediate future after the merger is complete?

Define the desired corporate culture and compare it with the cultures of the two merging companies. Look at the workplace style and employee value propositions that are currently in place. How are they compatible with the envisioned future culture? Is the way the employees are being treated now consistent with the stated employee value propositions for their respective companies? Or will there be a need to rebuild trust and commitment once the merger is complete? Are the performance and incentive systems in alignment with the behaviors that each company wants to promote? Are they aligned with each other? Or do they somehow conflict?

Again, looking at both companies separately, are they committed to treating their people with the same service philosophy that they expect their people to treat their customers? What gaps need to be closed in those areas?

Compare companies: Is one company a seat-of-the-pants swashbuckler when it comes to making strategic decisions and the other company a slow mover that takes years to make a simple staffing choice? Does one company welcome innovation and suggestions from throughout the ranks? And the other only from officially designated subject matter experts? Are the value statements aligned with each other? How different are they? How different are the customer-facing communications that reflect what the attitudes might be internally? What do the org charts look like? How do the two dress codes compare? What is the buzz on social media about these two companies and their reputations as employers?

What do the customers say about each company? Do the two cultures support go-the-extra-mile customer service? Or is one more interested in rate of immediate conversion driven by technological efficiencies, at the expense of potential customer relationships that last over time and result in repeat sales? This is not an exercise in passing judgment on the business models themselves. This is about thoroughly understanding the philosophies that are the foundations of each business, how they're different, and how they're compatible.

Who are the most influential people within each company and why? This is not about who is at the top of the org chart, but who is a connector. Who is the trusted source of news or inspiration? Who will motivate when others can't or won't? Who are the opinion drivers in the organization and why?

What are the generational factors that will present themselves as the companies merge? Do you have good reason to be concerned about potential age group conflicts? Where are the key contributors in their own individual career cycles? As the companies merge, will you have an out-of-balance population that needs to be addressed?

Compare engagement surveys. Naturally you will want to see the scores and their history of improvement trends (or lack thereof). But you will also want to study the questions themselves. Is each survey an off-the-shelf product? Or are they custom designed after thorough research into the company culture and values? If the companies have invested in custom-designed surveys, you will learn a lot about what's important to both the companies as employers and the people as employees. See if the survey questions reflect values that either match or at least coordinate with each other. Where do they diverge, and what do those instances tell you?

Study the C-suites equally thoroughly. The senior-level people leaders might be tempted to focus their study downward throughout the organization. But they shouldn't neglect an upward examination. Who runs the separate companies now? Who will run the merged enterprise after all is said and done? What will be the exit strategy of the stakeholders? What is their stated philosophy regarding their long-term obligations toward the individual contributors and the workplace culture? How does that philosophy compare with their actual track records of leadership? Can you reasonably count on them to facilitate the integration? Or are you seeing subtle signs of resistance?

Create an integration dashboard. You need to be able to tell at a glance that you are headed in the right direction, hitting on all your integration objectives. There will be plenty of data created throughout the integration process that needs to be organized so that it's ultimately useful to you.

This dashboard transforms all those numbers into a visible, systemized report that you can quickly grasp and keep track of those things that are most important to you.

A good dashboard will provide you with both quantitative and qualitative data. You can set it up so that it reveals those stories behind the objective measures. You can custom design it to suit your objectives. It can be as simple as a red, yellow, green construction. Or you can provide opportunities to elaborate on responses so you can get the color commentary as well. You decide the frequency periods when the dashboard is refreshed with updated reports.

Develop it in collaboration with your senior team. You want to make sure that there's agreement about the best people measures, talent measures, human capital measures, whatever the entire team finds to be worth monitoring, studying, and reporting to each other about.

You are creating a culture of collaboration in this way. And the participants are trained to understand the dashboard's nuance as early in the process as possible. Let's say, for example, your dashboard reports that your new integration is experiencing 10 percent turnover. In most cases, this might be interpreted as very bad news. But then another manager asks the question, "What percentage of this turnover was voluntary? What percentage represents people we didn't want to lose? What percentage are people we can afford to let go?" When you involve your senior team in the development of the dashboard, they will take active interest in using it. And they will ask themselves the questions about the results that really provide the value of understanding that the whole company is looking for.

Peter Drucker once said, "What gets measured gets managed." By developing this dashboard as a senior team, you are deciding together what are the important data points, how they should be interpreted, and what issues of lesser importance can be set aside for now. Some of the metrics you might consider including are:

- Aggregate retention
- Retention of critical talent flight risks identified during this early phase
- Retention rates by department

- Retention rates by location
- Exit interview data
- What should your company start, stop, or keep doing to accelerate integration?
- What is being said in public forums; what are the common themes of the comments?

I am presenting the dashboard as an essential component of the due diligence phase of the integration. But the dashboard will be a tool that you will carry with you throughout the entire process. And, hopefully, you will incorporate it into your management strategy well into the future.

Step 2: Take Action Based on Your Findings

What you do next will be very much based on what you discovered in your due diligence. You should now know where the gaps are between the condition of the two companies and the ideal merged culture—and what metrics will most efficiently track the progress in closing the gaps. You know what potential cultural elements could become barriers to the new company's progress. You also have a good estimation of what cultural disconnects are truly worth focusing on, versus what is simply fleeting cultural noise.

As you move forward into your action steps, it's important to remember that this is an iterative process that you will be monitoring and adjusting as you go. Feedback mechanisms are essential, as well as openness to necessary course corrections. You are setting the tone for your new culture by your own behaviors. People will be watching how you carry yourself, handle your department, and treat people. HR is the role model for the rest of the new organization.

Integrate your HR department quickly. You are setting the tone in terms of not only cultural behavior attributes but also a sense of urgency. You may not have everything organized or operationalized exactly the way you want your department, but as long as you're a step ahead of the rest of the company, you're leading.

Likewise, look for ways you can keep your outgoing counterpart in relationship with you and the newly merged company even after he or she has left. Offer a retainer relationship for a few months so that you have a sounding board with someone who could be the only person in the world who knows what it's like to be you.

Treat the departed with respect and dignity. Lay-offs will most likely come in waves, so people who remain after each wave are watching how the freshly laid off colleagues are treated throughout the process, and even in their absence. Give them the chance to complete projects if you can. Whenever possible, give them fair warning so that they can begin their job hunt from the position of strength of having a current title and position. Give them the opportunity to say good bye to their coworkers. Make sure their records show that their terminations are "no-fault" so that their careers don't suffer in the long run for this change in corporate strategy.

Look for ways to keep your laid-off employees associated with the new company. The budget for their position might run out before your need for their services does. If it makes sense to do so, engage them as consultants to do project work after their formal full-time employment comes to a close. Encourage your current employees to stay in touch with them. You never know when you might want to hire them again, either for this new company, or the company you move on to yourself after the integration process concludes. In the meantime, people will be watching how you treat all employees—past, future, present—which will be an essential example of corporate culture in action. Make sure your behaviors are consistent with the company's stated values.

Identify and implement ways of encouraging desired behaviors quickly. An across-the-board culture shift will take several years to completely settle in. But you can start right away to build up a workplace culture that reflects the desired behaviors. Look for cultural fit from the new hires, for instance. Establish appropriate behavior changes. These behavior modifications will build up over time.

Re-recruit your current employees. It's not enough for them to know they still have a job to be willing to volunteer their efforts and talents to the new organization. You need to make an active effort to invite them to rededicate themselves to the company and its new direction. You have kept your A Players for a reason, and it's the same reason that makes them supremely desirable to headhunters and your competitors. Make an effort to get to know them, tell them what their new job is, perhaps create custom retention strategies on an individual or team basis.

Create retention, compensation, and team-building budgets to correct salary anomalies and bring in special training. They don't have to be across-the-board salary increases for those who have managed to survive the merger process. But you need to have enough leeway to provide incentives for your highest-value performers to stay. And, the larger the organization, the more likely it will be that you will come across disconnects between compensation and desired outcomes.

Give your employees the chance to get to know each other in meaningful ways. A reorganized company means reorganized departments, with newly configured teams grafted together from a motley collection of employees, often from around the world. Shared objectives and dovetailed job descriptions won't necessarily create the bonded workplace culture that will help yours operate at its best. Look for ways they can have shared experiences both within their departments and cross-functionally that will reconstitute a new company culture that is quickly ready to operate at full capacity.

Communicate, communicate, communicate. Whether your company culture is embedded in a single location or throughout the world, you need to hear from your people. And they need to hear from you. And they need to hear from each other. Technology facilitates town hall meetings; Facebook-type social media platforms can create virtual communities of team far flung among continents. Team collaboration tools bring people together in virtual rooms where they can participate anonymously in focus group type conversations.

However, don't simply hide behind your computer monitor. Get out into the field as much as your time and budget will allow. Different geographical regions within your company, as well as different departments closer to home, have their own micro-cultures, too. So they need to be exposed to the new vision for the newly merged company. And they deserve to see the person who is driving the culture change.

If your company is in a variety of international locations, make sure all official communications to them are in their first languages. Everyone needs to know the same thing at the same time. This way you avoid the false impression that headquarters cares about one group over another.

Hold top of mind exactly what the vision is for the new company. Be as clear as you can possibly be when you imagine it yourself and in how you articulate it to the rest of the company.

Step 3: Track Your Trends and Results

By now your metrics dashboard is filling up with data. You have gotten your key stakeholders into the habit of referring to it in preparation for essential, high-level meetings. And they have come to own the responsibility of incorporating talent considerations into their decision-making process and communications strategy.

There is no end-point to your metrics gathering activities. But as the integration process reaches certain milestones, you would do well to re-visit your dashboard with a distinct set of objectives, beyond the essential tracking of trends that you had been doing all along.

Update your set of metrics to be the most relevant to your current phase of integration. It's likely that some of the most pressing issues that had been before you at the outset of the integration process are no longer the most relevant now. For instance, you may have moved beyond worrying about the voluntary departure of key talent at a certain point. And now you would like to replace that metric with one that tracks how many new candidates come to your company as a result of employee referrals.

Measure the correlation between stated employee value proposition and actual employee experience. Your newly integrated organization is building up a culture track record. Administer an employee engagement survey within twelve to eighteen months of the merger to begin to track the progress that the company is making toward the desired culture.

Don't be misled by an overwhelming positive report or a negative one. What you are looking for is an accurate snapshot of employee attitudes and experiences regarding the company. Employees who are apathetic or even mistrusting might report positive experiences just to get the survey completed and out of the way. Seemingly negative results could actually be a positive indicator that your people care enough about the progress of the new culture that they are willing to take the time to report honestly. Your goal is evidence of progress, not an indicator of having arrived at some ideal.

Use the results for training, not punishment. The leaders whom you have retained through the merger are learning new behaviors and management skills to align with the new ideal, merged culture. They're human; they're not going to deliver uniformly and perfectly from Day One. There will be an adjustment process. The results of your surveys and dashboard should be used as indicators for where additional training or, perhaps, team building is required.

Gather stories. Behind each new change in the dashboard, there is probably a multitude of stories about how the employees of the merged company are courageously taking on the transformation. The wisdom and insight you'll be gathering from these stories will help you breathe life into the metrics as you help the senior leadership understand the results of the culture transformation—as well as quickly grasp what has worked and what hasn't.

Conclusion

As you move through this process, the one cultural integration story that you should not overlook is your own. No matter what kinds of industries are being blended as a result of your merger initiative (even if it's not a professional services type combination), every company today depends substantially on its most mobile of assets—the high-value talent.

The experience that you will have successfully ushering two company cultures through a successful merger positions you to provide this exceedingly valuable service as companies form, combine, and recombine in the upcoming years and decades. This experience will be your differentiating factor, a niche that will put you in great demand.

Mark leads People, Culture, and Change Delivery for Crowe Horwath LLP's Merger & Acquisition Integration practice. These services include due diligence, organizational design, change management, leadership selection, employee communications, and cultural transformation across a broad array of industries. He has managed or advised leaders and their organizations on over two dozen M&A integrations ranging from emerging companies to leading global organizations with transaction values from $5 million to $5 billion.

Mark has over 30 years of combined industry and consulting experience with deep functional expertise in human resources strategy, organizational culture, leadership effectiveness, and change management. His career includes global human capital leadership roles with American Express, Ernst & Young LLP and Thomson Reuters, and he has served founding entrepreneurs and private equity firms and their portfolio companies as a human capital advisor. He earned an MA in Organizational Psychology from Columbia University of New York.

Contact Mark at mark@markwalztoni.com or call 847.400.7504.

Chapter 13

Democratizing HR: The Coming Shift in Power to People

Dean Carter
Head of Human Resources, Legal, and Finance
Patagonia

Every few years, HR professionals get riled up around the latest release of the "I Hate HR" message and are regularly indignant to see it get so much play time. The answer may not lie in the torrent of retorts spawned by such articles, but in the unspoken truth: Much of HR still clings to aging philosophies and systems better fit for eras long past. The Chinese, for instance, were using the annual performance review around the 3rd Century. And most American companies have been using the current "modern" version since 1960.

With the advent of IT and HRIS systems, HR chest-thumped its progress into the era of technology by paving the long-hallowed processes with silicon. All these updates may look like we're doing things differently (and therefore, it is presumed, better). But they really are just a fresh repackaging of the same old same old. I'm reminded of an old anonymous poem where the path of a meandering calf is paved, with no improvement of efficiency:

They follow still his crooked way,
And lose one hundred years a day,
For thus such reverence is lent
To well-established precedent.

HR's role has become a mash-up of spiritual intercessor, protective parent, and bureaucratic police officer. We have made ourselves indispensably important by making ourselves unavoidable. Instead of making a better way for the performance of our companies through our people, HR has merely continued to do what it does best: Get in the way.

Having our hand in the middle has somehow come to mean being essential. We have to be involved with the employees and their performance; the employees and their healthcare and wellness choices; the employees and feedback to each other; the employees and their relationships with their jobs, their careers, their company, their bosses, and each other. Those programs come out of our profession, we drive them. We are proud of them. Therefore we have to stay directly involved in every possible way. In fact, we set it up so that there could be very little progress in any of these areas without our direct intercession.

We haven't done ourselves and the HR profession any favors by staying on this path. So many of these programs and initiatives are automated now, the HR function has managed to relegate itself back into the administrative function, rather than use its added experience to continue developing new people programs that move the company forward. So really, when you think about it, our pursuit of significance as a profession has really been counterproductive.

Here's the new paradigm: Get out of the way altogether. Become imminently valuable by becoming seamlessly unobtrusive. And return human resources to the humans in a way never before possible.

The time has come for HR to break free from the well-tended paths of the past, to leverage new science and new technology to do what we intended to do all along—enable the power of human potential and performance. By embracing new alternatives, we can unleash control, exponentially improve the conversation, put the terms on an open platform of performance and truly transform HR for the future.

Consider one of our era's favorite metaphors for just about everything: Apple and all its products. Let's look at the pre-Apple world first: Depending on how old you are, you may remember big, clunky computers, pre-Windows. The hulking, yellowish, ugly computers themselves took up a tremendous amount of room on everyone's desks (assuming they had their very own computer assigned to them). Their operating systems instantly got in the way of your work. You had to know DOS almost fluently to even open a new document. You could never forget it was there as you tried to use the tool for getting your work done. All that coding had to be addressed to open a new file, insert a word in bold, switch paragraphs around.

There was just an awful lot of machinery and functional noise that stood in the way of your objectives. And heaven help you if you didn't know how to communicate with it in exactly the way it needed to be communicated with. Save that precious document in the wrong drive and your day was toast.

Compare that experience with Apple's philosophy of seamless and elegant integration that lies behind all its products. The physical nature of all the products is sleek and unobtrusive. But more to the point, the *experience* of implementing them to their highest potential is so intuitive that you can accomplish what you need to do practically anytime, anywhere, from your desktop in the office, on the beach, or from your pocket at a base camp on Mount Everest. The world of possibilities is accessible from that pretty little thing that fits in the palm of your hand wherever you go—unleashing you to live and work at your fullest potential. The only time you think about the machine itself is when you stop to appreciate how cool it is.

HR can be that for its company and all its stakeholders: Available as needed and delightfully innovative to unobtrusively enrich the performance and experience of all its democratized clients. Gratifying and meaningful to work with. Uniquely indispensable. And maybe even pleasurable.

Like the example of the Apple suite of products, HR can accomplish many of its essential objectives by almost invisibly helping people connect with each other, to perform independently but with the seamless support of their colleagues even a world away, and to get what they want and need now. (Without having to go to or through HR first.) And even at times have fun doing it, which, in turn, can promote even higher levels of engagement. We can do that through the use of technological platforms that already exist, moving into more crowd-based interactivity, leveraging social networking, and capitalizing on immediately available data that gives us the instant feedback we need to be instantly responsive, imminently valuable, and relatively unobtrusively.

How? By changing our posture altogether, democratizing the role of HR and leveraging three tools that have recently come into our lives, and are readily accessible (in fact, we're already using them):

Technology: Mobile technology is probably the biggest game changer of all the technological advances in recent years. We can receive essential information literally in our hands easily and instantly—from weather alerts to reports on the engagement levels of a division 2,000 miles away. The hundreds of thousands of apps that can reside in that mobile technology open up every conceivable possibility.

Additionally, technology is also enabling our understanding of many more humanistic aspects of the HR profession. Take, for instance, neuroscience. Now, with the marriage of technology and neuroscience, we can actually see what kinds of conversations light up the brain, which engage thought, and which actually shut down engagement. (Imagine the implications on the performance review conversation.)

Social networking: Time was once that our day-to-day circle of influence was limited to the person within shouting distance of our desk. Now we take it for granted that we are on friendly basis with someone halfway around the world who can help us with a business problem. Because of social networking, we are no longer bound by geography, nor are we constrained by hierarchy. It's the ultimate open door policy on the social network. Not only is everyone's door always open, but in truth, everyone is in the same room. And that where the answers can be found to any business question you may have.

Remember the Gallup Q12 question about whether you have a best friend at work? With the emergence of social networking, your employees can probably confidently say that they have multiple "best" friends at work—people they might not have even personally met but whom they can trust and turn to for best practice sharing and other support that promotes high performance and enhances their own engagement experiences on the job.

Easy availability of data: Data is information. And information is power. The hipster anarchists are fond of saying "Information wants to be free," which has some untenable ethical, legal, and financial implications. But a case can be made for the fact that data can be more freely—and more widely—shared, more rapidly, and in a format that is both delightful and easily applied to inspire immediate behavior shifts for the good of both the individual and the company.

It is free of all once-unavoidable constraints of time, distance, and hierarchy. Combined with mobile technology, data is immediately available in the palm of your hand, on your wrist, in your ear, even while you're asleep. As we'll see later in this chapter, the easily availability of data can now deliver a full company report of the mood of all employees *at that very moment* with a simple log in.

With this new power of knowledge, employees throughout the org chart have the ability to draw conclusions, make decisions, and act on them without the direct intervention of HR.

Getting Out of the Way at Sears

Opportunities for HR to get out of the way will expand as technology, social networking, and easy availability of data continue their sleek progress in seamlessly integrating the employee experience with organizational effectiveness. Here are three examples of how Sears Holdings is activating these three developments to put more power in the hands of employees—and getting undeniably valuable results in the process.

Health and Wellness

Over the last half century or so, we in HR created a phenomenon of learned helplessness when it came to making employees directly responsible for their health care. We chose the carriers, we chose the limited plan selection for our people, we even designed our healthcare communications around only health conditions that cost us the most—neglecting the vast array of diseases and preventative measures that were most meaningful to individual employees. The company's healthcare activities were rarely about the individual employee; they were about cost-benefit ratios regarded from the ultimate standpoint of what would be best for the organization.

Of course, the employees and their families benefited from these programs. Lives were saved by spreading the costs of healthcare across the population of employees and providing first-class healthcare. But at what cost to the overall value of equipping employees with the knowledge, skills, and tools they need to make adult, independent decisions about the way they manage their individual lives healthcare-wise?

While we in HR certainly had no malicious intent, our determination to be as valuable and functional as possible in containing healthcare costs across our employee populations had the effect of disconnecting the individuals from the knowledge *they* needed and self-sovereignty that must come with being personally responsible for being healthy. Up until recently, the technology and information weren't sufficiently democratized to put personal healthcare coverage decisions directly in the hands of the employees themselves. It all had to be done centrally—e.g., in the HR department. And employees had to go through HR to activate any of the healthcare benefits available to them. HR was in the way.

Now because of data and technology, and social media where people can comment about the quality of care they receive, a new world is emerging. Let's look at technology first.

Because of *technology*, we can build a system where individuals can make their own decisions around who their insurance carrier will be, according to their desires and priorities. And it enables employees to do it annually, rather than every three years during an exhaustive HR-managed RFP. As a result, a competitive marketplace for medical and dental insurance has emerged, also known as a private healthcare exchange. The carriers must now appeal to the direct consumers themselves. HR is out of the way. And the consumers—your employees—are asking better questions and becoming more actively informed purchasers of healthcare, and, consequently, managers of their own health decisions overall. HR is no longer the healthcare hero. The individual is his own hero.

Then with *social networking* in corporate health and wellness programs, employees can independently tap into the crowd of like-minded colleagues for peer support and even some friendly competition. For example, during Year One enrollment for the healthcare exchange at Sears, informal networks were popping up throughout the entire organization, all over the country to share information. Our early adopters began using portable devices such as Jawbone, Nike FuelBand, and FitBit, and they formed communities to bring a measure of fun and support to their new health objectives.

With HR out of the way, the healthcare conversation at Sears is a more personal, more of a mass-customized wellness community of individuals equally passionate about taking responsibility for their own healthcare—which is a system far more effective than any brochure corporate communications could have produced. Our role is to help facilitate the platform for these types of communities, not to be the gatekeeper.

The *ready availability of data* becomes immediately obvious in this new, self-directed healthcare environment. From the individual's perspective, data-based reporting is dynamic and instantly usable at a consumer level. The more immediately aware the employees are of the impacts of their behaviors on their performance, their health, and subsequently their wallets, the more quickly they can make their own decisions to change for outcomes they prefer.

Employees can now see plainly that they will pay more if they have higher healthcare costs. At Sears Holdings, we have transformed from a defined benefit model to a defined contribution model. When employee choices impact their pocketbooks in a more direct, more transparent way, the data helps them see that their choices are obvious ones—assuming they want to save money by staying healthier.

We're now on the threshold of such extreme accessibility of information. Employees can be equipped with the knowledge necessary to not only commit to 10,000 steps this week, but also perhaps taking more aggressive measures now that can prevent cancer that has been identified as statistically likely to occur several decades from now. Naturally, ready availability of data in the health care arena brings with it essential moral questions and ethical challenges around such issues as privacy. But as these issues sort themselves out in the public policy arena, and no doubt through litigation and legislation, the outcome for individual employees will hopefully be to continue to increasingly empower individuals to take direct responsibility for their health care and lifestyle choices. And because individuals are unlikely to stay with one company their entire careers, companies must be willing to work together to create platforms of data gathering and healthcare practices that easily transfer throughout the individual's working years from one company to the next.

Performance Management

Conventional performance management practices are not only outdated, they're also largely counterproductive—especially in the area of the performance review. Because there is so much information already available on the subject of how performance reviews fall short of the mark, I will simply remind us that such meetings

- Are universally dreaded and not value-add
- Are almost always irrelevant because of the passage of time
- Are almost always administered by someone whom the employees believe doesn't know the true value of their contributions
- And almost always have the opposite effect of shutting down the employee who is under review, rather than inspiring that person to higher levels of achievement.

There's also the matter of the fact that individual bosses carry less direct power over performance than they used to. While they still have a huge impact, their influence is eroding as the rise of social interactions make the entire "crowd" more impactful on the way a single employee performs. Not only is the answer to the question, "Who is my boss?" increasingly unclear, the important sources of performance quality inspiration and information are increasingly coming from surprising places: Far-flung geographic locations; other, unrelated departments; even lower down the org chart than any given employee.

Technology and *social networking* empower the democratization of performance management, making it more relevant to each of the employees and driving organizational objectives across the landscape of a large company like Sears far more efficiently than any individual "boss" would. While that binary relationship between employee and supervisor is still in place, we at Sears have implemented social networking as an even more valuable tool to drive quality in performance across the entire organization. Again, the result is that HR intervention is moved into the background, while the crowd steps forward to support everyone's individual accountability to their jobs and to each other.

At Sears, we have installed a robust, internally built social network that combines the best features of Twitter, Facebook, and LinkedIn. Employees can pick who they want to "follow," and others, in turn, choose to follow them based on the quality of their contributions to the conversations on the network. So there is an expectation that each employee gains a following, as well as carefully cultivates the "garden" of people they follow.

While there is no expectation of the topics that are discussed, we have analyzed the data around who appears to have greater social influence on the company and who doesn't. And then we lined up the results against historical performance reviews. And we have found an unmistakably high correlation between social influence, as scored using the network, and employees' performance reviews.

Separating out the possibility for manager bias, we then looked at social scores as compared with straight performance measurements—such as who sells the most appliances. And we found an even higher correlation. Then, we re-cut the analysis to align social networking scores with engagement scores. Again, a freakishly high correlation. We had undeniable correlations, but wanted to understand more about causation behaviors.

So we surveyed 6,000 people who were using the system. The top performers reported that they use the social networking system to keep up with what's going on in the company and get quality information quickly. Lower-performing individuals used the network for simple social reasons, such as wishing someone a happy birthday.

We also learned to identify highly valuable employees who might have otherwise gone unrecognized by more outmoded performance measures—active and influential social contributors who make everyone around them better, as opposed to high-scoring individuals who don't exert a positive influence on the people around them. These people have been with us all along but without the *easy accessibility of data* that accompanied our social networking platform, we wouldn't have been able to spot them before.

Now we know who is influencing whom; who has a community of 500 followers who are informed and inspired by their influence. The long-established conventions of performance management might have caused us to overlook these individual contributors who might have been graded B Players at best. But now with the social network platform, we can identify them and leverage their influence to the benefit of the entire community and company. Their influence goes both recognized and custom rewarded.

Employee Engagement

Finally, let's look at employee engagement as a third way that HR can use dynamic data availability, technology, and social networking to get out of its own way and achieve the desired results.

Up until most recently, the entire employee engagement process—however well-meaning its origins—risked being disengaging itself. Extensive surveys were developed at great cost, with sometimes questionable relevance to the employees' experience of the company to begin with, and then administered once a year or once every 18 months. Employees may or may not take the time to fill them out, and then everyone would wait for the slow churning of data analysis. And then hear...nothing.

Even under the best of circumstances and practices, the conventional employee engagement survey is a snapshot in time, taken well over twelve months before the results are delivered. In any dynamic company, so many changes will have already taken place in the interim, the results are outdated. Or, in the case of an especially disengaging manager, that would be a year's worth of further damage done to the culture while HR patiently waits for the numbers to come in. It's like taking a photo of

Chicago on a day in February—and spending the entire year planning on how to deal with that snowy day when the weather in August is quite different. Engagement—like weather—is fluid and changing…and the systems to respond to it should be just as dynamic.

With the confluence of *technology*, *social networking platforms*, and *readily available data*, HR can take the pulse of a company's engagement every morning, practically from the instant that the lights are turned on or off across the nation. On the belief that mood absolutely influences organizational performance, we at Sears created what we call the Net Mood Score (NMS), and we actually ask our people every day, "What is your mood?" Positive net mood correlates with engagement, which, in turn, correlates with "contributions per hour," such as the rate of sales. It may seem intuitively obvious to believe that better the mood the higher the performance, but now we can prove it.

Using our punch-out system, employees voluntarily and anonymously answer the question, "What is your mood today?" Their options range from "I'm unstoppable" to "I'm exhausted." We can then use the results (millions of data points over the course of a year) to capture the mood of our people. In mood heat maps by location, when the score is net positive, the visual report is a blue dot. When the mood is negative, it's a red dot; neutral is represented by a gray dot. Then we can animate the scores, moving those colors over time and what how and where they flare red, blue, gray, change, or don't change.

Then we can refer back to what was going on during that time, and what might have accounted for the change. For instance, when a generally positive district suddenly flares red, we can then see that the flare coincides with a change in district managers. And now it becomes a change management issue. Instead of guessing how things might be going across the country, we can directly and immediately measure the impact on organizational mood. And we can instantly make changes.

Instant and dynamic data reporting also helps us understand—and to some extent, control—the drivers. We know now that general mood escalates through the week, peaking at Thursday and dropping again through Saturday. On the busiest days, both mood extremes go up. There are people who are energized by busy-ness and others who are exhausted by it.

And we can follow up our initial question with, "We notice that you're unstoppable today. What's causing that? Here are six options to choose from." Then we can understand whether the drivers are within our control or not. We have a baseline for understanding the foundational elements of engagement on a store level, on a district level, and then across the nation. We expect that this will help us understand what the hot spots are for later investigation, what's going on in a particular region, whether we need to initiate an EAP intervention, even predict potential problems on the horizon.

Does this kind of measurement make HR responsible for *making* employees happy? Not necessarily. But there are two indisputable facts of life in any retail setting: People who are in better moods sell more, and retail is known for high levels of turnover. So if we can use any mechanism for measuring mood and infusing teams with that feeling of being "unstoppable," it's to the company's advantage ultimately. You can't train happiness. But you can certainly hire for it, and put elements in place that sustain it.

And we can do it quickly, rather than wait for a year or so to discover what happened after it was too late to do anything about it.

Conclusion

As we start to look at how dynamic data reporting can benefit both the company's employee engagement experience, as well as the employees' experience of the company, it's easy to start thinking of this as employee engagement 2.0. We are using technology, social networking, and readily available data as tools to unleash high performance in our company at all levels.

The same can be said of HR overall. These tools, likewise, unleash us from the low-value activities that bind HR and prevent us from providing an even more superior contribution to the company. As we begin to embrace the world of readily available data, social networking, and technology, what we do becomes exponentially more impactful, more interesting, more connected, more relevant to our organizations and the individuals and their own career interests.

But this means we have to let go of those intervention-level activities that we believed communicate our value to the organization. As a profession we need to be open to that feeling of discomfort as we release our grip on activities and initiatives that have long since been dismissed as being of limited value.

Let the crowd take more control, sustain itself, inform itself. Let your own value to the organization be the creation of the platforms that will empower employees to do what they do best on their own without needing to turn to you as their intercessor.

Once you untether yourself from those old beliefs of where your value lies, you will no doubt find the changes to be deeply gratifying, deeply rewarding, deeply stimulating. And well worth the risk. Because you will see that finally you have become the one who really is setting the stage for individuals to change their lives, improve their health, and build rewarding careers.

And you will have created the thriving organization that reinvents itself to serve its people as we all expand our capability to flourish and perform on ever-growing platforms—rather than sustain outdated organizations that constrain their people to stay small in how they show up in their lives and work.

Thomas Jefferson once wrote:

> …Institutions must go hand in hand with the progress of the human mind. As that becomes more developed, more enlightened, as new discoveries are made, new truths discovered and manners and opinions change, with the circumstances, institutions must advance also to keep pace with the times. We might as well require a man to wear still the coat which fitted him as a boy as civilized society to remain ever under the regime of the barbarous ancestors.

Time for a new coat.

Dean Carter is Head of Human Resources, Legal, and Finance for Patagonia. Before joining Patagonia in 2015, Dean was the Chief Human Resources Officer for Sears Holdings Corporation (SHC), a Fortune 50 company and is made of iconic retail brands including Sears and Kmart, as well as leading consumer brands, Kenmore, Craftsman and DieHard. During his tenure, Dean took an increasingly progressive approach to the application of HR Analytics, led the transformation of healthcare through the pioneering adoption of corporate private exchanges, and drove innovation in areas such as dynamic engagement and the gamification of performance management.

Dean was named among the Top Ten Global HR Breakaway Leaders at the 2013 Global HR Summit. His innovations in HR have been recognized and featured by organizations such as the CEB Corporate Leadership Council, SHRM/SIOP, The Annual McKinsey Summit on Healthcare, Boyden International's Global Leadership Series, i4cp, The Economist, and NPR's Morning Edition.

This chapter was written while Dean was still at Sears.

Dean can be reached at deancarter@me.com.

Chapter 14

The Data Connection: How Keeping Current with Your Impact Players Drives Your Competitive Edge

Sanjay Sathe
Founder and CEO
Risesmart, Inc.

Consider for a moment this question: Who knows more about your most essential talent and their capabilities than you do? (Setting aside, of course, their spouses, other key family members, and friends.)

The most likely answer would be: LinkedIn. It hardly seems possible, does it? A remote information portal where the relationships are virtual and participation is voluntary? There is no centralized governing process to ensure consistency, accuracy, and completion. It's just a variety of dashboards and dials to *influence* and *attract* a voluntary ongoing, incoming stream of updated information. It's not even human. And, unless your business is based in Silicon Valley, the chances are excellent that the humans who work at LinkedIn don't actually know any of your people.

And yet LinkedIn is one of the biggest threats to your secure position as your most-valuable employees' employer.

So how can LinkedIn be better than you are at staying absolutely current with your own people? When you think about the storyline of your relationship with your talent, it makes sense very quickly. Here's how it goes:

You have an opening that requires a certain, defined set of skills and experiences. About the same time you begin your search process, a wonderful candidate updates his LinkedIn profile to include his most recent career experience and educational credentials. In that fortuitous intersection where need (yours) meets availability (his), the selection, interview, offer, onboarding process begins. Your need is filled. He has a new job. And the interests of your business strategy, as it currently stands, are served.

Excellent. But the story isn't over.

This is where two pathways (yours and the employee's) begin to diverge again. You have opened a file for your new hire: His skills, background, educational credentials. And you now focus on putting him to work to help him be successful in helping your company be successful. This is what you do, and, as far as you're concerned, this is what he does. No more, and, hopefully, no less.

But that file is merely a snapshot in time, already out of date after the employee's first day at his new job. Your new employee's professional development lives on, as does his continually updated LinkedIn profile. While he is focusing on doing a stellar job for your company, exactly according to your mutual agreement about what the expectations are, he's continuing to build his credentials: Adding experiences, developing within the role, going back to school for additional degrees and certifications. In less than a year's time, maybe a little longer, the employee's qualifications have completely blown past the defined scope of abilities he came to you with. And now he's looking for new ways to put these abilities into action—to benefit both himself and whichever company is lucky enough to spot his offerings on, you guessed it, Linked In.

Did *you* know about his expanded scope of abilities? Very likely not. He has been measured for the work he had been hired to do. And he's been doing it well, perhaps even surpassing all expectations. Maybe his boss is loath to let him capitalize on his professional development because that would result in possibly losing him to a better opportunity within the company. Whatever the reason, your valuable employee sees no avenue through which to inform your company how he's been developing himself in his off-hours. And, likewise, there is no tool for you to capture that data in a way that will be easily accessible later with just the entry of a few keywords.

The employee decides that he has outgrown the potential offered by your organization. He sees no other opportunities internally. He has lost faith in his boss's ability to help him move his career to the next level. And so he starts to accept calls from recruiters who have found him on, of course, LinkedIn, using keywords that match his updated skill set. He eventually tells you he's moving on. Even if you do happen to see that his profile includes all those new skills and credentials that you're looking for in your own updated business strategy, you might be tempted to tell your recruiters to pass on them. There is still that belief in circulation that once someone decides to leave your company, there's no point in trying to hang onto him. You'd be just postponing the inevitable. He's already resigned in his heart (you assume), so any better deal you could offer will only keep him for a short while longer. So you're convinced that it's best to let him go. Better to start fresh. With new talent. A clean slate.

This scenario is not about how LinkedIn is your worst enemy when it comes to your efforts to retain your best talent. The point here is that there are new data tools at your disposal right now that can help you attract—and keep and redeploy—your most valuable people at a time when mission-critical "impact players" are essential to develop, retain, and maybe even re-recruit.

LinkedIn is an example of the approach to data collection (even data *attraction*) that can be used to thoroughly serve your strategies—not only the strategies of today but well into the future. What's the difference between LinkedIn's approach to data and what might be yours at the moment? Think of LinkedIn's data flow as an ever-moving river, always changing, always updating itself as conditions change, always filling new wells of information with new ways of organizing that information.

In contrast, if your data collection system is consistent with the vast majority of HR departments' out there, your system is more like a stop-action camera. Each moment in time is frozen with a single click to lock in the data. Once that data is locked in, it's already outdated. While LinkedIn's information river keeps rolling along, its current powered by an engaged membership that voluntarily contributes updated data.

Your company needs and deserves that same level of engagement. Its destiny rides on the back of your talent and how dedicated they are, which increasingly depends on how confident they are that your company is a good investment in their own professional development journey. This confidence, in turn, is tracked and measured by the information you are able to acquire and organize at a moment's notice. A shift in your approach to not only how you *collect* data on your employee population but also how you *use* it will accelerate your company's ability to keep up with its changing strategies and implement them using the best talent available to you. This chapter will help you retool your data management systems to make the most of your people, even your alumni, and their own thirst for professional development and growth.

The rest of this chapter is based on four organizing principles:

Data is most efficacious when it's fluid. As demonstrated in the opening LinkedIn example of this chapter, circumstances change so rapidly today that we need to install data collection and analysis processes in such a way that we can understand our talent population in real time, at a moment's notice. This way we see who we have right now and what they're capable of doing now (or soon). We can also reasonably forecast who might be beneficial to our companies' changing business strategies further down the proverbial stream.

True employee engagement is in constant motion. It wasn't that long ago that reports on engagement surveys could be reasonably expected twelve to eighteen months after the survey was administered. Pulse surveys filled in the gaps, but their scope was typically extremely limited to one or two questions. Today, especially with the influence of Millennials and their unique sets of workplace expectations, change is the new constant. And immediacy is the new standard. Today's talent demands ongoing feedback. They need to trust that they have the best possible mentors.

They need to know that there is always a next step inside the organization—or they will go elsewhere. They need to know this *all the time*.

Employee engagement drives—and is driven by—career empowerment. Top talent needs to know that they are constantly building their skill sets and laying down the path to their next development milestone and beyond. While the need to be constantly mentored and developed is most definitely a Millennial trademark, it affects the anticipations and expectations of all your employees, older and even younger. No one expects any job to be secure or predictable anymore (your own LinkedIn profile is up-to-date, right?). And the aggressive energy that the Millennials invest in making sure that they are always on the move adds pressure to their colleagues to be competitive as well. Therefore, you, as the HR leader, are on the spot to build your engagement factor by demonstrating your organization's commitment to the professional development of all your employees.

When employees see a linkage between what they do for their company and what they're doing for their careers by way of tapping into developmental opportunities you present to them, you as the employer are most likely to enjoy the business interest benefits of employee engagement.

And career empowerment drives business empowerment. Anxiety-ridden employees are not going to be equipped to provide their best work contributions to your organization. They're distracted at best. Resentful at worst. And it's a small step from being passively not engaged in the company's mission-critical priorities to actually being actively disengaged where the employees retaliate against a company by exposing intellectual property, sabotaging the company's reputation on sites like Glassdoor, even destroying physical property in extreme circumstances. There was once a time when employers could assume that employees were focused on their work so much they didn't notice the signs on the horizon that foretold almost certain layoffs (if you haven't been blindsided yourself by the unexpected conversation that concluded with you handing over your card key, you surely know someone who has). But those days are gone. Even the most sublimely contented employee has one eye on the open door. Single-minded loyalty to the current job has its limitations. Employees know that. And you know it too. Engagement isn't about keeping all employees; it's about sustaining a mutually advantageous relationship where trust and commitment benefit both employee and employer. And a very valuable component of that relationship is the employee's relative confidence that the employer is actively engaged itself in responding to all employees' drives for professional development and expansion of career potentiality. Even if that next step might be external to the immediate company.

This simple adjustment in the employer's philosophy about employees' professional development results in easily obvious benefits:

One of the top three reasons people leave an organization is the lack of challenging and meaningful developmental opportunities. According to Aon Hewitt, 74 percent of employees are actively searching for new jobs at any given time, and 69 percent report that searching for new opportunities is part of their regular routine. Employee turnover costs U.S. businesses an estimated $11 billion annually.

According to Gallup, actively disengaged employees represent $450 billion to $550 billion in lost productivity every year. This figure does not take into account the direct cost to the company in terms of harm done, such as equipment damage or compromised intellectual property.

An Accenture study reports that while 55 percent of employees report being under pressure to develop additional skills, only 21 percent report that companies provide the training for those skills. Additionally, a SuccessFactors survey reveals that 83 percent of employees don't feel that their current skills and experience are being fully utilized. And Accenture further showed that only 34 percent report that it was easy to move to another job within their own companies, and 49 percent said that their employers provided adequate information regarding what additional skills and knowledge would help employees progress to the next level.

Clearly, companies that take the simple, additional steps of creating a tightly woven matrix against which employees can confidently plot their entire array of skills development and deployment stand to benefit where their more detached competitors just won't.

In short: High-value employees—the so-called "impact players" who make the most significant difference in your company, the ones you want to keep for as long as possible—are most likely to stay with your enterprise when they can see a valuable connection to their future prospects.

Data is no longer for merely capturing employee information. It's to equip companies to stay current with their impact players—even the ones who have entered the ranks of alumni. Use data to keep engagement alive, to build bench strength for both the immediate and long-term future, and to build a healthy employer brand beyond your immediate circles of influence. This will position you well for attracting key talent in upcoming years to fulfill business strategy that you haven't even developed yet.

There are two ways to break down your approach to using data as a talent management enrichment/career empowerment tool: To retain key employees and to sustain a living relationship with them even after they have left your company.

Retention

When you lose a key employee, what do you suppose the cause may be? It may be natural to assume that the employee left for a better job or better paycheck. But increasingly employers are discovering that their best people are leaving because they are dissatisfied with their prospects for development. Maybe your training opportunities aren't as robust as they need to be, or there is a lack of mobility. Maybe your people are craving a broader array of developmental opportunities across the various departments so that their own bucket of capabilities is more comprehensive. Or perhaps they have lost faith that their immediate supervisor has anything new to teach them.

In any of these scenarios, your best people no longer see that your company is invested in their future.

On your side of the talent ledger, you believe the developmental opportunities that you can extend your people are limited. You see that your current business strategy (the one for which all your people are geared up) has an extremely limited shelf life. And you worry that all these people on your staff will need to be replaced—either gradually or abruptly—

as your company's new strategy shifts directions. True, you will probably lose some talent eventually—talent that was once mission critical but will become mission obsolete. But you recognized that there are extremely valuable employees who are worth the investment of developing, maybe even retooling. Your job is to figure out who they are and what they'll need to meet your company's future strategic needs.

A re-engineered data collection strategy will help your organization fully understand the psyche of the employees in terms of where they are, where they want to go, what are the skills they have, and where they want to grow. With that data, you can make informed decisions on how to empower employees so that you can stop whatever stagnation and disengagement there may be. You can also play an essential role in helping the organization realign its strategies using the talent that is already onboard, reducing the expenses associated with reductions in force, and ultimately sourcing and onboarding new talent.

If you must prepare yourself to onboard new talent anyway, use that energy and those resources to help your current talent onboard themselves in the form of career development. Employees who are satisfied with their career development are significantly more likely to stay for at least three to five years. Those are three to five years that you can leverage to keep them engaged partners in your company's future.

Data-enabled tracking and programming technology places critical tools at your disposal to extend multiple developmental opportunities to your essential talent to help your company develop itself from within, rather than depend on the constant, expensive, risky churn of sourcing and recruiting new employees:

Short-term developmental opportunities: These projects—increasingly referred to as *gigs*, give your key talent the opportunities to expand their scope of experiences while helping your company fill short-term needs. Maybe someone on family leave—or who has been assigned to another project—creates an opening for a short-term fill-in to help bring a project to completion in the resulting absence. Or a special project brings members from a variety of internal teams together to collaborate on a limited, defined objective. These opportunities give your people the chance to "test drive" career options they had not yet had the opportunity to fully explore, or investigate other departments or business units that might represent longer-term opportunities down the road. This can fundamentally increase their breadth and depth of experience.

Short-term developmental opportunities—especially those with specific, defined outcomes, also give employees the extremely valuable opportunity to tell a story about a project from start to finish. As many workplaces are increasingly based on the so-called *gig economy,* where you are only as good as your last completed project, an employer who is able to continuously offer its people an array of gigs to choose from is the employer most likely to keep those ambitious, high-talent impact players.

A culture of data-driven internal gigs benefit your organization beyond redeploying tried and true talent into short-term needs. They also prepare the next generation of managers and leaders within the organization. They allow you to give these people developmental exposure, driving the richness of their experience, therefore giving them the chance to grow. Ultimately, with every opportunity to lead—even for a short-term project—you are helping them develop the skills to become future leaders, qualifying them for their next full-time opportunity because they have proven themselves within the context of your company.

Cross-team collaboration also works very well in this gig approach to talent redeployment. When you create teams from across the company to address some specific needs where they can learn from each other, know each other better, and just increase the collaboration within the organization, you're creating a unified fabric of relationships and bringing together fresh ideas from unexpected sources. This is probably one of the most critical ways to fundamentally impact the growth of an organization and its impact in the marketplace. Very good communication and very good collaboration go hand in hand.

Long-term opportunities: Even today, with the benefits of the internal applicant tracking systems, the most sophisticated Fortune 500 companies still don't have a clear, well-defined internal mobility strategy. Quite often, the job openings inside one business unit within a large corporation may not be shared with another business unit, or, if they are, the path to transition isn't clear. It's not uncommon for a company to be laying off a group representing a certain skill set in one unit, only to be hiring the same talent in another business unit. The missed opportunities to hire from within during a layoff can be extremely costly, from outright talent acquisition and onboarding costs, to employer brand perception, reputation, and future referrals and rehire opportunities.

And even in those instances where the skill sets of the outgoing talent don't quite match up with the skill sets required of the new ramp-up, companies would do well to give all employees advance notice as to what skills they will be looking for in the foreseeable future. What are the attributes that will be needed as the organization grows in its new strategic direction? Are those skills within reach of current employees, given the time to complete their development toward those goals? You have a cadre of talent who fit the culture, who have institutional knowledge. Wouldn't it be wiser for you to give them the chance to develop themselves to meet your new required profile of capabilities?

This leads us to…

Forecasting: These needs don't simply jump out at organizations overnight. While some business units may appear to go live inside a very short time-frame from the public's point of view, the behind-the-scenes runway necessary to create the enterprise is a long and gradual one. No one should be caught by surprise that a certain set of abilities are in demand. Letting people know in advance that a certain demand is around the corner gives them the time necessary to volunteer for taking on that skill set and start accumulating the necessary knowledge, experience, and credentials.

Maybe your existing workforce already has those skills. A robust, data-based internal mobility solution equips you to know which skills already exist within your company, who has those skills, who can teach them to others, who would be an excellent mentor, and which skills need to be introduced into the organization from an external provider—either in the form of training or an entirely new population of talent.

Transition

Even with the best of developmental programs, companies still lose their most valued talent. But the relationship on pause doesn't have to be permanently broken. You can continue to re-engage talent at different points over the course of their careers by leveraging the data that you have kept on each employee, as well as tracking their progress as they develop their careers apart from your company.

Using data, you can always have access to valued talent—even the talent who is transitioning out through layoffs, voluntary terminations, and retirement. Your prospects for successful ongoing relationships with your alumni are driven by 1) how well you helped them land their next position quickly and 2) your ability to keep up with their ongoing career development story, which would include the ongoing acquisition of new skills and experiences that may come in handy for you at a future date.

It is at this time when it's especially important for your organization to treat your departing employees well. To begin with, you're protecting the employer brand. (With the proliferation of social media, careers and corporations can be brought down. Your company isn't immune to the damaging effects of negative word of mouth.) Organizations need to reinvent their thinking about their relationship with employees and ex-employees. Their relationship should not end, even if the tenure of the employee ends.

This puts you in an excellent position to have a well of talent to recruit from later, from gig assignments to full-time work. If you are looking at your alumni as talent that you can bring back again, build a database of these people and their associated skills. This is a living database, capturing the skills they had coming into the organization, the skills they acquired along the way, and the skills they have been accumulating since leaving the organization. As your needs evolve over time, requiring you to reach beyond the walls of your current employee population to source talent, this is the database you come to first.

Employees have a lifetime value to organizations, and you should make a point of building and nurturing an alumni network. Today there are a variety of tools that can be leveraged to keep your network alive and well-nourished, providing rich and current data on talent that can be re-activated at will.

Remember that your goal here is business empowerment through the career empowerment of all your employees. You're empowering alumni to succeed in their careers whether they are going to return as re-hires in the future or not. You are demonstrating that, as an organization, you're open and supportive of all your people, whether they are current employees or they are departing talent. Whatever their status, you are wise to keep your relationship with them healthy and mutually supportive. Alumni could eventually be your customers, your vendors, and your partners in the future. They could be the parents of a child you hire later. They will remember how you treated them.

Look at your transition strategies in terms of career empowerment, and consider elements of your separation process more holistically—from a long-term perspective, rather than just making a list, laying people off, and moving on thinking that everything is okay, just because you're saving money right now through a reduction in force.

Focus your efforts on helping your employees get their next job quickly (don't simply rely on the traditional outplacement firms' approach of merely training them how to be job seekers). As much as organizations have invested on the front-end of an employee's tenure with the company, they should invest on the back-end as well. The effort that you invest in helping your departing employees land quickly will come back to you financially, as well as in your reputation among both employees and customers.

Leverage the relationships that you have with other companies. There are tremendous opportunities, for instance, for employers of all companies across a given community, a geographic region, or a professional or industrial sector, to share resources and help employees transition from one company or another. All employers benefit from having this shared sense of responsibility to the extent that it's appropriate to build a community of talent.

Don't overlook the benefits of virtual career fairs. Enable organizations to present themselves online so that potential employers can meet directly with these people in transition. This is a win-win arrangement for everyone because the organization that is letting them go wants to land them fast. The organization that is hiring is able to fill the position fast. And you are able to sustain a relationship of goodwill with your talent that is transitioning out.

Conclusion

There was once a time—and unfortunately in many circumstances, it's still the case—when, for many companies, talent management was treated as little more than a speed bump in the fast traffic of market competition. The fortunate companies had the benefit of an energetic and creative HR professional who relished the challenges of making the best matches between immediate company need for a specific set of skills and the immediate availability of candidates with the skill sets that approximated that wish list. But more commonly, companies clumsily cycled through waves of employees, bringing them in as needed, washing them out when their skills apparently no longer matched the business strategy. I say *apparently* because, as we have seen in this chapter, employers commonly don't keep records of their employees' growing collection of abilities. And so they risk jettisoning the very talent via the left hand that they are spending vast sums to attract and acquire via the right hand.

Decade after decade of employers and employees alike experienced the hard knocks of layoffs, caused by all manner of reasons. The conventional outplacement services soothed the rough, sharp edges of regret, perhaps guilt, and worry over long-term reputational implications. That solution had its place while employees still assumed a more passive stance regarding their own career trajectory.

Some outplacement services and their consultants nobly and authentically concentrate on helping outgoing candidates make their next best career match. But the drive for business efficiencies being what it is, and human nature being what it is, the outplacement world has become somewhat commoditized. And success is all too frequently measured by speed rather than quality.

Today, as you walk through the corridors of your workplace and consider your employees, you're looking at workers who have taken active ownership of their own career trajectories. Quite independently, as a matter of fact, of whatever plans your company may have for them. They are using the various social networks and databases to their own personal advantage. Which is why, as we discussed in this chapter, LinkedIn very likely knows more about your employees than you do. It's all about the timely, to-the-moment, even voluntary updating of relevant data—organized and stored in a way that is most beneficial to both the individuals and employers.

This caliber of data collection is within your own grasp as a private employer. When you take up the resolve to actively gather essential data on your employees' developments, several benefits occur:

You gain strategic insight and are better able to reinvest in your current employees and potentially even alumni.

You reduce expenses associated with recruiting, onboarding, training, unemployment, and severance. Don't overlook the intangible expenses, such as reputational and brand-negative impacts on your company.

You are best equipped to align your workforce strategies with business strategies, well in advance of actually needing the abilities in place. With a robust data collection strategy, you can quickly identify who already has the heretofore untapped abilities that will be essential in the near future. You can also identify who is best positioned to perhaps take on new training to acquire those necessary skills. And, you can even tap your alumni, inviting them to return because in the intervening years, they have become exactly what you will be needing very soon. And you know this because your data collection system has presented them to you for your consideration.

In its simplest iterations, this dedication to a robust data gathering program could be easily seen as mere "career empowerment." It's always healthy for employee engagement, good will, and your employer brand to be seen as an organization that takes an active interest in your employees' career well-being.

But in this context, career empowerment is a critical component of *business empowerment*. It is *always* to the company's best strategic and competitive advantage to know exactly what skills and abilities are available to it at any given moment. Whether your most compelling need at the moment is a redeployment of talent from one business unit to another, or a temporary stand-in for a gig that offers developmental opportunities to the employees, the more insight you have in the talent that is closest to you, the more agile you are—ready to stay ahead of your market needs and competitors' challenges.

After going through a layoff himself, Sanjay Sathe founded RiseSmart to deliver higher quality career transition services via cutting edge, proprietary technology to forward-thinking and compassionate employers who wanted their employees to land the right new jobs—fast. RiseSmart, now the nation's fastest-growing outplacement firm, was led by Sathe as CEO and President from startup to the 2015 acquisition by Randstad, one of the world's largest HR services providers.

Prior to founding Risesmart, Sanjay served as vice president for enterprise data management for Sabre Holdings, the parent company of Travelocity and a $2.5 billion global leader in travel commerce. Before Sabre, Sanjay was senior vice president of marketing for Brierley & Partners, a CRM and loyalty management company that serves global brands such as Hilton HHonors, Hertz #1 Club Gold, Sony, and Nokia. He also has worked in marketing management in Europe and Asia with Lufthansa, HSBC, and other major corporations.

Sanjay holds a Master of Business Management degree from the Asian Institute of Management in Manila, Philippines, and has completed an executive education program at the Wharton School of the University of Pennsylvania.

Contact Sanjay via ssathe@risesmart.com.

Chapter 15

Building Leadership Capability: How the Suitability Model Simplifies the Way We Think About Talent

Susan J. Schmitt
Senior Vice President, Human Resources
Rockwell Automation

Let's start by burying a myth.

There is no perfect candidate for any job, especially for a leadership role vital to the future success of your company amid global competition. Yet our priority in human resources is to lead our organization in finding and selecting the right talent for these key roles—individuals who will succeed and thrive as leaders and employees for the organization.

Sometimes in finding the right match, luck has too much to do with that hire. We've all been burned once or twice after thinking we've found the perfect candidate whose background checks all the right boxes. Then only to find out, six months later, that person wasn't a perfect match after all.

These mistakes are costly. According to a study by the Society for Human Resources Management (SHRM), it could cost up to five times a bad hire's annual salary. SHRM also found that the higher the person's position and the longer they remain in that position, the more it will cost to replace him or her. Not to mention the cost to the company of poor decisions made by the individual in question.

Over the years, I've learned to trust my instincts about candidates, even when I am the last hold-out on the hiring team. I've drawn from the rigorous research by psychologist Dr. Elliott Jaques, who proved that selecting the right people isn't as hard as we think. The real mystery is why more organizations haven't adopted his *Suitability Model*, a proven framework that simplifies the leadership talent dilemma.

Developed by Jaques and further advanced by his colleagues and contemporaries, the Suitability Model offers a simple, yet comprehensive, approach to assessing employees in current roles, as well as selecting and placing candidates into new roles at all levels in the organization. It improves the accuracy when assessing talent for current needs and succession planning, and it's been implemented in large companies throughout the world. His work is so highly regarded, the United States Army has used the model to predict, with uncanny accuracy, who is destined to become a five-star general based on the subject's ability to process the complex elements critical in the role of master strategist.

This chapter introduces you to the Suitability Model and its four components, which will guide you in acquiring, assessing, developing, and keeping talented workers and leaders. Your company will be able to:

- Identify and hire internal and external candidates ideally suited to your immediate needs and your future strategic requirements.
- Better assess talent and match talent to key roles—any role, at any level.
- Retain valued employees who might otherwise be lost through a series of flawed assumptions.
- Create a succession plan with talented individuals identified as most likely to thrive given the opportunity to develop their leadership skills.

- Accurately identify an employee's weaknesses, determine whether those weaknesses warrant remedial action or cannot be addressed, and create a plan to keep the employee and their colleagues functioning at optimal levels.
- Coach employees in their career management and development plans.
- Explain to employees why they were not selected to receive a promotion.
- Confidently create a pipeline of candidates for upper management leadership and defend hiring decisions that might go against the prevailing opinion of a work team.
- Develop an overall staffing strategy that will meet immediate performance requirements and position your company for the future.

In addition to exquisitely simplifying the entire talent management process, Jaques' breakthrough findings cast a fresh light on the ultimate efficacy (or lack thereof) of the conventional competency model, one that has been cherished within most corporations. So, before diving into the Suitability Model and its four components, let's put the conventional competency model in its rightful place.

Limitations of Your Competency Model

For decades, competencies have been developed and fine-tuned with the goal of identifying the skills and knowledge that are essential for the performance of any given job. Professional groups developed their own competencies for career-long performance. SHRM, for instance, has a relatively modest list of nine competencies for the entire HR profession. But when companies turn their focus to the competent performance of each job, they can spend hundreds of thousands of dollars codifying the multiple duties of each role within their ranks. Page after page of competencies reduces the effectiveness and relevance of employee assessment and performance review. Much of the language used in the current competency assessments is meaningless and superficial.

Moreover, it doesn't explain why people all too often fail even though they check all or most of the competency boxes.

Over time, competency models began to drive the performance management process, rather than support it. Managers are burdened with the obligation of assessing each direct report according to the rigid delineation of the job's competency set, one that has been divided and subdivided into minute judgment calls (does the employee *always, almost always, sometimes, rarely, never* demonstrate proficiency in the myriad competencies identified as essential to the job?). The competency assessment has taken over, causing HR and managers to lose sight of what's really important: Identifying, hiring, and developing talented leaders for today's business and reaching strategic goals in the future.

The primary flaw here is that the competency is limited in its ability to explain why some people succeed and others fail. Plus it almost always overlooks the person's capability to manage the complexity requirements of the role, i.e., Information Processing Complexity (IPC), which we will discuss later in this chapter, and whether the candidate accepts the role requirements of the job at hand.

Granted, it's difficult to abandon a system that has drawn so much investment in time, money, and research. Set aside your organization's attachment to the system for just a moment, and consider these questions:

- How effective is your current competency model in predicting who will succeed in bigger, more complex roles and who will stall or be asked to leave the company?
- How often do you make costly mistakes in filling senior management roles?
- How useful is your competency model in helping employees understand why they're moving up...or not?
- Are you losing an unacceptable number of talented, valuable employees who would have remained with your company if they had a clear understanding of their career path?

It might make sense, at first blush, that if you find employees who have the skills, knowledge, and experience necessary to do a job, and meet certain behavioral competencies, all you need to do is find them a workspace and assign them their employee ID and password. The assumption is that they'll be off and running, performing at a high level.

Yet, it doesn't take long for that first blush to fade. We soon recognize that an employee's performance is impacted by the totality of who they are, not just the sum of the parts on their resume.

This is where the standard competency skills model leaves you empty-handed. Every time. When was the last time you had to terminate an employee because he or she lacked skills, knowledge, or experience? It is most often about something else.

The Suitability Model helps you identify and organize all those "something else" elements before it's too late.

The Suitability Model Simplified

There is a universe of considerations that go into how successful an employee is at any given job, and how successful the employee will be in more demanding roles as you consider them for more promotions. As taught to me by Ken Wright, President, Ken Wright and Associates Ltd., Nancy Lee, President, Requisite Organization Associates, Inc., and Mark Van Clieaf, Managing Director, Organizational Capital Partners, the Suitability Model organizes all those elements into four components that are applicable to individual contributors and leaders alike: 1) Skills, knowledge, experience, and education; 2) information processing capability; 3) temperament; 4) accepts the role requirements.

With these components as your guide, you can reasonably assess your talent, help your employees assess themselves, and create a pipeline of well-chosen candidates with high potential for your succession planning.

You will be able to explain, using a common language, why someone has stalled, has been asked to leave the company, or continues to be promoted.

Skills, Knowledge, Experience and Education

The first element of the Suitability Model is the one that is easiest to understand, primarily because it is easy to describe and recognize: Skills, knowledge, experience, and education (SKEE). Here we match what the employee brings to the table regarding their background.

This element too often carries an inappropriate amount of importance when matching a candidate to an opportunity for advancement. There is a tendency for people to think that the perfect candidate for the assignment must have the exact skills, knowledge, experience, and education that have been defined for the job. These are often the skills that get candidates the job offer at the outset. But they aren't the skills that will guarantee their success at the job. (I can't think of a single instance in my career when someone was terminated because they didn't have the skills required to do a job.)

The other three elements of the model, in particular these next two, explain more about the individual's career path and that person's chances for success: Why that person gets promoted and at what point does the person stall or is asked to leave the company. These elements, when considered carefully, take the emotion and mystery out of any staffing decision and increase trust, as well as transparency, throughout the organization. They prevent reputation damaging assumptions, minimize the emotion around staffing decisions, and help you keep high-value talent.

Information Processing Capability

A person's capacity to manage the level of complexity in a job is described as their information processing capability (IPC). While every other element in the Suitability Model can be improved through additional education and developmental opportunities if the employee is willing to address them, IPC is a given. No amount of coaching, training, or experience will bring an employee beyond their "maximum height" or level of processing capability. However IPC does grow over time for everyone, just at different rates.

This helps us understand why some people struggle beyond their top level of capability. Traditionally, we assume that once employees have mastered their current jobs they are ready to be promoted to the next level. They deserve the promotion. It's only fair.

Soon, however, it becomes obvious that they have been promoted one too many times. It's not that they're lazy, stupid, unreliable, or undisciplined. They are simply in over their heads. Their work has taken on a level of complexity that has exceeded their ability to manage, and they could be making decisions that cost millions of dollars in investment, labor, and potentially shareholder value.

Consider the executive managing one plant, one manufacturing facility, or one department. There is a level of complexity to that role. If that leader is promoted to a job managing ten plants, ten facilities, or a number of divisions, the scope and scale of the complexity has jumped considerably. And it's incumbent on those making the hiring decisions to match a person's information processing capacity to that increased challenge. Can the person conceptualize what needs to be done to make that larger operation succeed now and in ten or twenty years in the future? It requires a different mental model and level of thinking to manage complexity, as well as more strategic decisions with consequences and impacts years into the future. Managers and those charged with hiring decisions can assess current information processing capacity by reviewing an employee or prospective employee's past work and its level of complexity. For example, has the employee demonstrated his or her capacity to manage effectively increasing complexity?

Transferring the principles behind the IPC component to your own business, you can probably think of several highly placed and valuable employees who hit their ceiling through no fault of their own. Corporate culture places such a high premium on the upward trajectory of a career path that when employees are promoted beyond their capability, they are loathe to take a step in reverse, even when they find themselves floundering. It can be perceived as a humiliating demotion to return to an earlier role. If you want to keep these stellar individuals, your understanding of the information processing capability component will guide you in their placement and can help you identify if that might be the problem hindering their performance in a new role. Such analysis also helps you rectify matters before an inappropriate role match leads to a career-ending failure or losses to the company.

In contrast, people who demonstrate a high level of information complexity can handle the higher degree of thinking required to synthesize all the paths and alternatives available in any scenario, project, or problem. They come back with suggestions that are often better than what even their managers might have conceived originally. People with high levels of information processing capability see things that nobody else sees because they're processing input at extraordinary levels. They can see connections that no one else can and discover complex patterns of variables, scenarios, and circumstances, bringing options that only they can add to the strategic discussion. They can also anticipate downstream consequences further out in the future.

Temperament

The third component is temperament. Is there any behavior that is getting in the way of the employee's ability to be effective in their role? Jaques described this as a negative *temperament* or *-T*. With very few exceptions, there are no absolutes in temperament that are universally wrong, regardless of the role. But even your outstanding employees could be sabotaging themselves because of some aspect of their nature that hinders their ability to do the job. It's not always a negative behavior. It could just as easily be a positive behavior that, when overplayed, limits effectiveness in a particular role.

For instance, there was a director on my team who had masterful relationship-building skills, and she worked to create harmony in her team. She moved through the ranks smoothly, until she pursued a vice president position she was confident she was ready to fill. It was a natural step up, one that she had earned. There was more prestige, increased salary, a bigger office, and an impressive title.

We gave that promotion to someone else. She was terribly disappointed. And who could blame her? To her credit, the director came to me for an explanation. She set her emotions aside and allowed me to fully describe the particular temperament the role required: A ruthless negotiator, someone who could drive a hard bargain and not blink, while also accepting the criticism of those who disagree with such an approach. This could potentially create a lot of conflict. That wasn't her temperament, and she knew it.

Did she really want that position, even if it was the natural next step up for her in her career? Most certainly not. She left the meeting relieved to know that the person who didn't promote her to that role knew her well enough to know that her temperament would doom her to failure. And she trusted me to wait until a more suitable opportunity came along, which it did.

Or consider the example of a brilliant manager who had all of the skills and information processing ability to be a successful leader, but he was volatile and bullied people. Through coaching, he was able to see how his behavior was problematic for his success and the success of his team. When he improved his approach to working with people, he rose to become a top executive in his function.

Temperament is something that is coachable, only provided that the employee is willing and open to change. A hair-trigger temper, for instance, could make a leader impossible to work for, no matter how brilliant. But there would come a time when their star power doesn't overcome the fact that no one wants to work with them. As Toni Lynn Chinoy, President, Harlan-Evans, Inc., says, their behavior becomes a distraction to their value and contributions. If they are willing to be coached to manage that element of their temperament, they might stand a shot at shining in another role.

Accepts the Role Requirements

Finally, there is the component of accepting the requirements of the role. Are there reasons—personal or otherwise—that would cause a person to not want a particular assignment? What naturally comes to mind, of course, is whether the employee believes in the mission of the company, department, team, and the particular assignment. But it can also be more personal than that. Family circumstances, for example, might prevent someone from taking a role that requires extensive travel.

This can play out in other scenarios, too. Some people, for instance, are great individual contributors and their success suggests they should be promoted to where they are managing people. What if they don't want to manage and develop others? What if they thrive as individual contributors who want to be left alone to do what they do best? Should they be invited to leave the company because they're not leadership material and are showing resistance to development? Or should they be left to do the work they were initially hired for and that they love?

When employers and employees get their wires crossed around accepting role requirements, companies risk losing valuable talent. Traditionally, high-value employees who demonstrate disinterest in advancing in their profession are often left feeling less valued or pressured to leave the company.

By following the Suitability Model and understanding how role requirements play into an employee's interest in available opportunities, the answer may often be *yes*. One exceptional leader in my company, for instance, was ready for the next step—a relocation to Hong Kong. Her reply: "No thanks."

So a few months later, we offered her the opportunity to open a business unit in another part of the United States. Her reply again: "No thanks."

In any other company, two strikes and the employee would be out. But because I had been applying the Suitability Model, I decided to meet with her to learn more about why she turned down two highly valuable opportunities.

The answer was readily revealed: She had two children whose lives she didn't want to disrupt with either a major move or the long absences necessary for her to perform her duties and a husband who was well established at a local company. We absolutely wanted to keep her, no question about that. But we also needed her to recommit to her development so that she could be a relatively reliable member of our succession planning pipeline. We agreed that we would continue her developmental activities in her current role through the next three years' time, seeing her through this sensitive period in her children's lives. In the meantime, we also upgraded her current responsibilities to leverage her capacity for more complexity.

The Rockwell Automation Story

Throughout the world, human resources professionals are constantly searching for the best way to define and identify leadership potential in a complex environment. In my years studying the work by Jaques and others, the Suitability Model is the one construct that sustains its utility and relevance, no matter the circumstances.

Rockwell Automation, a 113-year-old company built on innovation and customer focus, is the world's largest company dedicated to industrial automation and information, with customers in more than eighty countries.

When I assumed the role of senior vice president of human resources at Rockwell Automation in 2007, the company was undergoing a radical transformation. At that time, one third of our global workforce was relatively new to the company.

There were three HR initiatives in play (creating strategic clarity, designing a culture of inclusion, and building leadership capability). And HR's greatest opportunity for influence centered on leadership. The mission was to create a culture in which people could do their best work and build their best futures. Yet the company's performance management system, in its current state, was not helping us achieve the mission.

The existing process centered on a very complex and cumbersome organizational competency model that was customized for most jobs in the company worldwide. Each job was coded with the competencies, along with a large number of behavioral anchor scores that measured whether the employee was demonstrating them. By the time the manager finished assessing each employee on their goals, there would be pages and pages of competency measures. With that onerous complexity, the manager was serving the performance management system, rather than the system serving the manager and his or her needs.

Additionally, there was a lack of substantive conversations about leadership and what kinds of leaders the company needed. Our leadership assessment capability was lacking. We weren't able to clearly and succinctly articulate what it means to be successful in the organization, or what we look for when assessing people for senior leadership capability.

The time was right to start over. One of our key tasks was to create a clear description of what Rockwell Automation needed in its leaders that would serve the transforming company into the future, and help us fill a pipeline with qualified individuals who would be well-prepared candidates for leadership positions.

Introducing the Suitability Model

I saw an opportunity to bring the Suitability Model to life in a way that would move us toward our mission, provide clarity to help make decisions about leadership, and enable us to determine the best candidates for long-term succession planning.

The first step was to work with the senior leadership team to develop an understanding of what we mean when we talk about leadership and who we think has the potential to become a vice president or senior vice president. Using the Suitability Model, we were able to begin creating clarity, and we were on our way.

In 2009, we created the Leadership Capability Advisory Council, made up of high-potential senior leaders with the vision to define leadership capability. Looking at our existing process and our history with competencies, how do we help people understand what we're looking for based on the four components of the Suitability Model? It was a process. While the leaders still relied on some of the language of the competency criteria, they were open to embedding it into a framework that supported the suitability criteria.

As the leaders became more familiar and fluent with the Suitability Model, they could see how it could be applied to jobs throughout the company, not just the senior leadership positions. Additionally, because of its elegance in simplifying conversations around performance and potential, we are using the Suitability Model as a tool for individual career coaching.

In 2010, after introducing the four elements of the model to the larger group of top company leaders worldwide, our next challenge was deciding how to use it in a dedicated, organized way. While developing the succession planning process, we built tools to guide understanding of the Suitability Model.

An assessment guide was designed to help leaders understand the four components of the Suitability Model, with a special focus on the complexity of their leadership roles in the company.

The *User's Guide for the Suitability Criteria* was then created to supplement the assessment guide to help managers determine whether those reporting directly to them are underemployed, over-employed, or properly engaged with the company. It's a meaningful way to look at talent and assess capabilities for roles, once again illustrating how the unwieldy language of the competencies doesn't help us define what drives career success within Rockwell Automation.

The result? Now that the framework has been in place for several years, we are finding that our senior leaders are providing truly useful feedback on who is likely to be a great candidate for future senior leadership roles, as well as better clarifying how to develop future leaders.

When we started looking at high performers through the lens of the suitability criteria, honest conversations followed. All of us are more aware that we have different levels of information processing ability, different temperaments, and different reasons why we and our employees accept or reject roles based on role requirements. The emotion is taken out of the discussion, and the conversations are more productive, realistic, meaningful, and strategic.

Another important result is the ability to help people understand how leadership decisions are made. We have a formalized framework to explain why they're not being promoted despite their skills and experience, why they are being accelerated in one track instead of another based on their information processing capacity, or how temperament issues are impacting their promotions. Such clarity can help guide further development for some and enable retention of talent through increased understanding of leadership role requirements.

We completed the first phase of the work involved in rolling out the Suitability Model to all people managers and our global HR team. Managers across the globe received training and tools to help them understand and integrate the model into their everyday work. The next steps include transitioning to the use of and language of suitability within all our performance, selection, and development tools. Our global HR team continues to support their managers in using suitability to help assess employees in their current roles and for ongoing coaching and feedback, as we involve them in the change management process.

As we look to adapting the model throughout more talent management processes at Rockwell Automation, we understand that the next phase will be an evolution. Is there still an attachment to our original competency model? Yes, in some parts of the world especially. But we find that more and more, as our managers and employees fully understand the Suitability Model, they come to value it as an insightful tool to assess the match between an employee and a particular role.

There is an increasing receptivity to the Suitability Model because it's intuitive, it's what good managers are doing already, and it's applicable throughout the cultures represented in our company's more than eighty countries. We believe the model will move us closer to our mission of creating a culture in which people can do their best work and build their best futures at Rockwell Automation. We also believe the model will better enable us to select our future leaders who will make wise decisions on behalf of our shareholders leading to long-term health and well-being of our company.

Susan J. Schmitt, Senior Vice President Human Resources at Rockwell Automation, is a seasoned executive with over 25 years of HR and business experience across several industries, including industrial automation and technology, consumer packaged goods, consulting, and banking. As a guest speaker and author, Schmitt is known for her insights to build greater long-term value through leadership, talent, and corporate culture. Her published articles include: "Improving HR Performance–Leading HR Executives on Overcoming Performance Challenges," "Resolving Conflicts and Creating a Culture of Development," *and* "Transforming and Improving HR's Value in the Midst of Economic Uncertainty."

Contact Susan via sjschmitt@ra.rockwell.com or 414.382.8113.

Chapter 16

Positioned for a Successful Future: Syncing Human Capital Planning With Business Strategy

Marianne Jackson
President
3g Human Capital Consulting

As companies renew their strategy, reorganize themselves, and take on new marketing offerings, the rush to deliver on new business imperatives may cause the human side of the business to be out of step with the transformative vision. Yesterday's people strategy was created to match yesterday's vision. Not tomorrow's objectives.

This chapter will give you the essential tools to master strategic shifts ensuring that the business has the necessary talent in place to meet new business objectives. This will no doubt be the most sophisticated work an HR practitioner will ever do. You will be calling into action all the gravitas that you have accumulated over your years as an HR professional: Your business acumen; your consulting skills; your organizational development skills; your credibility with senior leadership, based on both your knowledge and your track record of accomplishments to date.

This work is where you will be stringing together all your areas of HR expertise to translate those business objectives into needed organizational capabilities and turn them into an actionable people strategy or a human capital plan (HCP).

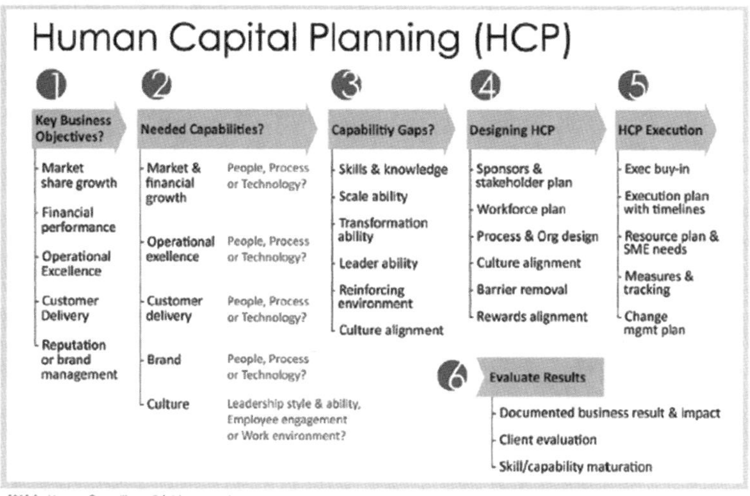

When a New HCP is Essential

At periodic intervals, businesses go through market analysis that will eventually challenge the HR department directly, perhaps even to the point of revolutionizing it. This exercise of market analysis can result in an updated or entirely new strategic plan. HCPs should be pressure-tested each time strategy changes and/or new business objectives are set.

All the great, transformative ideas coming out of those executive meetings sound fantastic at first blush. But unless the HR executive is contributing in those meetings, the people implications of those strategic changes could be the last thing on the minds of the strategic planners.

Without an expert specifically tasked to own the human capital portion of the new strategy, the other stakeholders can easily fall into what psychologists refer to as the *normalcy bias*. If the deployment of skills and talents have worked so far, it's easier to assume that, even with a new strategic direction, the day-to-day work environment will continue pretty much as it always has. All the company needs is just a talent tweak here and there. Right?

Not likely. Whether you are the HR leader for the entire enterprise or the HR leader of a business unit or department, you are exquisitely aware of all the interdependencies embedded within a strategic plan, especially as it relates to the people.

- Do you have the necessary skills and talent to activate the new strategy?
- If you don't, can you acquire them in time to meet the commitments being proposed?
- Do you have the necessary leadership style to inspire the new performance standards and objectives?
- Does your comp plan support the new behaviors that you want to reward?
- Are employees inspired by the vision set by their leaders?
- Are your senior leaders actually and sincerely onboard with the changes necessary to activate a new plan?
- Will your company be able to create or reinforce a culture or work environment that enables the strategy?

Without input and influence from the people side of your business as early in the process as possible, strategies created and argued for in a C-suite vacuum can result in substantial capability disconnects when the time comes to activate the new strategic iteration. It usually is obvious for leaders to check that technology; legal, and financial functions are in shape to support the business. But it is much less common to check for human capital alignment.

At what point will HR be included in the conversation? Ideally in the same series of meetings as other executives are involved. But regardless of what phase you're brought into the transformation process, you will own the responsibility of breathing life into the new strategy with the reconfiguration and redeployment of your human capital—otherwise known in other circles as the *talent* or *people strategy*.

The point when you're brought into this discussion and the value you add in the process will combine to position you as the indispensable partner in the earliest exploration of strategic planning. Without a process to follow in a form-follows-function approach, it can be daunting for you and your clients. There is, happily, a six-step process that can be right-sized at any level of organizational transformation. You can use it locally, within a single department, or business unit. Or you can use it globally on a corporate level, marshaling multi-dimensional demands in an international context. Same process. Different setting.

The Six-Step Human Capital Planning Process

Effective execution of any human capital plan in the service of the strategic plan is dependent on the alignment of talent, leadership, and culture. The work of HR is to design and execute a plan that delivers the human capacity and capability required so that the business achieves its objectives.

And, in turn, every time an organization experiences how the HCP performs to efficiently meet the new requirements, the leadership will naturally integrate it (and you) into the most important phases of strategic transformation from then on.

The repeated experience of human capital planning positions you as the ultimate expert in organizational effectiveness and performance. If you discipline yourself to go through this repeated pattern, you'll get better with practice. And you'll brand yourself and your team as the catalyst for much better business planning.

This six-step process organizes diagnostics and execution into logically separated and sequenced parts, components, and phases, so you and your organization don't become overwhelmed. Just work through one step at a time, and the HCP will begin to materialize in a logical and executable way that is appropriate for any scope and scale of planning that you are undertaking.

Step 1: Identify key business objectives

The business plan will likely include strategies that affect the entire organization and initiate some significant changes that will impact your employees. The company will probably be addressing market share or revenue growth, sales goals, and new products. There will also generally be some attention to customer satisfaction, operational excellence, and reputation or brand management.

As mentioned earlier, without HR input, strategic planning can take place with no understanding of the impact of the company's human capital footprint that's already in place. Leaders can say, "Let's scale as fast as we can!" Or "Let's grab market share!" without addressing the fact that there will be an impact on the talent that you may or may not have available yet.

Ideally, you will be part of the entire strategic or business planning process from the very beginning so that you understand not only what the forward vision is, but also the reasoning why the leadership team arrived at that vision. At the very least, you must be on the same kind of observational platform in order to gather information real-time for the translation of the business interests into talent strategies. You must know what's behind the interest of the business endgame or timeline that you've been presented with. Knowing the context of the business changes will keep you in a strategic planning mode yourself, instead of being relegated to response mode only.

Whichever your ultimate method for identifying business objectives may be, make sure you test your understanding of each one with other relevant leaders. Break down the major company objectives into their logical parts and seek alignment for clear outcomes expected with each one. What is sales saying they're going to do toward the objectives? What is finance doing? What are the product development people going to do to grow this new revenue level that's now on the table? You can facilitate important conversations that aid the leadership team in agreeing on what success looks like by way of establishing clear outcome statements. Keep asking the questions designed to get specific about what particular outcomes will look like, and even how they will be measured. This will help you accurately identify needed capabilities.

Step 2: Assess needed capabilities and cultural imperatives

Once you understand what the successful outcomes will look like in a measurable fashion, you can then drill down to identify what talent you need to achieve those outcomes successfully. This is the time when you start analyzing what skills and knowledge you will need for each business objective.

The clarity regarding business outcomes you achieved in Step 1 is the basis of what you need for Step 2: To identify which human capital abilities are necessary to achieve those outcomes. For example, if one of the key business strategies is to grow market share in Europe, capabilities that would be required might be:

- The ability to rapidly open legal entities in foreign countries
- The ability to establish brand identity in each location
- The ability to hire sales professionals in each region
- The ability to adequately compensate talent in each market.

Remember that at this stage of the process, you're identifying the capabilities that you believe underpin the identified outcomes. Even though you may be a novice at this, you can easily test your ideas by asking colleagues to validate your work and make changes along the way. The only way you can end up with a wrong diagnosis is to perform this task in a vacuum. The best HCPs have a lot of tested input in a collaborative environment.

Do an analysis for each of the business objectives as they relate to your organization's talent. What skills, knowledge, employee location, essential business processes, or supporting technology/tools are necessary to achieve those stated goals?

Now is also the time to start identifying culture-related capabilities as they pertain to the company's success profile. Do we have execution excellence? What leadership style and skills will easily enable the achievement of both the business and the human capital plan? Leadership has a major influence on company culture. And the company culture can accelerate or slow company performance.

Which culture characteristics could help each employee perform at her or his best? For example, if your company is in hyper-growth, what culture conditions enable speed, autonomy, and agility? If your business plan mandates execution excellence, you want a leadership style that establishes a commitment for accountability or achievement. Or, if the strategy is dependent on employee creativity, you need a culture and environment that encourages new ideas and risk taking.

Step 3: Identify the gaps

At this point, you have a draft schematic of essential capabilities needed to achieve the business strategy: Skills and knowledge, cultural conditions, and leadership style. More seasoned professionals performing HC planning often also evaluate needed key technology systems and core business processes. However, many first time HCPs focus only on talent needs.

Once completing Steps 1 and 2, you should feel confident that you have a solid draft of what the HCP will have to produce. Now you need to identify any gaps currently existing in your company versus those identified in Step 2.

An easy way to assess the depth of each capability is to conduct a qualified opinion rating. Do this by first gathering your team's opinion of the capability. Is it at *mastery, sufficient,* to *challenged* levels? Then, share your draft ratings with key stakeholders and confirm or adjust the ratings as needed.

For example:

Business Outcome	Needed Capabilities	Capability Status
Maintain a 100% customer satisfaction score	1. Able to maintain best in class call times	1. Challenged
	2. Able to maintain high trust quotients with customers	2. Challenged
	3. Maintain zero defect rates	3. Sufficient
	4. Culture of *customer first*	4. Mastery

You should be prepared to refer to recent performance facts to back up capability ratings. Obviously if the capability is brand new for the organization, there is no past performance to examine. In that case, you can use industry competency models as a reference guide to describe the gap.

After you have an agreed-upon capability gap analysis, work with a few key stakeholders to put the gaps in priority order. Most organizations can't tackle all the gaps simultaneously. So they need to be staged over time.

You want to make sure to check in with appropriate stakeholders along this journey. Have you articulated the business outcomes in a way that they recognize? Are they aligned with you on the creation of a human capital plan? Do they all agree on the gaps identified? This constant conversation continues among all stakeholders to create the HCP that the leadership owns; not just a plan for the HR department. Executing an HCP is highly dependent on successful change management. And successful change management begins with engaging stakeholders—not just as input givers but as owners of the process and outcomes.

Stakeholder commitment is never more important than in doing culture work. It is quite common that some amount of culture work is necessary in each iteration of the talent strategy. Leaders especially must commit to culture attributes that support the new direction and human capital plan. Do they understand the connection between culture, employee engagement, and performance? Do they hold the value of other peoples' success? Are leaders willing to make necessary changes even in their personal leadership style to help employees be at their best and thoroughly enjoy the experience?

Even the physical set-up of the workplace contributes to how employees experience the real culture. Are your offices closed-door cubicles that promote solitary, unilateral thinking? Or are they wide open workbench areas where everyone works elbow to elbow—even the CEO? Is there too much bureaucracy, or just the right amount of infrastructure? Would employees say the policies aid or slow getting things done? There is no right or wrong. Only what is right for your organization. This is where you find out what's what: What to emphasize, protect, or remove as part of the human capital plan.

Now that you have identified the gaps and gained an aligned view of those gaps with key stakeholders, you are ready to design the implementation strategy to close those gaps.

Step 4: Design the HCP implementation plan

Unfortunately, human resource organizations get little training in project management and execution excellence. Doing these well can make or break a successful human capital plan. It can be well worth it to train your team in these skills and processes.

The HCP implementation plan must be organized and managed by tracking milestones, understanding key decision points, and knowing when resources need to be onboard to get the work done. It is also critical to integrate stakeholder and change management plans into the project plan. Part of good execution management is to have regular progress review meetings when the leaders of each initiative area discuss what is accomplished, what is up next, and what might be any risks to the next set of milestones. Therefore, appointing a project manager to keep the plan organized and anticipate interdependencies is a very good strategy.

Generally, a key part of a HCP is the **workforce plan**. A workforce plan is designed to close talent gaps, either by hiring, developing, or borrowing needed skills. The decision will be highly dependent on how fast your company needs this talent or what might be the best method to bring those skills to your company. It can even end up being a merger/acquisition strategy. What will be your strategy? And does it time realistically with the outcomes that have been envisioned further into the future? Will you be able to attract the outside talent that you will need and integrate them effectively with your current employees? Perhaps you need to implement training and development to reinforce your current bench strength and bring them up to speed with their new deliverables.

Next, what initiatives should be on the HCP that reinforce or will modify an enabling culture? Do your company's practiced values line up with the stated values, and do they indeed align with the business environment you are in? What other cultural barriers do you need to account for as you design your human capital plan? How is your employee engagement? Employee engagement information can tell you almost everything you need to understand about your real company culture.

Another area to evaluate is the condition of your employer brand. Do you have an easy time competing for talent? Does your culture well satisfy the talent market preferences of today? Today's workforce wants very different support from their leaders. No longer is it adequate to just be good at setting direction and delegating duties. Do your leaders inspire employees? Are they great at generating self-direction and collaboration? Getting culture right, having strong employee engagement, and great leadership are essential ingredients of corporate success. We can no longer focus on just getting the talent in the door. These can be material sections of your human capital implementation plan.

What about your current **rewards structure**? Does it support your new objectives, desired culture, and business model? Or does it reward past behaviors that may be embedded in the company's legacy culture? Sales compensation and company bonus plans can easily get out of sync. Make it a routine practice to check them for solid alignment.

The actual design of the company can be a reinforcing factor when you are closing gaps identified through human capital planning. If you are experiencing global expansion decisions about distributed versus central organizations, frank conversations may be well worth the tension such talk can elicit. When you are changing the business model, consolidating some of the business units, or simplifying product lines, to respond to changing regulations and laws, you may find yourself challenged to rearrange the proverbial deckchairs, reducing headcount in one business unit while adding in another. Organization structure and design can accelerate decision-making, speed, and collaboration if they align well with how the work needs to get done. It is worthy of review. If your company is not ready for reorganization, it doesn't have to be fatal for the success of the HCP. Make sure there is an open dialogue about working with the current construct, especially if there are known challenges, like silo barriers.

The HCP is a "systems model." It's very helpful to use one of those models to check that you have a balanced HCP, ensuring you have not introduced risk to success because a key interdependent element was missed. The five-point Star Model by Jay Galbraith, for instance, effectively demonstrates the interconnectedness among strategy, people, rewards, structure, and processes. (See www.jaygalbraith.com for a thorough explanation.)

At this stage, your HCP should be composed of seven to ten key initiatives that close the priority capability gaps along with a reinforcing surround made up of culture, structure, and leadership. The next step in this process addresses stakeholder support, securing resources, and creating solid project plans to lead and track execution.

Step 5: Execute the HCP

You now have designed a systems approach to your HCP. You have seen to it that there is a shared vision for what needs to get accomplished. The team knows what to do and how it will impact the various stakeholders. Now is the time to make sure that you have all the resources and planning done that are needed to execute the company's human capital plan.

Confirm there is executive buy-in for the HCP and its implementation. It is highly recommended that the HR executive sit down individually with senior executives to walk them through the plan and ask for their continued support. The HCP must be owned by the collective leadership, een though the execution will most likely fall on the HR team.

All the critical leaders must be aligned with the components of the plan that will ultimately execute the larger strategy. Not only will some portion of this work likely be paid for out of their budgets, but you will also need their explicit support in promoting the changes among their teams. It is too easy to let the forward-moving momentum of this activity distract you from subtle indicators that you might have a non-supporter. Not noticing you have an outlier can have a disastrous effect on the success of the HCP.

Executive buy-in also requires that leaders are willing to free up their critical talent to help execute HCP initiatives. Have you negotiated with them effectively so that you're confident that they will lend you their best employees for whatever percentage of their schedule you need to activate the new strategy? A risk to the implementation plan often happens when it becomes difficult to get stakeholders together to align on key decisions or deploy solutions.

Communication throughout the company must be an essential part of the HCP implementation plan. Segment your stakeholder groups and design a communication strategy to not only keep them informed but also keep them engaged. Each stakeholder group may have their own resistance or pace in getting the changes launched and solidified. Take the time to understand what each group needs, cares, or worries about and pragmatically build that into your plan.

Enterprise-wide communications are easier and more effective now with the advancement of enterprise social media. Integrate a variety of communication media into your plan. Videos, blogs, chat sessions, and group meetings can all have a place in involving every last employee in the company's human capital strategy.

Step 6: Evaluate the results

Now you're in the execution phase, and you're tracking your forward movement. Be mindful of what you measure. It's not sufficient to point to the accomplished milestones as evidence of results achieved. Those milestones are designed to get you there. They are the destination themselves. There is a difference between objectives and results. You want to know now if you are predictably on track to deliver the outcomes.

As you hold progress reviews, assess whether the initiatives are beginning to yield results. Too often results are examined at the very end of the execution phase, allowing no chance for redirection or recovery strategies if something has not met expectations. There are a variety of ways to assess whether in-process efforts will yield. One approach is to establish baseline views of the starting state, then conduct periodic surveys to see if you are getting change at an acceptable pace. Checking your change management plan against adoption continuum is also a great way to assess progress. Has the organization successfully transitioned from awareness to understanding to accountability to ownership?

Ownership

Accountability

Understanding

Awareness

If everything is activated properly, in sync with all the components, and with realistic expectations, objectives achieved will create the desired outcomes. Be sure to not only look at typical HR metrics, such as time to hire, but rather measure outcomes expected from the HCP. Does the organization now successfully possess the necessary new capabilities? Has there been an improvement in leadership effectiveness? Are you now seeing evidence of an aligned culture?

Be consciously competent (or at least consciously incompetent) in evaluating your results. Did the human capital plan yield what you wanted within the time you wanted? What were the essential elements that facilitated that success? What created failure or disappointment?

The most recent human capital plan that you have designed to serve the business strategy of your company will not be the last one you ever do. It will only be the most recent one. So treat each cycle of these six steps as a learning process, preparing you to take on an ever-more complicated, more elaborate, more critical round of human capital strategies the next time. So treat each iteration as a learning journey in your HR career, as well as for the leaders of your organization.

Every time you cycle through human capital planning, you're that much smarter, more realistic, and more experienced with using good hypotheses and assumptions, an improved sense of timing, increased ability to secure resources, as well as designing an effective change strategy—and your contribution to a successful company will be evident to not only yourself but also leaders and most employees.

Conclusion

Earlier in this chapter, I made the point that human capital planning will be the most sophisticated work you will ever do. You'll be called upon to pull multiple levers; fully understanding how each lever interacts with the others on multiple levels—locally, globally, departmentally, corporate-wide. And, as you advance in your own career, the scope and scale of your HCP projects will increase with each new phase of strategic planning at the C-suite level.

This will not only be the most sophisticated work you will ever do, but it will also probably be the most important work you will do in your capacity as an HR leader. Only you and your HR colleagues can fully understand exactly how essential correct and innovative HCP is to a successful strategic re-engineering.

As you repeatedly implement this six-step system to breathe life into your organization's strategy, your own acumen will deepen and broaden and prepare you for the next round of constant change.

Marianne Jackson has devoted her career to providing effective human capital strategies that aid numerous companies in achieving their business objectives. She has over twenty years' experience as the Chief Human Resources Officer in some of California's best known corporations. Her experience spans both healthcare and technology industries, including Cisco Systems, Palm, Sundisk, Sun Microsystems, and Blue Shield of California. She is well known for her practical approach to organizational effectiveness, executive/leadership development, workforce optimization, strategic planning, human capital planning, and culture shaping.

Marianne is now the president of a human capital company that assists organizations with improving competitiveness. Her approach effectively links the business strategy with a targeted people strategy ensuring the right capabilities and culture have been invested in such a way that they propel performance, increase engagement, and strengthen the employer brand.

Marianne's business, 3g Human Capital Consulting, is located in Northern California.

Contact Marianne via email at 3ghumancc@gmail.com.

About Martha I. Finney

Martha Finney is the author, ghostwriter, and co-author of over 23 books on HR, leadership, employee engagement, and career management. Her bestsellers include *HR From the Heart: Inspiring Stories and Strategies for Building the People Side of Great Business,* which she wrote with Libby Sartain.

She is also a publishing and platform consultant and coach, helping an exclusive clientele expand their professional thought leadership brand by leveraging publishing and social media.

Her clients and interviewees come from such companies as Intuit, Yahoo, JetBlue, Southwest Airlines, Avery Dennison, Marriott, Starwood Hotels and Resorts, Kenexa, Caterpillar, Sears Holdings, U.S. Marine Corps, H-P, SAS Institute, etc.

Her own original research into employee engagement has been featured in *The Wall Street Journal, The New York Times, The Washington Post, Miami Herald, The San Francisco Chronicle, The San Jose Mercury News, Time Magazine, The Huffington Post,* CNN, and NPR, among other business media outlets.

To learn more about Martha and to contact her directly, visit www.marthafinney.global.